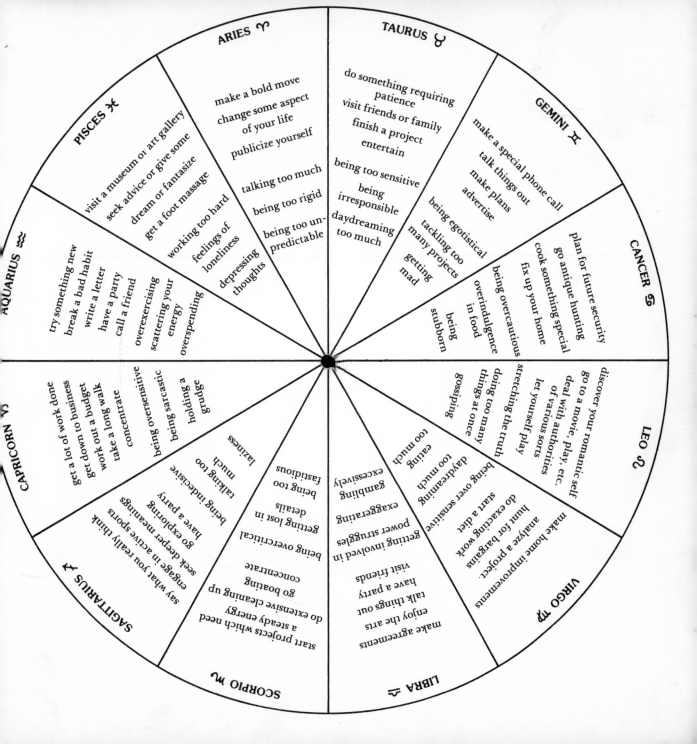

Mary Orser

Rick and Glory Brightfield

PREDICTING

with

ASTROLOGY

by the authors of INSTANT ASTROLOGY

HARPER COLOPHON BOOKS
Harper & Row, Publishers
New York, Hagerstown, San Francisco, London

PREDICTING WITH ASTROLOGY. Copyright ©1977 by
Rick Brightfield and Mary Orser. All rights reserved. Printed
in the United States of America. No part of this book may
be used or reproduced in any manner without written per-
mission except in the case of brief quotations embodied in
critical articles and reviews. For information address Harper
& Row, Publishers, Inc., 10 East 53rd Street, New York,
N.Y. 10022. Published simultaneously in Canada by Fitz-
henry & Whiteside Limited, Toronto.

First HARPER COLOPHON edition published 1977
LIBRARY OF CONGRESS CATALOG CARD
NUMBER: 77-87157
INTERNATIONAL STANDARD BOOK NUMBER:
0-06-090572-7

Contents

What astrology can predict

What does the future hold? This is a question that has intrigued and fascinated mankind throughout history. Few of us, however, if given a chance to read the future like an open book, would really want to. A zest for the unexpected is part of being human. Nevertheless, most of us would like some guidelines for what's coming up.

In past and present cultures all over the world human beings have studied astrology, connecting the positions of the sun, moon, planets, and stars with conditions here on earth. It was observed that nature and human life followed definite cycles and that these were reflected in the predictable cycles of the heavenly bodies. For example, we predict the seasons by forecasting the regular yearly changes in the axis of the earth with respect to the sun. We also predict the tides by the positions of the sun and moon relative to the earth. Going beyond these obvious interrelationships, astrology has, through the ages, collected an organized body of knowledge that makes it possible to make other predictions about natural phenomena and human behavior.

However, future events are not predetermined and irrevocable. Just as the "science" of economics, for example, works with probabilities and trends, so astrology tries to delineate areas of probability and possibility. It is somewhat like weather predicting. When the local weather forecaster predicts a ninety percent chance of rain and it doesn't rain, he can always say, "Well, that's the ten percent chance for you." To come to the weatherman's defense, if it doesn't rain, then obviously some unforeseen factor must have intervened at the last moment to keep what must have seemed like a virtual certainty from happening. In the case of an astrological forewarning, it seems that an act of will power, or sometimes simple caution, can often prevent something untoward from happening or can tip the balance in our favor.

The basic importance of the positions of heavenly bodies at any given time in respect to the earth is that they indicate the *present relationship among various energies,* similar to the way a musical score indicates the wavelength relationship of the various notes being played. To use another comparison, the positions of the sun, moon, and planets at any given time may indicate *current conditions surrounding us,* just as taking a blood sample determines the current condition of the body as a whole. For convenience, however, we speak of "the effects of planets" or "the effects of a zodiac sign" in the same way that we say "the sun rises," although we know that it is really the earth turning to meet the sun.

Astrological predicting can cover a wide range of phenomena. Sometimes if the astrological conditions are very clear-cut, actual "events" can be predicted, both on a personal level and on a world scale. However, the more usual case is where *possibilities* and *atmospheres* are what can be anticipated.

We must also recognize what events are really important. Many things that seemed relatively insignificant at the time are seen eventually (usually much later, in retrospect) to be turning points in people's lives or in world history.

Modern science in earlier stages of development, with its initial enthusiasm for absolute proof, seemed to rule out the possibility of connections between cosmic phenomena and human activity. However, science today, with its broader perspectives, is reinvestigating what are emerging as definite connections between heavenly bodies and conditions here on earth.

Are certain events inevitable?

Winter is inevitable in the north when the sun takes its yearly journey south. The outside temperature and the weather conditions seem beyond our control. But we *do* have some control over how we prepare for the winter, how cold our houses and our bodies are, and our attitude toward the weather.

It's exactly the same when you predict what's going to happen in other ways by using the positions of the sun, moon, and planets! Certain general conditions are inevitable, but we can make preparations for our proper use and often enjoyment of these general conditions. In other words, *knowing about coming conditions can help you put them to positive use.* You can learn to distinguish between the "inevitable" astrological conditions (like winter) and the "controllable" astrological conditions (like your preparation for and response to winter). Guidelines for the future give us *more* freedom rather than *less*. If we had no idea when to expect the seasons, we would not know when to plant our gardens and when to prepare for the cold. Knowing the future weather can help us plan picnics for sunny days and closet cleanings for rainy days.

For each type of planetary influence you will find suggested best uses and cautions. The better you understand what to expect, the better you can create your own preferred response to the condition.

How astrology predicts daily and long-range changes in your life and in the world

This book explains the simplest and yet most widely practiced astrological techniques for predicting how the coming positions of the sun, moon, and planets can affect both you and other individuals, as well as organizations, activities, nations, and the whole earth. In addition, we describe how astrologers predict the weather, the timing of gardening activities, and earthquakes. Astrologers are busily testing these methods, discarding the ones that don't work and improving on the ones that do. Also, modern techniques can predict with great accuracy the future positions of all the heavenly bodies.

You will discover that what affects you personally can be expressed in many different ways—in other words, that you can often *work with* astrological effects rather than be unconsciously controlled by them.

In fact, as mentioned earlier, you are already doing this with one astrological effect: the seasons. You consult your calendar, which tells you it is fall, the time to get out warm clothes and do other "acorn gathering" in preparation for colder weather. Or, your calendar will tell you it is spring, the time to get out lighter clothes and plant your garden.

Just as you allowed for seasonal changes by knowing the angle of the sun, you can also make preparations in other areas of your life by knowing what changes are coming in the positions of all the heavenly bodies. And that's the way astrological prediction works!

Personal important points

The zodiac positions of the sun, moon, and planets (as well as certain other zodiac points) at the time of your birth are your **personal important points**. The movements of the heavenly bodies in connection with these **personal important points** indicate what conditions surround you personally now as well as what conditions you can expect in the future.

This book gives (without complicated mathematics) the approximate *zodiac positions* of some of the planets for any date from 1901 to the year 2000. The faster-moving planets are given for shorter periods. This information will enable you to determine (from your birthdate) many of your **personal important points** and will help you to know when to expect movements of the heavenly bodies in connection with these points. We will also give what astrologers have found to be some of the *meanings* of changing zodiac positions of the sun, moon, and planets, both for general world conditions and also for you personally as they interact with the positions of the heavenly bodies when you were born.

Knowing about coming astrological conditions in connection with your **personal important points** can help you decide the best times to plan social activities, get a lot of work done, start a new project, take a vacation, communicate with others, enlarge your family, and many things with deeper personal meaning. Astrology can give you help in deciding the best times to start short-term projects and also to pursue long-term goals.

Sun energies around the zodiac

Every year the sun goes through each of the twelve signs of the zodiac. As it travels through a sign, the energies of that sign are activated. We see these energies manifested in many different ways, both in the world in general and in our individual lives. The diagram below shows the sun's yearly trip through the zodiac. (For time and date the sun enters each zodiac sign in a specific year, see the sun and moon calendars beginning on page 82, since the actual date of entry can differ by a day or so from year to year.)

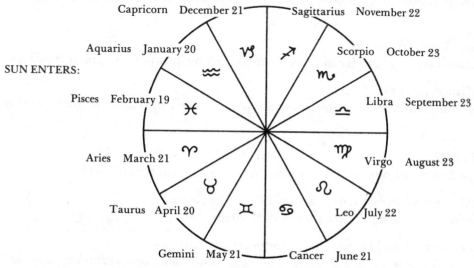

Astrologers have also developed certain general categories that characterize various groups of signs. Understanding these will give you a sense of the basic energies of each sign.

EXTROVERTED AND INTROVERTED SIGNS

EXTROVERTED (Aries, Gemini, Leo, Libra, Sagittarius, Aquarius)
Every other sign, beginning with Aries, is considered to be extroverted, meaning that the energy flows outward, as in a positive electrical pole. When the energies of these signs are activated, you will tend to be more outgoing, social, and assertive.

INTROVERTED (Taurus, Cancer, Virgo, Scorpio, Capricorn, Pisces)
The introverted signs are associated with an inward flow of the energy, as in a negative electrical pole. This influence is toward reception, introspection, being somewhat more in yourself.

THE ELEMENTS

Each sign is classified under one of the four *elements*. The nature of each element indicates a *type of approach* that seems more natural during the influence of this sign.

FIRE (Aries, Leo, Sagittarius)

Enthusiasm, creativity, fulfillment, enjoyment, stimulation: a time when everyone gives off more sparks.

EARTH (Taurus, Virgo, Capricorn)

Emphasis on the practical and concrete, stabilization of activities, a time for getting "down to earth."

AIR (Gemini, Libra, Aquarius)

Ideas and communication: a time for making contacts, getting information, and spreading it.

WATER (Cancer, Scorpio, Pisces)

Emotions, sensitivity, atmosphere; a time when everyone is more tuned into the "feel" of things.

THE QUALITIES

Each sign is classified under one of the three *qualities,* which means *types of action.*

CARDINAL, or generative (Aries, Cancer, Libra, Capricorn)

Under the influence of these signs it is easier to *start things moving*.

FIXED, or concentrative (Taurus, Leo, Scorpio, Aquarius)

This influence works best toward *holding the line, sustaining, concentrating,* and *following through* an action that has already been started.

MUTABLE, or distributive (Gemini, Virgo, Sagittarius, Pisces)

The emphasis here is on *keeping an action moving* and *steering it* resourcefully through its changes.

Remember that the sun's zodiac position is only one influence, although a most important one. The zodiac positions of the other planets modify the general energy flow. Following are characteristic influences of each zodiac sign. At this point we are thinking of these influences as they combine with sun energies, but they may also be applied to the moon or any of the planets in their travels around the zodiac.

Sign classifications

	Element	Quality	Extroverted or Introverted	Planetary Ruler
Aries	fire	cardinal	extroverted	Mars
Taurus	earth	fixed	introverted	Venus
Gemini	air	mutable	extroverted	Mercury
Cancer	water	cardinal	introverted	Moon
Leo	fire	fixed	extroverted	Sun
Virgo	earth	mutable	introverted	Mercury
Libra	air	cardinal	extroverted	Venus
Scorpio	water	fixed	introverted	Pluto & Mars
Sagittarius	fire	mutable	extroverted	Jupiter
Capricorn	earth	cardinal	introverted	Saturn
Aquarius	air	fixed	extroverted	Uranus & Saturn
Pisces	water	mutable	introverted	Neptune & Jupiter

Fire: operates mainly from enthusiasms.
Air: focused on the need to understand.
Water: operates from emotions.
Earth: oriented toward practicalities and concrete results.

Cardinal: initiates action.
Fixed: follows through on action.
Mutable: keeps the action moving and steers it through changes.

Extroverted: more outgoing, social, and assertive.
Introverted: more introspective, sometimes shy, less assertive.

Aries ♈

EXTROVERTED, FIRE, CARDINAL, RULED BY MARS

(Sun in Aries every year approximately March 21—April 20)

This is a time of *new beginnings,* when the emphasis is on *action.* The energy level is generally high. If you have been encountering resistance toward tackling something (either in others or in yourself), this is a time when the sun position can particularly help you push through, although be wary of high ego energies (your own included).

This "power boost" period can be used either physically, emotionally, or mentally, as you will find that energy on all levels is more volatile and flows stronger. Therefore it's a good time for physical exercise, for cutting through emotional complexities, and for anything requiring mental work.

The cautions to be observed are just what you would expect in a high-energy period: You may start too many things and have trouble finishing them. If you try to do too much too fast without pacing yourself, you could be accident-prone or get overtired. Observing these precautions, however, you will find that this period is a time to enjoy *being spontaneous* and *doing.*

Keywords: taking initiative, courageous, assertive, adventurous, breaking through, beginning, acting with outrushing force, active, daring, pioneering, exhibiting fast action in bursts

Avoid: being egotistical, foolhardy, selfish; displaying temper explosions; not finishing what you start.

Taurus ♉

INTROVERTED, EARTH, FIXED, RULED BY VENUS

(Sun in Taurus every year approximately April 20-May 21)

This is a time to slow down from the faster, more erratic speed of Aries. Try to settle into a *sustained rhythm* in whatever you are doing. In Aries the energy is more suitable for spontaneity, hatching ideas, and getting things started, while in Taurus the rhythm is better for more regular, getting-down-to-business activities. This is a time for practicality and an emphasis on the right routines in your life. Taurus, being an earth sign, is also a good time for becoming interested in nature, animals, growing things, preparing food.

However, Taurus is not all work, as the Venus influence brings a strong appreciation of beauty and the good things of life.

In Taurus (as in any fixed sign) the energies tend to be sustained in one direction beyond the point where they ought to have made a change. Be careful not to overeat or overindulge in other ways (such as overworking). Try not to be too stubborn. Enjoy what you are doing, but be conscious of when it's time to stop.

Keywords: practical, reliable, persistent, affectionate, patient, sustaining steady action, concentrated, following through, artistic

Avoid: being stubborn, opinionated; holding grudges.

Gemini ♊

EXTROVERTED, AIR, MUTABLE, RULED BY MERCURY

(Sun in Gemini every year approximately May 21-June 21)

Gemini is a time of *variety* (in activity) and *communication*. This is true in the world in general and in your own activities. You will find that your mind tends to be more active and curious, with a tendency to hop from one topic to another. Gemini is the monkey of the zodiac, and if you will visualize a monkey's normal way of doing things, you will get a pretty good picture of what Gemini rhythms are like. It is a particularly good time to communicate with others, think, study, learn something new.

The challenge of Gemini, as of the other mutable signs, is to center and steady your energies and not to get spread too thin. Since Gemini is a mutable air sign, this spreading is particularly likely to happen in the areas of thinking and communication. Use the energies for contacting people, any form of communications, and new ways of thinking, but keep aware of how your specific activities fit into your life as a whole.

Keywords: inquisitive, changeable, talkative, ever-active, adaptable, spontaneous, intellectual, thinking

Avoid: being scattered, impatient; overthinking.

Cancer ♋

INTROVERTED, WATER, CARDINAL, RULED BY THE MOON

(Sun in Cancer every year approximately June 21-July 22)

The keynote of Cancer is *sensitivity on the feeling level*. This does not imply that your feelings will be either positive or negative, but merely that you (as well as everyone else) will naturally tune in more to how you *feel* about things rather than what you *think* about them.

It is a time when emphasis is on the home, the family, nuturing people, animals and plants, and preparing good food.

Avoid being supersensitive and also treading on the supersensitive feelings of others. Don't brood about the past. It is a good time to take a look at your emotional patterns, how you have been indulging your feelings and how you have been ignoring them as well as how they flow in your life pattern as a whole.

Keywords: sensitive, sympathetic, nuturing, receptive, cautious, reflective

Avoid: being moody, illogical; brooding on the past.

Leo ♌

EXTROVERTED, FIRE, FIXED, RULED BY THE SUN

(Sun in Leo every year approximately July 22-August 23)

This is a time of *warmth*, not only of the weather but also of the heart. Leo should be a time for doing what you enjoy, a time for sharing activities with friends and family. It can also be a time of work, although if you are trying to do things in scattered bits and pieces, your efforts will go against the steady, smoother rhythm of this fixed sign. Leo relates to children and play; it is a time to reestablish your connection with the child in yourself and in others — not the selfish child, but the sense of adventure and wonder.

Leo can bring out the self-centered and self-indulgent nature in all of us and is therefore a time to be wary of ego confrontations and everyone's heightened potential for hurt pride. Try to get into the deeper center in yourself (other than the ego center). Increase your potential for relating from the heart.

Keywords: self-expressive, creative, dramatic, proud, optimistic, broadminded, generous

Avoid: being self-centered, unadaptable, uncooperative, self-indulgent.

Virgo ♍

INTROVERTED, EARTH, MUTABLE, RULED BY MERCURY

(Sun in Virgo every year approximately August 23-September 23)

Virgo is a time for *perfecting* whatever you are doing. As with the other earth signs, this sign is a good time to "get down to brass tacks"; Virgo is particularly good for working on the practical details. Since this sign is ruled by Mercury, it is also favorable for study, research, or communication. Cleaning and reorganizing, whether physical objects or the contents of your mind, are also activities that are aided by the Virgo energies.

Virgo can bring out the supercritical side of all of us, so it's important to be conscious of the need to be somewhat tolerant of human faults (your own included). It's not the best time for making a lot of major decisions because you may find it a little harder to judge from the perspective of the total picture. The best uses of Virgo energy are for *sorting everything out* in your activities and in your mind.

Keywords: analytical, practical, orderly, perfecting details

Avoid: being over-critical.

Libra ♎

EXTROVERTED, AIR, CARDINAL, RULED BY VENUS

(Sun in Libra every year approximately September 23-October 23)

During Libra the emphasis is on *balancing things out to establish harmony.* Relationships are highlighted, and this means that it's a good time both for social life in general and for one-to-one relationships. If things are going well in your relationships, they should be even smoother during

Libra. If you feel there is an imbalance between yourself and another, this is a good time to work it out. The connection of Venus with Libra means there is emphasis on the arts, either the fine arts or merely redecorating your home or adding to your wardrobe.

Libra is not the easiest time to make clear-cut, firm decisions. It is also not the best time to get at the hard facts, because the emphasis is more on diplomacy than on what's really happening. The best use of Libra is to establish more peace and beauty in your relationships and your surroundings.

Keywords: diplomatic, seeking harmony, artistic, friendly, tolerant, peace loving, considerate

Avoid: being indecisive, indirect, inconsistent.

Scorpio ♏

INTROVERTED, WATER, FIXED, RULED BY PLUTO AND MARS

(Sun in Scorpio every year approximately October 23-November 22)

Scorpio is a time of *particular intensity* and often involves bringing to the surface things that have been hidden. Since Scorpio is a water sign, this refers especially to the emotions. However, this "getting to the bottom of things" can be applied in many ways, which is why Scorpio is a good period to do almost any kind of research. A certain amount of solitude is natural, and you are likely to find that decisions come easier. This period is particularly favorable for physical exercise.

The emotional intensity of Scorpio needs careful handling. It can bring to the surface grudges, paranoia, and various other repressed feelings. It is well to look at yourself and others with a certain humor during Scorpio's influence. The best use of this period is to apply Scorpio's emphasis on getting at the truth in order to take a good, hard look at whatever elements of your life need an overhaul. Then go about doing it.

Keywords: intense, passionate, determined, courageous, ambitious, mysterious, energetic

Avoid: being unforgiving, secretive, uncooperative, undiplomatic.

Sagittarius ♐

EXTROVERTED, FIRE, MUTABLE, RULED BY JUPITER

(Sun in Sagittarius every year approximately November 22-December 21)

Sagittarius is an *expansive* time, with an emphasis on moving around and "good fellowship."

Thanksgiving, which comes when the sun is in Sagittarius every year, is one typical manifestation of this sign, a sociable time when people feel warm and open to each other. It is generally a good time for contacting people and, often, for traveling around. Sagittarius is also connected with philosophy and religion—in other words, getting an overall perspective on things. This applies not only to life in general but also to the direction of your own life and work.

Sagittarius, like the other mutable signs, indicates a certain restlessness. You may have to work harder on concentration. Also, during this time people seem impelled to speak their minds, and this, of course, may need careful handling. The expansive quality of Sagittarius can also mean overindulgence. The best use of Sagittarius is in getting perspective on your life and in making contacts with others.

Keywords: expansive, enthusiastic, optimistic, independent, friendly, farsighted, athletic, loving the outdoors

Avoid: being unrestrained, irresponsible, tactless, lacking fixity of purpose.

Capricorn ♑

INTROVERTED, EARTH, CARDINAL, RULED BY SATURN

(Sun in Capricorn every year approximately December 21-January 20)

Capricorn is a natural time to *organize*, plan, and get down to work. This contracting and centering influence follows the expansion of Sagittarius and can impel you toward more concentration, rather than diffusion, in your activities and also toward more solitude. In Capricorn the emphasis is on usefulness, practicality, and no nonsense. It is also a good time to get a clearer look at your goals and be able to see, more realistically than usual, what progress you are making toward achieving them. Capricorn does not have to be all work. It is good to get some recreational exercise, although probably this sign is more conducive toward slower exercises, such as hiking or yoga.

Don't get so involved in what you are doing that you resent any intrusion on your plans. Express the sobering Capricorn energies in dedication, not depression. The best use of Capricorn energies is to get yourself realistically organized.

Keywords: serious, cautious, economical, realistic, ambitious, disciplined, methodical, dependable

Avoid: being overserious, pessimistic, fretful, overly hardworking.

Aquarius ♒

EXTROVERTED, AIR, FIXED, RULED BY URANUS AND SATURN

(Sun in Aquarius every year approximately January 20-February 19)

Aquarius is a sign whose emphasis is on *communication*, working with others, and *new ideas*. Following Capricorn and Sagittarius (relatively conservative signs) Aquarius is a time when people tend to be somewhat more open to new ways of doing things. The emphasis is more on cooperation than on individual work. However, if you are doing work of a more individual nature, you will likely find that you are getting some new ideas on how to go about it.

Everybody seems to be more opinionated during Aquarius, and they aren't shy about voicing these opinions. Even though there is interest in new ideas, the fixed-sign influence means that any strong opinions will be maintained stubbornly. The best use of Aquarius energies is in breaking through to new perspectives, both in relationships with others and in your own life.

Keywords: independent, individualistic, friendly, detached, interested in new ideas, original

Avoid: being tactless, unpredictable, opinionated.

Pisces ♓

INTROVERTED, WATER, MUTABLE, RULED BY NEPTUNE AND JUPITER

(Sun in Pisces every year approximately February 19-March 21)

During Pisces it is natural to dream and to get more deeply in contact with your own *feelings* and those of others. It is a time in which sympathy is emphasized and people are more likely to listen to what others have to say. The emphasis is more toward feelings than on thinking, which means that it's not the best time for hard, realistic, concrete reasoning. All of the last four signs of the zodiac have to do with perspectives, and, in a sense, Pisces brings the broadest perspective of all.

During Pisces keep conscious of the "hard realities" of what you are involved in. It is easier to be enchanted by an enticing dream that might not hold up in reality. Also, everyone's feelings are more sensitive now than during any other sign, so tread lightly. The time is best used for dreaming and planning (with a foot on the ground), for relating on a deeper level, and for contacting deeper levels of inspiration in the arts, nature, and life in general.

Keywords: sympathetic, understanding, imaginative, emotional, receptive, compassionate

Avoid: being impractical, indecisive, unrealistic, illogical.

General predictions and personal predictions

The sun, moon, and planets all appear to move around the earth in the zodiac. This is a relatively narrow band across the sky's background pattern of "fixed" stars. As we saw in the last chapter, different kinds of energy changes are to be expected as the sun moves through each zodiac sign. This is true also of the moon or any of the planets as they move through the signs.

Astrologers have observed that the sun, moon, and each planet correspond to different functions and future possibilities in a person's life. For instance, the sun indicates your *consciousness*, the moon your *instinctual reactions*, Mercury your *way of thinking*, and so on. The basic influence on you is shown by the planet positions in your natal horoscope. The *consciousness* of a person born when the sun was passing through the sign of Capricorn, for example, is colored by the combination of characteristics that astrologers call Capricorn and is therefore experienced differently from the consciousness of a person born with the sun in Libra. The *thought patterns* of a person born when Mercury was in Aries are different from those of a person born when Mercury was in Taurus.

Note: Although the sun and moon are not planets in the technical sense of heavenly bodies that orbit the sun, astrologers for convenience refer to them as planets. Any reference hereafter to the planets will include the sun and moon.

Further on in this book, in the simple-to-use planet calendars and diagrams, you can look up the zodiac positions of not only the sun but also the moon and outer planets when you were born.Each of these positions is a *personal important point*. You probably already know what sunsign you are. (A person who says, "I'm a Taurus," or, "I'm a Libra," is referring to his or her sunsign.) The place (degree) within your sunsign occupied by the sun at the time of your birth is one of your *personal important points*. Each planet position in your natal horoscope (a chart of all the planet positions at the time of your birth) describes certain elements of your basic personality. In addition, it is affected by planets that either pass by it or form certain other angles to it after your birth.

At any given time the planets form a pattern in the sky. If we could hear it, this pattern would be a kind of "cosmic chord," linking all the planets' individual positions in the zodiac. This cosmic chord is a combination of the *zodiac position* of each individual planet and the pattern of *connections* (called *aspects*) among the planets in the circle of the zodiac. The planetary pattern of a particular moment, as it relates to the earth's position, affects all of us, both in general world conditions and in the rhythms of our individual energies.

Of course, the positions of the planets at the moment of your birth formed a cosmic chord, too, and when an astrologer interprets your natal horoscope, he or she is interpreting this pattern.

If you looked east for twenty-four hours, you would see all twelve signs of the zodiac rise, one after the other, because of the earth's rotation. Besides the points marked by each planet position, another *personal important point* is the place in the zodiac that was *just coming up over the eastern horizon* when and where you were born. This is called your *ascendant*, or *rising sign*. The zodiac point that was passing highest in the sky when you were born is also a **personal important point**. This is called your *midheaven*, or *M.C.* (*medium coeli*, which is Latin for "midheaven"). These two **personal important points** can be calculated accurately only with fairly complicated astrological tables.

With this book you can find the exact zodiac position of many of your **personal important points** and the approximate position of others. If you have had your horoscope made, you will have the exact positions of all your **personal important points** available. If not, for a small price you can order your personal horoscope, which will give the exact zodiac degrees of your ascendant, midheaven, and each planet, as well as other **personal important points**. To order your horoscope, see page 159.

Here are examples of the cosmic chords on two different days:

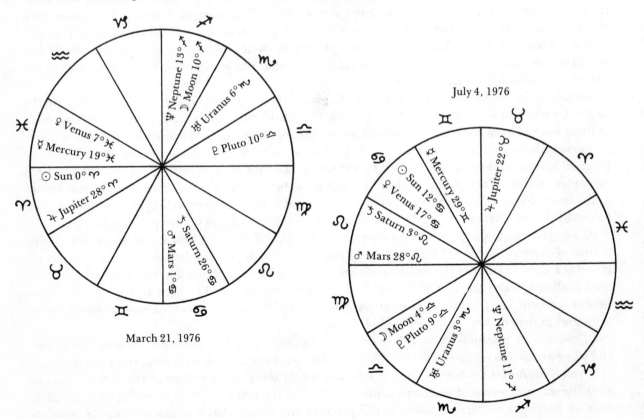

March 21, 1976

July 4, 1976

Transits

Particular personal effects for you are to be expected on any date in which one or more of the planets are passing over (forming a *conjunction* with) one of your ***personal important points***. These effects should be considered in addition to those effects felt by everyone at this time. Personal effects are also to be expected if any planet is opposite on the circle of the zodiac (forming an *opposition* with) one of your ***personal important points***, or *square* (at a right angle) to it. Certain other angles between a planet today and a ***personal important point*** are connected with particular effects for you personally. The effect of each such angle is different. (Further on you will find out how to locate not only your ***personal important points*** but also the places in the zodiac from which planets make transiting angles to your ***personal important points***.)

In other words, when making personal astrological predictions, you should look for connections between the *position of an important point in your personal horoscope* and the *position of a planet at a particular time since your birth*. This is called a *transiting aspect*, or *transit*. A transit is similar to something moving past the fixed point where you are standing. You may be aware that it is coming before it actually gets to you, and you may also be aware of its presence for a period after it has passed you, but potentially its strongest effect is just when it is passing by you.

Certain transits are like big trucks going by: You are aware of them while they are some distance away, both before and after they pass. Other transiting planets can sneak through without your being consciously aware that something has passed close by, but the effect is going on in unconscious levels.

Transiting planets also pass by at different speeds. The moon zips totally around the zodiac once a month, so it will pass a ***personal important point*** quickly, within a few hours. On the other hand, Pluto (the slowest-moving planet) takes 248 years to circle the zodiac, and therefore its transiting effects can last several years. In general, transits of the faster-moving planets indicate more superficial effects, such as changes in mood or happenings of a fairly unimportant nature. Transits of the slower-moving planets mark major changes in your life.

The slower-moving planets (Uranus, Neptune, and Pluto) can be likened to the bass rhythms, while the faster-moving planets (sun, moon, Mercury, Venus, and Mars) carry the melody. The intermediate speeds of Jupiter and Saturn can be said to tie together the rhythms of the faster and slower planets.

The potential effect of a transiting planet begins when the planet arrives within around 2 degrees on the zodiac circle of a ***personal important point***. (Remember that there are 360 degrees in any circle, so 2 degrees is fairly close to the actual position of the ***personal important point***.) The transiting planet is considered to be effective (called *in orb*) until it is about 2 degrees past the exact position. That means, for example, that if your natal (birth) sun is at 8 degrees of Scorpio, the effects of a transiting planet will begin to be felt when it arrives at about 6 degrees Scorpio. The effects are likely to be strongest when the transiting planet is at 8 degrees, and they will be on the way out when the planet passes 10 degrees.

This range of effectiveness is also true for *angles* between a transiting planet and a **personal important point**. Of course, this 2-degree orb is only an astrologer's rule of thumb, as the influence of certain planets seems to have a wider range. Also, some people seem to feel the transits of certain planets over a wider orb than do other people. With some planets you can be aware of their influence during the whole period they are within orb, whereas others are effective only at a specific time somewhere within that period.

Different angles between two points on the zodiac have different effects, and when the transiting planet is passing in a part of the zodiac where it is not making an effective angle (called an *aspect*) to a **personal important point**, its influence on you personally is not so strong. See the aspect chart on page 108 for an easy way to locate effective aspects to your **personal important points**.

Here are the most important transiting aspects for prediction, with an example of each:

Conjunction

Symbol: ♂

Distance apart: Together (0°)

Example:

In this personal horoscope
Mars (♂) was at 5° Cancer (♋)
at the time of birth.

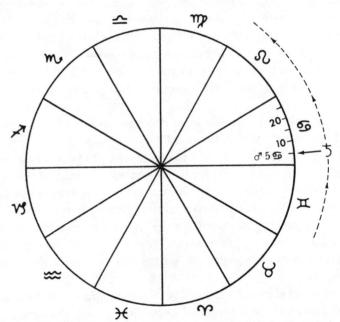

On May 19, 1974, Saturn (♄) arrived at 3° Cancer (♋), in orb of natal Mars (♂). The transit was exact (5°) the first week in June. The effects continued until around June 28, when Saturn went into 8° ♋ , thereby passing beyond the orb of influence, which spans approximately 2° either side of the point where the transit was exact.

Meaning of a transiting conjunction: *Joining together* of the energies of the transiting planet and the ***personal important point***. The conjunction symbolizes a *new beginning* in the relationship between the two energies.

Opposition

Symbol: ☍

Distance apart: Opposite (180°)

Example:

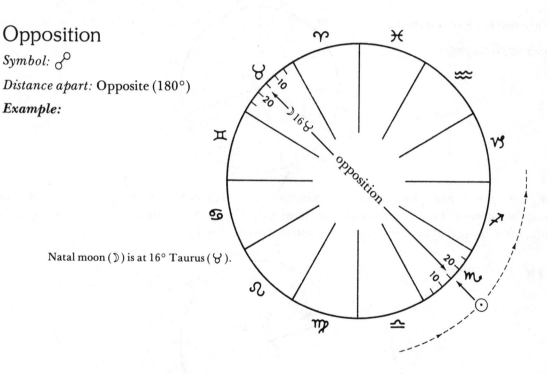

Natal moon (☽) is at 16° Taurus (♉).

On November 6, 1976, the sun (☉) reached 14° Scorpio (♏), in orb of an opposition to natal moon (☽) at 16° Taurus (♉). It was exact (180°) on November 8 and in orb through November 10, when it moved into 18° ♏ .

Meaning of a transiting opposition: *Awareness* of the contrast between the two energies, a confrontation that can be expressed either as conflict or as a fulfillment and integration between the polarized energies.

Square

Symbol: □

Distance apart: Right angle (90°)

Meaning of a transiting square: *Contrast* between the two energies, a *challenge* of your ability to make the right relationship between the two energies.

There are two kinds of squares:

Example of first square:

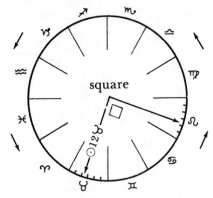

The first square takes place when the transiting planet reaches the first right angle after conjuncting the ***personal important point*** it is transiting. The square marks a testing of elements in your life, often those that began around the time of this conjunction.

Example of last square:

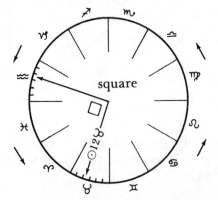

The last square takes place when the transiting planet reaches the last right angle before a conjunction with the ***personal important point*** it is transiting. This square challenges your ability to adapt to a changing situation.

Trine

Symbol: △

Distance apart: One third of the circle (120°)

Meaning of a transiting trine: *Harmonious flow* between the energies of the transiting planet and the **personal important point,** in which you are best able to *combine creatively* the two energies.

There are two kinds of trines:

Example of first trine:

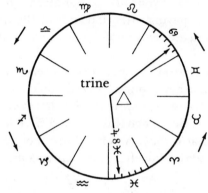

The first trine marks a time of creativeness and smooth flow, particularly in connection with elements in your life which began around the time of the last *conjunction* between the transiting planet and the **personal important point** it is now *trining.*

Example of last trine:

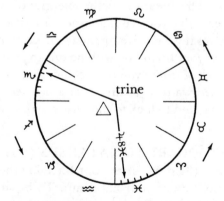

The last trine is much like a first trine. It is also a good time for using the smooth flow between the transiting planet and the **personal important point** that it is transiting in order to ward off possible future problems between the energies they represent.

How the sun "affects" you personally

As the sun goes around the zodiac every year, it acts like a spotlight, focusing on each of your *personal important points*. The sun indicates your *conscious awareness* and your *will*. As it contacts a *personal important point*, you will often find you are paying particular attention to an area of your life represented by this *point* and the parts of your horoscope to which it is related. Often some outside event will bring this area of your life to your attention in a specific way. Or, you may simply feel particularly interested in paying attention to it at the time of the transit. In any case, a sun transit marks *a time when you are better able to focus and concentrate your energies on the area of your life that is spotlighted.*

Each sun transit takes place around the same day every year, since the calendar was constructed to follow the sun's regular journey around the zodiac. Therefore you can expect to receive the effects of each particular sun transit at *approximately the same date every year*. This will not be true of any other transiting planet, since each travels at a different speed.

Sun transits are in orb (that is, have an effect) for about 3 to 5 days. This includes the day they are exact, the day before, and the day after. Let us first consider sun transits to your natal sun.

TRANSITING SUN CONJUNCT NATAL SUN (☉T ☌ ☉N)

Each year on your birthday the sun passes over the same place where it was when you were born. Thus, expressed in astrological language, *the transiting sun is conjunct your natal sun*. Astrologers would write this: ☉T ☌ ☉N. This means that the energies of the day (and to some extent the day before and the day after) can give your consciousness a particular boost. Certainly we all feel the focus of attention on ourselves if we receive birthday gifts or a party is given for us. But even if you should find yourself alone on your birthday, with no one to give you attention, it is a natural time to look at yourself and take stock of where you have come from and where you are going. Like all conjunctions, it is a *new beginning*, a time to turn over a new leaf, to let go of anything from the past that is no longer right for you, and to look to the future with a positive attitude.

TRANSITING SUN FIRST SQUARE TO NATAL SUN (☉T □ ☉N) — *challenging transit*

Approximately three months (91 days) after your birthday the sun will be making its first square (90° angle) to the zodiac position of your natal sun. To be sure of the date, see the Date-Degree Chart on page 29. The energies are flowing at right angles to each other. It is possible that these energies are working at *cross purposes*. On the other hand, this contrast can put a *particularly sharp focus* on some area on which you are concentrating your consciousness and your will. This time marks, in one way or another, a *conscious challenge*, a *testing* of something you are trying to do or of some element in your personality. Often, but not always, this testing is related to something which began around the time of your last birthday. Sometimes the challenge comes in the form of another person, and you will find yourself tempted to engage in ego confrontations because you feel that someone else's energies are frustrating your own direction. The best use of this energy is to make a *sharp appraisal* of the important areas in which you are directing your consciousness and will.

TRANSITING SUN FIRST TRINE TO NATAL SUN ($\odot_T \triangle \odot_N$)—*flowing transit*
Four months after your birthday (about 122 days) the sun will be trining your natal sun. Unless there are challenging transits at the same time, these three days are a period when you should feel particularly well, have more energy, and find that things flow easily for you in any form of creative self-expression. Because your self-confidence will be high, it's a good time to make contacts with anyone with whom you want to relate smoothly. Entertainment, travel, and cultural activities are all favored by this transit. Because a smooth flow in your activities is likely, it's a good time to correct anything that might cause a problem later on.

TRANSITING SUN OPPOSITION TO NATAL SUN ($\odot_T \, \sigma^{\!o} \, \odot_N$)—*challenging transit*
Six months after your birthday (about 182 days) the sun will be opposing your natal sun. This is a time when you have the possibility of being more strongly aware of where you have been directing your consciousness, your creativity, and your will. It can be a period of fulfillment for you, particularly if your energies have been flowing in directions that are right for you. If, however, you have let your energy flow in directions that go against your basic self, this can be a time of obstacles or ego confrontations. These can be between your ego and that of another person or between competing ego drives within yourself. This period presents an opportunity to use your heightened, objective consciousness to find solutions to some of the conflicts in your life.

TRANSITING SUN LAST TRINE TO NATAL SUN ($\odot_T \triangle \odot_N$)—*flowing transit*
This period consists of the three days around eight months after your birthday (about 243 days). Like the first trine, it marks a time of energy and easy flow in your activities. Therefore it is a period of self-confidence, a good time for making contacts and for entertainment, travel, and cultural activities. It's also a good time for "preventive maintenance" in any areas of your life that are running smoothly now but might not continue to do so if you don't prepare for possible problems.

TRANSITING SUN LAST SQUARE TO NATAL SUN (⊙T □ ⊙N) — *challenging transit*

This period consists of the three days around three months (or about 91 days) *before* your birthday. Like the first square, it can be a *testing* both of something you are trying to do and of some area in your personality. Often this testing can be related to projects you are trying to complete while, at the same time, you are looking ahead in future directions. Your challenge during this period is to leap the potential hurdles presented by the square as gracefully as possible and at the same time look ahead to the finish line.

SUN TRANSITS TO OTHER PLANETS

Each year the sun goes through the same series of aspects, not only to its own position in your natal chart but also to the rest of the planets and your other *personal important points*. The starting point of each cycle of transits is the *conjunction*, the time each year when the sun reaches the *zodiac position* of the natal planet or other *personal important point*. Finding this "sun conjunction date" for each of your planets and other *personal important points* is not difficult and does not require difficult mathematics. It is one of the first steps toward making your *Personal Prediction Chart*, which will enable you to keep track of future astrological influences affecting you personally. (We will give more details about constructing this chart as we go along.)

If you have not had your horoscope made, you can determine the approximate degrees of many of your *personal important points* with the charts beginning on page 82 of this book. For more accuracy, you will need a personal horoscope made either by a competent astrologer or by a computer service. You can order a personal computer horoscope for a small fee from the address given on page 159.

Don't be put off by all of the symbols that look like so much Greek on your horoscope. It's not hard to pick out the information you want. Here is a list of what the symbols mean and a typical horoscope that will show you how the information is usually set up:

♈ Aries	♎ Libra	⊙ Sun	♄ Saturn	M.C. Midheaven
♉ Taurus	♏ Scorpio	☽ Moon	♅ Uranus	I.C. Nadir
♊ Gemini	♐ Sagittarius	☿ Mercury	♆ Neptune	R Retrograde
♋ Cancer	♑ Capricorn	♀ Venus	(♀) ♇ Pluto	
♌ Leo	♒ Aquarius	♂ Mars	Asc. Ascendant	
♍ Virgo	♓ Pisces	♃ Jupiter	Desc. Descendant	

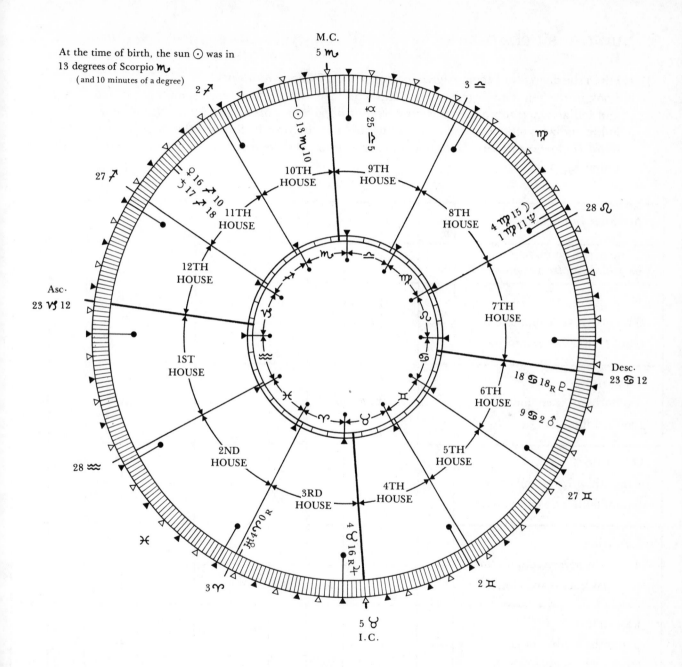

At the time of birth, the sun ☉ was in 13 degrees of Scorpio ♏ (and 10 minutes of a degree)

M.C.
5 ♏

2 ♐

3 ♎

☉ 13 ♏ 10

♅ 25 ♎ 5

27 ♐

♀ 16 ♐ 10
♄ 17 ♐ 18

10TH HOUSE

9TH HOUSE

8TH HOUSE

♏

4 ♍ 15 ☽
1 ♍ 11 ♆

28 ♌

11TH HOUSE

12TH HOUSE

♐

♍

♎

Asc.
23 ♑ 12

7TH HOUSE

1ST HOUSE

♑

♌

Desc.
23 ♋ 12

18 ♋ 18 R ♇

6TH HOUSE

♒

28 ♒

♓

♋

9 ♋ 2 ♂

2ND HOUSE

♈

♉

5TH HOUSE

27 ♊

3RD HOUSE

4TH HOUSE

♓

♅ 4 ♈ 0 R

4 ♉ 16 R ♃

2 ♊

3 ♈

5 ♉
I.C.

27

Sun transit chart

1. Fill in the degree and zodiac sign of each *personal important point*.
2. Look in the sun date-degree chart (opposite page) for the date corresponding to each degree and zodiac sign combination of your *personal important points*, and fill in second line.
3. Fill in zodiac positions and corresponding dates of sun transits for the other aspects to your *personal important points*. Note that in each column the degrees remain the same although the zodiac signs and dates change.

	☉	☽	☿	♀	♂	♃	♄	♅	♆	♇	Asc	MC
personal important point		4♍	25♎	16♐	9♋	4♉	17♐	4♈	1♍	18♋	23♑	5♒
Time of sun conjunction to **personal important point** ☌	11/5	8/27	10/18	12/8	7/1	4/24	12/9	3/24	8/24	7/10	1/13	10/28
First square, ☐ 3 months *after* conjunction	13♒	4♐	25♑	16♓	9♎	4♌	17♓	4♋	1♐	18♎	23♈	5♒
(count 3 lines *down* on chart)	2/2	11/26	1/15	3/7	10/2	7/27	3/8	6/25	11/23	10/11	4/13	1/25
First trine, △ 4 months *after* conjunction	13♓	4♑	25♒	16♈	9♏	4♍	17♈	4♌	1♑	18♏	23♉	5♓
(count 4 lines *down* on chart)	3/4	12/26	2/14	4/6	11/1	8/27	4/7	7/27	12/23	11/10	5/14	2/24
Opposition, ☍ 6 months *after* conjunction	13♉	4♓	25♈	16♊	9♑	4♒	17♊	4♎	1♓	18♑	23♋	5♌
(count 6 lines *down* on chart)	5/4	2/23	4/15	6/7	12/31	10/27	6/8	9/27	2/20	1/8	7/15	4/26
Last trine, △ 4 months *before* conjunction	13♋	4♉	25♊	16♌	9♓	4♑	17♌	4♐	1♉	18♓	23♍	5♋
(count 4 lines *up* on chart)	7/5	4/24	6/16	8/8		12/26	8/9	11/26	4/21	3/9	9/16	6/27
Last square, ☐ 3 months *before* conjunction	13♌	4♊	25♋	16♍	9♈	4♒	17♍	4♑	1♊	18♈	23♎	5♌
(count 3 lines *up* on chart)	8/5	5/25	7/17	9/9	3/30	1/24	9/10	12/26	5/22	4/8	10/16	7/28

Sun date-degree chart

This chart shows the approximate date each year that the sun transits each degree of the zodiac. There are slight variations from year to year, but this chart should not be more than a day or two off, which is adequate for general prediction. To find date the sun will be in a specific zodiac degree, follow column under number (top line) down to intersection with zodiac sign line. Reverse this process to find zodiac degree of sun for any specific date.

Degrees

Sign	0	1	2	3	4	5	6	7	8	9	10	11	12	13	14	15	16	17	18	19	20	21	22	23	24	25	26	27	28	29
♈	March 21	22	23	25	24	26	27	28	29	30	31	April 1	2	3	4	5	6	7	8	9	10	11	12	13	14	15	16	17	18	19
♉	April 20	21	22	23	(24) 25	26	27	28	29	30	May 1	2	3	4	5	6	7	8	9	10	11	12	13	14	15	16	17	18	19	20
♊	May 21	22	23	24	25	26	27	28	29	30	31	June 1	2	(3) 4	5	6	7	8	9	10	11	12	13	14	15	16	17	18	19	20
♋	June 21	22	23	24	(25) 26	27	28	29	30	July 1	2	3	4	5	6	7	8	9	10	11	12	13	14	15	16	17	18	19	20	21
♌	July 22	(24) 23	25	26	27	28	29	30	31	August 1	2	3	4	5	6	7	8	9	10	11	12	13	14	(15) 16	17	18	19	20	21	22
♍	August 23	24	25	26	27	28	29	30	31	September 1	2	3	(4) 5	6	7	8	9	10	11	12	13	14	15	16	17	18	19	20	21	22
♎	September 23	24	25	26	27	28	29	30	October 1	2	3	4	5	6	7	8	9	10	11	12	13	14	15	16	17	18	19	20	21	22
♏	October 23	24	25	26	27	28	29	30	31	November 1	2	3	4	5	6	7	8	9	10	11	12	13	14	15	16	17	18	19	20	21
♐	November 22	23	24	25	26	27	28	29	30	December 1	2	3	4	5	6	7	8	9	10	11	12	13	14	15	16	17	18	19	20	21
♑	December 22	23	24	25	26	27	28	29	30	31	January 1	2	3	4	5	5	6	7	8	9	10	11	12	13	14	15	16	17	18	19
♒	January 20	21	22	23	24	25	26	27	28	29	30	31	February 1	2	3	4	5	6	7	8	9	10	11	12	13	14	15	16	17	18
♓	February 19	20	21	22	23	24	25	26	27	28	March 1	2	3	4	5	6	7	8	9	10	11	12	13	14	15	16	17	18	19	20

How to make and use a sun transit chart

As you determine the zodiac degrees and signs of each of your *personal important points*, list them in the spaces provided below and complete the chart as shown in example on page 28.

	⊙	☽	☿	♀	♂	♃	♄	♅	♆	♇	Asc	MC
personal important point												
Time of sun conjunction to *personal important point* ♂												
First square, ☐ 3 months *after* conjunction (count 3 lines *down* on chart)												
First trine, △ 4 months *after* conjunction (count 4 lines *down* on chart)												
Opposition, ☍ 6 months *after* conjunction (count 6 lines *down* on chart)												
Last trine, △ 4 months *before* conjunction (count 4 lines *up* on chart)												
Last square, ☐ 3 months *before* conjunction (count 3 lines *up* on chart)												

Now that you know the dates each year that the sun makes transiting aspects to your *personal important points*, you will want to know what to expect during each period, which lasts approximately three days (the day before the aspect is exact, the day it is exact, and the day after).

Remember that each planet serves as a *function* in your life, or, in other words, shows *how a part of your personality expresses itself*. Here are keywords for each planet. The following two pages will show you how to put all this information together.

SUN
Will, creativity, center of consciousness (either your ego or a deeper center), men, authority figures, father

MOON
Feelings, instincts, subconscious, functions of the body, women, mother

MERCURY
Thinking, intelligence, memory, senses, written and verbal communication

VENUS
Affections, emotions, personal relationships, likes and dislikes, aesthetic sense

MARS
Forcefulness, vigor, passion, sex drive, initiative, sports, physical energy, anger

JUPITER
Expansion, enthusiasm, optimism, abstraction, wisdom, generosity, extravagance

SATURN
Organization, structuring, practicality, discipline, time sense, contraction, caution, limits

URANUS
Independence, inventiveness, originality, intuition, "out of the blue" events

NEPTUNE
Idealism, inspiration, vision, compassion, devotion, illusion, dreams

PLUTO
Basic change, regeneration, reformulation, collective energy

Following are rules for using the chart of transiting sun aspects to your **personal important points**. If your chart were the one shown on page 27, you would note that around November 26 the transiting sun will be making a first square to your natal moon.

1. Read the keywords for the sun and the moon on page 31.
2. Read the description of squares (page 22) and of a transiting sun first square aspect on page 24.
3. Read the description of sun in Sagittarius on page 14.
4. Read, on page 13, the keywords for Virgo, the sign the moon is in.
5. Think about how the foregoing fits together and the various directions in which the energy combinations could go. Put special emphasis, of course, on positive uses of the energies, since an awareness of these will make it easier to channel the energies in that direction.

For instance, you would note that a square can pose "a challenge of your ability to make the right relationship between the two energies" in this case the sun and the moon. Since it is a first square, the challenge may apply more to energy patterns that are beginning to develop rather than those that have been established. Keywords for the sun are: "will, creativity, center of consciousness (whether your ego or a deeper center), men, authority figures, father." Keywords for the moon are "feelings, instincts, subconscious, functions of the body, women, mother."

The description of the sun in Sagittarius is on page 14. This informs you that it is an expansive time, with emphasis on moving around and "good fellowship." It is a good time to travel and get an overall perspective on things, but the energies may be scattered and the general expansiveness can also mean overindulgence.

The keywords for Virgo (sign of the natal moon) are: "analytical, practical, orderly, perfecting details (and sometimes being overcritical)."

Since the sun is the transiting body, it is posing the challenge to the natal moon.

You can see that a transiting first square from the sun in Sagittarius to natal moon in Virgo has thousands of possibilities. To list a very few:

*   Your father or your boss (sun) might come up with some concepts (Sagittarius) that challenge (square) your instinctual feelings (moon) for how things should be done (Virgo).

*   You might overeat and get indigestion—the Sagittarian expansiveness would be out of step with the Virgo (digesting) moon (functions of body).

- You might be susceptible to an ego (sun) problem (square) with a woman (moon).
- You could focus your will and creativity (sun) on gathering together into an overall understanding (Sagittarius) the various (Virgo) feelings (moon) that you have been registering.

This last possibility shows that it could potentially be a very creative time, either for a project you are working on or for understanding yourself and your relationships a little better. That is, if you can be conscious of, and counteract, some of the less desirable possibilities. Since Thanksgiving comes every year about this time in November, a person whose natal moon is around 3 degrees of Virgo has to be more careful than the rest of us about the possibility of overeating or ego confrontations on Thanksgiving!

When you look ahead to transit conditions, it is important that you get a feeling for the basic energies involved and see how they can be expressed in many different ways. It is even more important that you concentrate on and project the constructive manifestations of the transit, since *every transit has constructive possibilities*. We are all somewhat open to suggestion, and if you let yourself be convinced that a certain transit is bound to be expressed negatively, you can make it do just that. Remember that *square and opposition transits are tests of your ability* to deal with life in some way or other; you might as well set your mind toward passing the test.

As you have seen, transits of the sun take place once a year. Now that you are getting a feeling for working with these transits, the next step is to find out what to expect when the moon, which travels around the zodiac once a month, transits your *personal important points*.

Moon energies

You no doubt have days when "everything's going your way" and other days when you "should have stayed in bed." Or, you may have scheduled a game of tennis, but, when the day comes, feel more like staying home and reading a book. There are days when you feel like diving in and cleaning things out, and other days when you can't stand the thought. Although sometimes a little momentum may get you into the swing of what you have set out to do, there are other times when carrying out your plans just simply goes against the flow of the day.

Can astrology predict the tone of the day? Not completely, of course, but in certain ways, yes. You might think of it as if astrology could tell you what musical numbers the cosmic orchestra was planning to play and just when each piece would begin. You would then be able to plan your own personal "dance" in step with the cosmic rhythms. Some of these rhythms are general to the whole earth, and others have a very personal effect on you because of the way they interact with the *rhythm of your personal astrological chart*.

Cosmic rhythms that change from day to day, or even during the day, are most likely to be moon rhythms. The moon moves faster than the sun or any of the planets. It is also closest to the earth, and it is the only heavenly body that goes around the earth. Besides this, it goes through the most noticeable changes. In actual size the moon is tiny compared with the sun, but since it is so much closer, the gravitational force it exerts on the earth is two and one-half times that of the sun.

It also seems as if the moon exerts more force than the sun in certain other energies that we have not yet learned to measure with scientific instruments. In primitive cultures all over the world the moon's influence is considered to outweigh that of the sun in many ways and there is much similarity in the kind of influences attributed to the moon deity, who is worshipped usually as a goddess but occasionally as a god. This deity has been called Isis, Eleusis, Luna, Selene, Diana, Mary, and many other names.

Until fairly recently the scientific community has paid little attention to lunar effects. Everyone understands, of course, that the moon is the chief cause of the tides. Most people are also aware that the moon has some influence on the breeding cycle of certain animals, the crime rate, and periods of excitement in mental hospitals. At the present time more scientific investigators are becoming interested in lunar effects, and they are continually uncovering further interesting—and often unexpected—connections between the moon and activities here on earth.

We will show you how to find the moon's position easily to the year 2000. Knowing the moon's position, you will learn to observe and work with different kinds of moon influence:

- **Moonphases:** new, crescent, first quarter, gibbous, full, disseminating, last quarter, balsamic

- *Eclipses,* of either the moon or the sun
- *Moonsigns:* the influence of each sign of the zodiac as the moon passes through it
- *Personal:* how the moon influences your personal astrological chart.

After you follow the moon for a few months, you will begin to feel—and flow with, in a positive way—moon rhythms.

Moonphases

From the viewpoint of earth the moon (which orbits the earth) as well as all the planets (which orbit the sun) travel along the "sky highway" we call the *zodiac*. Also, the sun appears to traverse this band. The moon goes all the way around the zodiac in slightly less than a month. It makes about thirteen complete circuits a year, the time the sun takes to make one circuit. (Actually it is the earth that traverses the zodiac as it goes around the sun, but we are not directly aware of our own motion.)

You could think of the sun as the hour hand of a clock and the moon as the minute hand. The two hands come together at twelve o'clock. In the time it takes the minute hand (moon) to go around the dial, the hour hand (sun) reaches one o'clock, and the two hands next come together at about five minutes past one. In the next cycle they conjoin when both hands are pointing toward the number 2, and so on.

Each time the moon passes the position of the sun, we see none of the moon's bright side, and we call this a *new moon*.

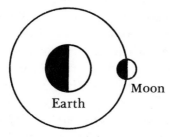

Earth / Moon

Sun

Two weeks after each new moon we again have a lineup of the sun, earth, and moon. This time, however, the earth is in the middle, and therefore we are seeing the moon from the same viewpoint as the sun is shining on it. This is a *full moon*; we see all of the moon's bright side.

The cycle of the moon (from new, to full, and back again to new) is a recurring pattern of *moonphases*. The new moon, which is the first moonphase, is a coming together of energies or a *new beginning*. The sun and the moon are *pulling together* in their influence on earth. Following the new moon is a buildup of energy (*waxing*) to the full moon, the moonphase of greatest intensity. At that time, from the standpoint of earth, the sun and moon are opposite each other.

The full moon is followed by a gradual lessening (*waning*) of this intensity back again to a new moon coming-together. The other moonphases occur during the waxing and waning periods. Workings of this pattern have been documented in the myths of many cultures, and scientific investigation has uncovered evidence that demonstrates, in a less poetic but more factual way, some of the effects of this cycle.

As you learn to understand the energies of the different phases of the moon, you will be more able to work with nature in applying them to your life. Naturally it is not always possible to postpone each activity until the most appropriate moonphase comes along, and you should never become a slave to this kind of routine. Nevertheless, things work better when you flow with the cosmic currents, and this principle can be applied in many areas.

In the next few pages we will tell you characteristics of each of the eight moonphases and what activities correspond to them. To use this information to best advantage, look up the moonphase for today (or any future date that interests you) in the sun and moon calendars beginning on page 82. Then check the moonphase description, its keynote, and best activities for this moonphase. With this information hopefully you can use the time (insofar as you have the choice) for the appropriate activities.

In addition to the moonphase, if you take into consideration the moonsign, (see page 42), you can coordinate the moon energies with your activities even better. The moonphase descriptions apply to the general atmosphere of the period, but in the moonsign section you will find more specific suggestions for use of the energies.

Each month when the moonphase is the same as the moonphase under which you were born, you are especially tuned into the moonphase rhythm.

New moon ●

The sun and the moon are in the same place in the sky, uniting their forces. This is a time when the sun, which represents consciousness, and the moon, which represents the instincts or the unconscious, operate on the same wavelength. In mythology this is when the sun, the male principle, gives to the moon, the female, its life energy. Now you are in touch *not* with the bright side of the moon, which is *reflected* sun energy, but with its dark side, energies of a more subjective nature. This is a time when your conscious and unconscious forces unite for a *new beginning*.

New moon keynote: Begin

Good time to: think about who you are and where you are going here and now. Start a new activity, hobby, relationship, job, trip, or study project. Turn over a new leaf; make plans. Plant seeds in the soil or in the mind.

Avoid: being impulsive or supersensitive.

Crescent moon ☽

The moon has moved enough ahead of the sun so that you can see, just after sunset, a sliver of its bright side, a promise of the fullness to come. That which was begun at the new moon begins to develop its individuality. Energy is beginning to rise, and you should be feeling urges to assert, to do, and to work out details.

Crescent moon keynote: Be creative

Good time to: be confident and inventive, assert new ideas, have faith in yourself. Develop a new activity and begin to work out the details.

Avoid: being overconfident, too assertive, egotistical, foolhardy.

First quarter moon °

You can now see half of the moon's bright side, since the moon and sun are at right angles to the earth (90° degrees apart). This is an energetic moonphase that creates a dynamic tension impelling you to action and challenge.

First quarter moon keynote: Be active

Good time to: work, launch a new activity, challenge the old, build for the future, overcome obstacles, try your skills.

Avoid: being impatient, too assertive, overactive, ruthless, determined to get your egotistical way.

Gibbous moon °

The moon is approaching fullness, and you can see most of its bright side, although it does not yet appear totally round. The energy is continuing to build, and you can instinctively sense the coming peak of energy and light. It is a time when you should begin to have a sense of understanding more clearly.

Gibbous moon keynote: Be aware

Good time to: think about how things relate to each other and what they mean. Clarify your goals, ask "why," and visualize your dreams. Tie the pieces together. Reach an understanding with someone.

Avoid: expecting too much, expecting not enough, being too skeptical.

Full moon °

Now the moon is round and filled with light. It rises as the sun sets, and earth is in the middle between the two energies. The dynamic tension and the energy reach a peak, and your instinctual self is likely to be strong and often restless. At the same time, since your sun-consciousness and moon-instincts are, so to speak, at opposite poles, you have the opportunity to *see clearly*, to be objective, to reach a sense of balance or wholeness about whatever you turn your attention to.

Full moon keynote: See clearly

Good time to: think about wholeness, fulfillment, the larger picture. Keep a balance between con-sciousness and instincts. Understand relationships and whatever you have been working on.

Avoid: Being too perfectionistic, losing track of realities, being pulled in opposite directions, overindulging or giving way to instincts you might later regret.

Disseminating moon °

The light of the moon has begun to wane, and although you can still see most of its bright side, it no longer appears totally round. The energies of this moonphase are conducive to tying together the insights of the full moon and *demonstrating*, or *sharing with others*, what you have realized.

Disseminating moon keynote: Tie things together

Good time to share with others, teach, learn, synthesize, demonstrate, advertise.

Avoid: Shoving your ideas down someone's throat, talking too much, drawing conclusions before you have all the facts.

Last quarter moon °

Now you can see half of the waning moon's bright side, since it again is at right angles to the sun. The energies of this moonphase tend toward *action*. This includes *applying* what you have learned as well as *reformulating* your plans with an eye to the future. In the last quarter you can consolidate what you have gained rather than strike out in new directions.

Last quarter moon keynote: Reformulate

Good time to: systematize, organize yourself, apply principles you have learned, build for the future, harvest.

Avoid: being unconventional just to be different, stubborn, oversensitive about criticism.

Balsamic moon ☾

The waning moon now appears as a crescent just before dawn. The cycle is ending as the moon approaches a new conjunction with the sun. The energy of this moonphase is to finish things up and to dream of, or begin to project, what might develop in the coming new cycle.

Balsamic moon keynote: Dream

Good time to: think about your deepest dreams and look to the future. Finish things up.

Avoid: being too unrealistic or fanatical.

Eclipses

SUN ECLIPSES

At the time of most new moons the moon passes by the sun without being closely in line with it. However, when the sun, moon, and earth are exactly in a straight line, the moon obscures the sun, from the vantage point of earth, and we have an eclipse of the sun.

The effect of a sun eclipse is in some ways like a particularly intense new moon. However, there is also a difference, especially if you happen to be in the eclipse path (that is, on the part of the earth where the eclipse is visible). As in any new moon, the sun (consciousness) and the moon (instincts) have come together on the same astrological "wavelength." In an eclipse, however, the light of the sun is temporarily obscured, and we receive its effects filtered, so to speak, through the moon. This puts increased emphasis on *instinctual reactions* and helps explain why in ancient times sun eclipses were associated with upsurges of instinctive reactions on the part of the masses. So far as we know, no one has yet tried to make physiological measurements of changes in instinctual reactions during eclipses, but there is scientific evidence of changes in blood samples taken from the same people before a sun eclipse, during the eclipse, and just after it. This test, the Takata reaction to determine speed of flocculation of the albumen in the blood, also changes at other times, such as dawn and periods of unusually large numbers of sunspots, indicating that certain changes in the human blood are directly connected with changes in the sun's radiation.

Since it was believed that during a sun eclipse a dragon or some other malevolent spirit was swallowing the sun, the element of fear was strongly emphasized and the mass instinctive reaction tended to be predominantly on the negative side. Among the dire effects believed to be caused by a sun eclipse were war, drought, death of great men or kings (represented by the sun), pestilence, famine, murders, dissension, and calamity in general. A great many eclipses seem to have happened during the great military battles of the ancient world. It is to be noted that whichever army kept its cool and was not panicked by the awesome apparition of the eclipse, usually went on to victory. And in some cases an eclipse actually halted a battle and led to peace being hastily concluded.

In modern times most people understand that an eclipse is a natural phenomenon; they know that the sun is not being eaten up by an invisible dragon but will be shining as brightly as ever when the eclipse ends after a few minutes. Since astronomy can predict eclipses with extreme accuracy and since they are widely publicized, mass fear of the unknown is not projected by human beings except possibly in remote and very primitive areas. Thus, the emotional "atmosphere" of an eclipse is different today, and we have more opportunity, both collectively and individually, to experience the instinctual upsurge of a sun eclipse *in a positive way*. In fact, many people today are *too* conscious, too identified with their sunselves, and can, potentially, use the opportunity of a sun eclipse to get back in touch with their deeper instincts.

The duration of a sun eclipse, particularly if you are in a part of the world where it is visible, is a special time for tuning into your own center as expressed through your intuition.

MOON ECLIPSES

At least twice a year (at full moon) the sun, earth, and moon are so exactly lined up that the earth cuts off the sunlight from the moon and we have a lunar eclipse, visible over half the earth.

A moon eclipse intensifies the normal full moon effects, adding a special effect at the actual time of the eclipse. The light of the moon, which we on earth are getting in its fullest force, is cut off for a short period. At the time of greatest intensity the light circuit is broken, and we are looking not at the moon's permanent dark side, but at its light side *temporarily dark*. The time when the moon is receiving no light from the sun is a time, like a sun eclipse, when the moon, representing our instincts and intuitions, does not transmit through the reflected light of sun consciousness. The moon's influence while it is eclipsed comes directly from its temporarily dark surface. During a sun eclipse the two energies come from the same place in the zodiac, the same "wavelength." During a moon eclipse, however, the sun and moon are on opposite sides of the earth, in opposite signs, and either the conscious (sun) and instinctual (moon) energies are balanced in a special equilibrium or else they will pull in opposite directions.

Ancient astrologers predicted various calamities as effects of moon eclipses, similar to what was expected for sun eclipses. Today, since we accept moon eclipses as natural phenomena, we are in a better position to turn the strong energies of a moon eclipse in positive directions.

Like a sun eclipse, a moon eclipse is a time to tune into your own center of consciousness as expressed through your intuition. (See sun and moon calendars for eclipses.)

Moonsigns

The sun spends a month in each zodiac sign, but the moon travels through it in only two and one-half days. If you follow the moon around the zodiac for a few months, you will learn to recognize the somewhat subtle moonsign influence, which works more on unconscious than on conscious levels. One good way to become conscious of moonsign differences is to compare the atmospheres of social gatherings in different moonsigns. In certain moonsigns everyone will be more reserved, and it will be harder to "break the ice." In other moonsigns the atmosphere can be warm, even exuberant, from the beginning. Of course, the zodiac signs and aspects of the sun and planets also have an effect on "atmospheres," but the moonsign is a major influence.

The general characteristics of each zodiac sign are described in the section beginning on page 10. Remember that the moon represents the instincts and the unconscious and therefore the influence of the sign will tend to be under the surface. See also the wheel in the front of the book for some suggestions for the kinds of activities that flow well with the moon energies in each sign.

Personal moon transits

The moon moves so quickly that moon transits in connection with your *personal important points* usually last only two or three hours. These are primarily expressed as mood changes, momentary contacts with other people, and unconscious or instinctual reactions in connection with the *personal important point* being activated. Here are some things to look for each month as the moon aspects your *personal important points*. Of course, different aspects (see page 20) will make these transits manifest differently. To determine the times of these contacts, see page 106.

MOON TRANSITING SUN

This cycle is somewhat like your own personal moonphase cycle, with the "new moon" coming when the moon passes over the zodiac position of your natal sun, the "full moon" when the moon is opposite your natal sun, etc. Emphasis is on consciousness.

MOON TRANSITING MOON

The time when the transiting moon passes over the zodiac position of your natal moon sets the trend to some extent for the emotional tone of the coming month. It's a time to pause and center your feelings in a good place.

MOON TRANSITING MERCURY

Your thinking and communicating are particularly tied in with your feelings.

MOON TRANSITING VENUS

You should have pleasant contacts. The time is good for social activities and the arts.

MOON TRANSITING MARS

You are likely to have a lot of energy, but sometimes you will be impulsive. Avoid irritability.

MOON TRANSITING JUPITER

You feel expansive and self-confident. Don't expand yourself by overindulging.

MOON TRANSITING SATURN

Your patience and ability to work should be good, but avoid temporary feelings of isolation.

MOON TRANSITING URANUS

Expect something exciting emotionally, quick mood changes, restlessness.

MOON TRANSITING NEPTUNE

You are particularly sensitive and sympathetic to what's going on around you, somewhat dreamy.

MOON TRANSITING PLUTO

This transit adds a passing intensity of feelings that should be kept in perspective.

MOON TRANSITING ASCENDANT

There will be an increased emotional element, whether positive or negative, in any relationship.

MOON TRANSITING MIDHEAVEN

There will be an increased feeling component in your work and/or your dealings with the public.

Predicting with the "other" planets

Each planet (as mentioned earlier) corresponds to different functions and future possibilities in your life. Astrologers may for convenience call the sun and the moon *planets*., However, in the older terminology these two bodies were known as *lights*; they refer particularly to your *conscious awareness* (the sun) and your *instinctual awareness* (the moon). The planets from Mercury on out relate to more specific functions in your life.

Mercury ☿ and Venus ♀ have orbits closer to the sun than that of the earth. Mars ♂ has an orbit just outside ours. These three planets are sometimes called the *personal planets* because their zodiac positions and aspects *indicate how you express yourself as an individual.*

Jupiter ♃ and Saturn ♄ whose orbits are beyond that of Mars, indicate more abstract elements in your makeup; and Uranus ♅, Neptune ♆, and Pluto ♇ indicate even deeper influences that you share with others born about the same period. The influence of these outer planets can seem to come from deep inside you or from events in the outside world. Of course, the natal positions of the planets indicate your basic makeup and their *transiting* positions indicate the current influence on you.

Retrograde planets

Unlike the sun and the moon, the planets (Mercury through Pluto) spend part of their time *retrograde*, which means that, *from the standpoint of earth*, they appear to move backward in the zodiac. Of course, all the time they are actually moving forward in the zodiac *from the standpoint of the sun.*

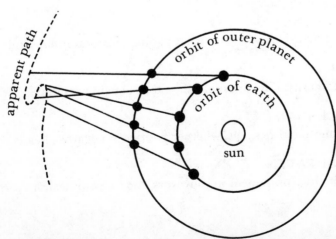

When a planet is retrograde, its influence comes from a particular area of the zodiac for a longer period than usual. The effect of a retrograde planet can be thought of as a kind of *reverse flow* of its normal action. This influences us all, but the effects are more marked for people who have a **personal important point** that the planet is aspecting during its retrograde period. If the transiting planet is *stationary* within 2 degrees either side of exact aspect to a **personal important point,** the effects are especially marked. A planet is stationary first when it comes to a stop (after going forward in the zodiac) and turns retrograde. It makes another station when it comes to a stop after going backward; then it turns forward again. You can find these retrograde periods in the planet charts beginning on page 108. In the chapter for each planet you can find some things to look for when the planet is making a retrograde transit.

A planet sometimes makes *three* transits within orb of one of your **personal important points**: first, it crosses the transit point before it turns retrograde; second', during its retrograde period it recrosses the transit point; third, after turning direct it again crosses the transit point.

Here are more details for each of the "other" planets.

Mercury energies ☿

The movement of Mercury around the zodiac is connected with *how we communicate* (both verbally and in writing), *how we think, what we remember,* and *how our senses are operating*. In society as a whole it is connected with such functions as *commerce, negotiations, the news.*

Mercury is the planet nearest the sun, and, from the point of view of earth, it never gets very far from the sun, appearing either in the same zodiac sign, the sign just before, or the sign just after. It usually stays in a sign about two weeks, but around its retrograde periods it can spend up to six weeks in a sign.

Retrograde periods of Mercury mean that thinking and communications tend to be slower and somewhat confused. It seems easier to make mistakes and harder to make up one's mind. It can be harder for people to come to agreements in negotiations, and if they do, misunderstandings are more likely to arise later. Although many astrology books advise against signing contracts or making other important decisions while Mercury is retrograde, we do not feel that everyone should avoid negotiations of any sort or that all lawyers should close up shop during these periods. However, during the retrograde periods of Mercury it is well to be even more cautious than usual in communications, negotiations, and contracts.

As Mercury moves through a zodiac sign, the sign's qualities seem to modify to some extent the manner of our communications, thinking, and other Mercurial activities. As you come more and more to understand the nature of each zodiac sign, you will be increasingly able to recognize the effect on each planet as it transits through the "influence field" of a particular sign. You can increase your understanding of these effects by rereading the descriptions of each sign beginning on page 10 and pondering on how these sign energies would apply to Mercury. To help you get a feeling for it, what follows are some things to look for as Mercury makes the zodiac circuit:

MERCURY IN ARIES
Communications and thinking tend to speed up, senses are keen, and what people say may have more of an edge to it. Use this mental energy for exploring new areas of thought. Avoid a tendency to argue and make snap judgments.

MERCURY IN TAURUS
Thoughts and communications may slow down somewhat but they usually can be followed through to practical conclusions. Visualization is easier. Avoid stubbornness in your ideas.

MERCURY IN GEMINI
Thoughts speed up again and go in many directions. Curiosity, cleverness, talkativeness, nervous energy are more marked. Avoid letting your mind get too scattered.

MERCURY IN CANCER
Minds are more impressionable, less logical. Senses and memory are sharper. Don't let emotional influences cloud your thinking.

MERCURY IN LEO
Thoughts get grander, more personally directed, sometimes with a touch of the dramatic. You can think creatively, but keep your ideas flexible.

MERCURY IN VIRGO
This position of Mercury is good for analytical, detailed, and practical thinking. Avoid being over-critical and losing track of the broader view.

MERCURY IN LIBRA
This is a time when judgment tends to be more balanced and communications pleasant. Avoid indecision and not saying what you mean because you don't want to rock boats.

MERCURY IN SCORPIO

Thoughts and senses are more penetrating and intuitive, although there is a tendency for reserve in communicating them. Avoid stubbornness and sarcasm.

MERCURY IN SAGITTARIUS

Thoughts and communications range wide, with emphasis on overall viewpoints. People tend to express themselves more frankly. Avoid jumping to conclusions and ignoring the details.

MERCURY IN CAPRICORN

Thoughts can be concentrated, methodical, and practical. Communications tend to be a bit on the serious side. Don't lose track of your imagination.

MERCURY IN AQUARIUS

Thinking can be unique and inventive, breaking new ground. More cooperation is emphasized, but care is needed to avoid being overabrupt and opinionated.

MERCURY IN PISCES

Senses and ideas have "softer edges," with imagination and poetry flowing more naturally. Sensitivity to all impressions is stronger. Avoid being too impressionable and letting your imagination go beyond a balance.

Personal predicting with Mercury

When Mercury makes a transiting aspect to one of your *personal important points,* it seems to activate thought, memory, your senses, or some kind of communication in connection with this *personal important point.* Sometimes this can come from the outside, such as meeting someone, a letter, or a phone call. Other times you may find that your thoughts seem to be drawn to an area of your life that is associated with the *personal important point* receiving the Mercury transit.

Mercury is the chameleon of the planets, and when it interacts with another planet, it seems, more than any other planet, to take on the characteristics of the planet it is relating with. However, in all transits there tends to be some distinction between which planet is doing the transiting and which planet is being transited. Since the planets move at different speeds, one difference is the amount of time the transit lasts. In addition, although basically you are dealing with an interaction between the two planets, remember that the transiting planet is *acting on* your natal *personal im-*

portant point. Of course, any transiting planet can also act on other *personal important points,* such as your ascendant or midheaven.

Since Mercury usually moves between 1 and 2 degrees a day, its transits to *personal important points* normally last around two or three days. If it is stationary in aspect to a *personal important point* (just before or after a retrograde period), the transit can last almost two weeks.

If Mercury is aspecting a *personal important point* while retrograde, particularly with a square or opposition, consider putting off major decisions (if you can reasonably do so) until it goes direct again.

You can find when Mercury will make transiting aspects to your *personal important points* in the same way you found the personal transits of the sun and the moon. First, look in the Mercury charts in the back of the book, beginning on page 108, to find where in the zodiac it will be at the time in which you are interested. Then, in the Aspect Chart on page 108, check the positions of your *personal important points* for aspects from Mercury's transiting position in the zodiac. Fill in this data on the Personal Prediction Chart on page 79.

To help you forecast what kinds of conditions to expect during Mercury transits, here are some hints as to how it combines with each *personal important point:*

MERCURY—SUN
There is conscious focus on thinking, communications, and sense impressions. Avoid expressions of ego.

MERCURY—MOON
Your thinking can be in touch with your feelings and memories, and you can express what you feel. Don't lose track of logic.

MERCURY—MERCURY
Communications, thinking, and planning are emphasized, and it's a good time for working with the specifics. Avoid overthink.

MERCURY—VENUS
Pleasant communications, thoughts, diplomacy, adaptability are all likely. It's a good time for discussions but not hard decisions.

MERCURY — MARS

There are energetic, sometimes excitable communications. The mind is keen, the wits quick; it is a good time for analysis. Avoid arguments.

MERCURY — JUPITER

Your viewpoint is broad; you can connect specifics to the larger picture. Avoid excessive talking and thinking, and repeating yourself.

MERCURY — SATURN

Thinking and communications can be disciplined and organized, with a good deal of realism. Avoid depressing thoughts or an unwarranted sense of isolation.

MERCURY — URANUS

This is a time for inventive, far-out thoughts, with a fast tempo. There are likely to be unexpected communications. Stay calm and keep your reactions in proportion.

MERCURY — NEPTUNE

These transits stimulate imagination, poetry, and fantasy. This is a good time for expression of artistic and subtle feelings. Avoid confusion, daydreaming, and overidealizing.

MERCURY — PLUTO

Thoughts and communications can be penetrating, sometimes bringing up hidden elements. Avoid compulsive thinking and unnecessary confrontations with the ideas of others.

MERCURY — ASCENDANT

These transits increase thinking about and communicating with other people; this is a good time for learning. It is also good for negotiations, but avoid debates.

MERCURY — MIDHEAVEN

These transits stimulate thinking and communications about career and home. Keep the two in balance.

INFLUENCE OF ASPECTS IN MERCURY TRANSITS

As you consider a Mercury transit to a *personal important point*, keep in mind the following differences between the aspects:

☌ **Conjunctions**   focus thought, senses, and communications

☐ **Squares**   contrast various thoughts and communications

△ **Trines**   smooth thoughts and communications

☍ **Oppositions**   emphasize either conflict or balance in thoughts and communications

As an example let us consider Mercury transits to Neptune (♆):

Transiting Mercury conjunct natal Neptune (☿$_T$ ☌ ♆$_N$) is good for studying or communicating in the arts, particularly those things that are subtle or mysterious. However, you might not express yourself very precisely, and you should watch that your imagination doesn't get out of hand.

Transiting Mercury square natal Neptune (☿$_T$ ☐ ♆$_N$) is also a good time for studying and communicating subtle or out-of-this-world subjects in the realms of ideas, art, religion, etc. However, you may be especially open to daydreaming, confusions and misunderstandings, and distortions of the truth.

Transiting Mercury trine natal Neptune (☿$_T$ △ ♆$_N$) is a transit in which your imagination, creativity, and understanding of the ideal and the mystical is increased. You are also likely to be particularly sympathetic. It's not likely to be a time when your discipline is good.

Transiting Mercury opposition natal Neptune (☿$_T$ ☍ ♆$_N$) is a time when your sensitivities to the subtle elements in life and nature are greatly increased. However, you must guard against things not being clear in your communications, either on your part or that of the other person.

For each transit of Mercury to your *personal important points* that you have forecast, think about:

1. the influence of the zodiac sign Mercury is in (page 46) and the influence of the zodiac sign your *personal important point* is in
2. how the energies of Mercury can combine in your life with the *personal important point* it is transiting
3. how the transiting aspect could modify these energies (page 19)
4. In light of the above, how the energies can best be used and what you should be careful of during this transit.

Venus energies ♀

As Venus moves around the zodiac, its transits indicate *what we are attracted to, what we draw toward us, how our creativity, our tastes, and our affections are being expressed.* Venus is particularly connected with *social affairs, relationships, beauty.* Generally its transits are pleasant and enjoyable.

Like Mercury, Venus is also nearer the sun than the earth is, and therefore it never gets very far from the sun's zodiac position. It is rarely farther away than one sign on either side of the sunsign. It usually stays in a sign slightly less than a month, but during its retrograde periods it can remain as long as four months. When Venus is retrograde, it is a time for reconsidering and reevaluating whatever and whoever is attracting you.

The zodiac sign through which Venus is transiting seems to have an influence on the atmosphere that surrounds relationships, whether two people or a group. It should also be connected with the kinds of things you enjoy doing, the music, art, colors, and forms you are attracted to at a given time. It is connected with the values you are currently emphasizing.

Think how the zodiac sign descriptions (beginning on page 10) would apply to the "Venus function."

Some thumbnail sketches of the characteristics of Venus in each sign follow:

VENUS IN ARIES
You feel like going after what attracts you, whether people or possessions. Don't go too far.

VENUS IN TAURUS

You particularly appreciate good food, good friends, and any other good or beautiful object or activity. Don't overeat.

VENUS IN GEMINI

You enjoy meeting more people and could crave more variety in food and entertainment. Don't spread yourself too thin.

VENUS IN CANCER

The emphasis here is on good eating, family, fixing up your home. Don't spend time needed for the present in reminiscing about the past.

VENUS IN LEO

There's a lot of warmth between people now, as well as a stronger need to express yourself creatively in some way. Don't overspend.

VENUS IN VIRGO

Increased appreciation of order may be evident, including cleaning things up and repairs. Your tastes may be for very specific things. Avoid being too finicky.

VENUS IN LIBRA

There is increased appreciation of anything beautiful and increased enjoyment of individual and social relationships. Don't be too diplomatic.

VENUS IN SCORPIO

The desire intensity gets stronger. Hidden feelings can come to the surface. Keep emotions in balance.

VENUS IN SAGITTARIUS

There is more openness toward all sorts of people and a tendency to be more outspoken. Tastes might run toward vivid colors. Another period to watch overindulging.

VENUS IN CAPRICORN

People are less outgoing, somewhat drawn to more serious pursuits, and sometimes seeking solitude. Don't curb your expression of affection.

VENUS IN AQUARIUS

This is another social time, with emphasis on the exchange of ideas. You may want to buy or try something very different. It might be okay, but think twice about it.

VENUS IN PISCES

Fantasy and daydreams are particularly evident. You may have increased sympathy for others. People may be oversensitive.

Personal predicting with Venus

Generally the transits of Venus to your *personal important points* are pleasant happenings. They normally last two or three days, but when Venus is stationary while transiting a *personal important point,* the influence can last up to two weeks.

To find when Venus will make transiting aspects to your *personal important points,* see the Venus charts beginning on page 108. Proceed with Venus as you did with Mercury by filling in your Personal Prediction Charts. Here are some hints as to how Venus combines with each *personal important point:*

VENUS—SUN

Attention may be attracted to yourself. This transit may mark a social occasion for you. You may hear from a friend. You may be particularly creative.

VENUS—MOON

You may be affectionate, or you may be dreamy. This occasion is good either for social gatherings or for staying home and enjoying good food.

VENUS—MERCURY

You can express yourself well and diplomatically. These transits are another combination for good communications and relationships.

VENUS—VENUS

Any transits of Venus to itself are good for personal relationships, social contacts, and the arts. You may enjoy pleasant and sympathetic feelings.

VENUS—MARS

These transits add a spark to your personality; they can be stimulating sexually, creatively, or socially.

VENUS—JUPITER

These are "lucky" transits, good for relationships, finances, social activity, creativity. However, watch for overindulging or overspending.

VENUS—SATURN

You might feel somewhat reserved in your relationships. These transits can add proportion and practicality to creative projects.

VENUS—URANUS

These transits can add an unexpected or exciting element to your personal relationships, social affairs, or creative projects.

VENUS—NEPTUNE

These transits add inspiration to your creativity and romantic relationships. They are better for fantasy and daydreaming than for practical work.

VENUS—PLUTO

This is a time of intensity in relationships, particularly sexual. There is also the possibility of tapping deep creative energies.

VENUS—ASCENDANT

These transits are good for personal relationships, entertaining, and fun. You are likely to make a favorable impression on anyone you are with.

VENUS—MIDHEAVEN

These transits are good for personal or group relationships and creativity, particularly in regard to your work.

Mars energies ♂

Mars is the energizer of the planets. You could think of its transits in terms of *where and how personal horsepower can be applied.* This power can work physically, emotionally, or in thinking.

Mars is the first planet whose orbit is outside that of earth, and it takes about two years to circle the zodiac. It usually spends about six weeks in a sign, but when retrograde can stay up to six months. Retrograde periods of Mars can be marked by a reconsideration of actions, a delving below the surface of anything, or delays.

The zodiac sign it is passing through will show you something about how Mars energy is currently inclined to manifest: quickly or slowly, in bursts or steadily, focused or diffused. Each zodiac sign description (beginning on page 10) will give you general material to apply to Mars as it moves around the zodiac. Also, here are some particulars to note about how Mars energy manifests:

MARS IN ARIES
Quickly and strongly, in bursts, focused.

MARS IN TAURUS
Slowly, steadily and strongly, relatively focused.

MARS IN GEMINI
Quickly, somewhat lightly, flitting from here to there, focusing briefly wherever directed.

MARS IN CANCER
Somewhat slowly, in rhythm or in phases, diffused, emotionally influenced.

MARS IN LEO
Slowly, steadily, focused, consciously.

MARS IN VIRGO
Fairly quickly and methodically but flexibly, practically, sharply focused.

MARS IN LIBRA
Cooperatively, rhythmically, influenced by both thinking and feeling.

MARS IN SCORPIO
Intensely, either quickly or slowly, steadily, strongly focused.

MARS IN SAGITTARIUS
Quickly, in bursts, diffused, physical activity strong.

MARS IN CAPRICORN
Slowly, steadily, methodically, focused.

MARS IN AQUARIUS
Slowly but with sudden and unexpected changes of direction, cooperatively, influenced by thought.

MARS IN PISCES
Slowly, variably, quite diffused, emotionally influenced.

Personal predicting with Mars

Mars adds *energy* to any *personal important point* it aspects. In one way or another it revs up the motor and increases the power available to you. If you are aware of this extra power, you can use it to get things done and to break through situations of inertia that have been holding you back. However, if you are not conscious that a Mars transit is activating you, the energy, which must come out somewhere, may be expressed in negative ways: you may be embroiled in ego battles or you may be accident prone simply through carelessness and irregular rhythm in what you are doing. If you have been bottling up anger, it is particularly likely to burst out during a Mars transit. This is especially true of Mars squares and oppositions to *personal important points*. Therefore, if you see a challenging Mars aspect coming, center yourself ahead of time and plan good uses of the energy gift.

Mars transits usually last four or five days, but when it is moving slowly in connection with a retrograde period, a transit can continue up to approximately a month. The transits of certain planets seem to have an influence through the whole period they are in orb, but sometimes the effect of a Mars transit will be focused at a certain time, usually before the aspect is exact, and not felt during the rest of the period it is in orb.

The charts that will tell you when Mars makes transiting aspects to your *personal important points* begin on page 111. You can fill this information in on your Personal Prediction Charts.

Here are some things to look for as Mars combines with each *personal important point:*

MARS—SUN
These transits are marked by high energies, initiative, and confidence. Watch out for ego.

MARS—MOON
This is a time of emotional intensity and restlessness. Avoid irritability and undue self-protectiveness.

MARS—MERCURY
These transits are good for working with your mind and for decisiveness. Avoid being argumentative.

MARS—VENUS
These transits are good for sports, sex, creativity. Don't be too impulsive.

MARS—MARS
The transits of Mars to itself are characterized by strong energy, self-confidence, assertiveness. Work off some of the energy in physical activity and don't be too rash.

MARS—JUPITER
This is a time of energy, opportunity, and enterprise. Don't overextend your activities, but do get some physical exercise.

MARS—SATURN
These transits are good for planning, patience, and exacting work. Don't feel frustrated if your energy level is lower.

MARS—URANUS
These transits are good for starting a new activity, but expect the unexpected and keep centered to avoid being accident prone.

MARS—NEPTUNE
This time is good for meditating or helping others, although your energy level may be low and you may feel somewhat inadequate.

MARS—PLUTO
Now is a good time to dive in and change conditions that need changing, but be wary of possibly strong ego struggles.

MARS—ASCENDANT
You are self-assured and can assert yourself, but don't overdo it.

MARS—MIDHEAVEN
These transits are good for work, courage, confidence, but again watch your level of self-assertion.

Jupiter energies ♃

A Jupiter transit will expand whatever it touches. This can range from enlarging your pocketbook to gaining weight in your physical body. The transit can also expand the frame of reference of your ideas. Since we humans seem to prefer abundance to restriction, Jupiter transits have traditionally been looked upon with favor, and the planet was called, in ancient astrological terminology, the "greater benefic." However, Jupiter can also bring too much of a good thing.

The transits of Jupiter and the planets beyond it (Saturn, Uranus, Neptune, and Pluto) are often connected with conditions and events that seem more impersonal than are transits of the "personal" planets (sun, moon, Mercury, Venus, and Mars), which we have talked about up to now. Certainly the slower-moving and farther-out planets are felt in specific ways for us as individuals, but the influences often seem to come from deeper levels of ourselves or from more general levels of our environment.

Jupiter takes about twelve years to travel around the zodiac, therefore spending an average of twelve months (from five months to a little over a year) in each sign. Its retrograde periods may delay whatever expansion it is making for you in the outer world, but the retrograde Jupiter can also mean expansion in your inner world, such as more dreams, an abundance of thoughts, etc.

Besides the general influence of each zodiac sign (beginning on page 10), Jupiter can increase these tendencies while transiting each sign:

JUPITER IN ARIES
You have more self-confidence and generosity. Avoid too much optimism or impulsive spending.

JUPITER IN TAURUS
These transits can expand opportunities for acquiring material resources as well as creative expression. Avoid overeating or overspending on luxuries.

JUPITER IN GEMINI
These transits expand broadmindedness and interest in everything, near and far. Avoid superficiality.

JUPITER IN CANCER
Opportunities can appear for increased security. You have more interest in the home. Don't overeat.

JUPITER IN LEO
Confidence, optimism, and affection can increase, but so can overconfidence and conceit.

JUPITER IN VIRGO
These transits are good for work, integrity, and cleanliness, but watch out for overcritical attitudes and overwork.

JUPITER IN LIBRA
You may feel an increase in cooperation, creativity, and sense of justice, particularly in relationships. Watch for laziness or expecting more than you deserve.

JUPITER IN SCORPIO
These transits intensify concern both for personal needs and social situations. Think twice about being uncompromising.

JUPITER IN SAGITTARIUS
These transits expand concern with ideals, optimism, and an interest in travel and sports. Don't be reckless and do be practical.

JUPITER IN CAPRICORN
Responsibility and integrity are expanded as well as drive, but don't be a miser.

JUPITER IN AQUARIUS

These transits expand tolerance, democratic ideas, and cooperation. Test your new ideas for practicality.

JUPITER IN PISCES

This is a time of more sympathy and generosity. You may tend to dream big, but keep your dreams in proportion.

Personal predicting with Jupiter

As you would have suspected, a Jupiter transit will expand opportunities connected with the *personal important point* it is aspecting. Like other transits, this can (to some extent) be planned for ahead of time. Good things can come from any transiting Jupiter aspect, but always remember that any potential problems with Jupiter will take the form of *over*optimism, *over*doing, waste, etc., rather than restrictions. This, of course, is particularly true of the challenging aspects (squares and oppositions).

A transit of Jupiter usually lasts three to ten days, but it can continue up to a month if it is near a stationary period. The transit is generally felt through the whole period. At the very least this should be a time of more optimism, although specific opportunities or "increases" may be pinpointed within the transit period.

The charts that will tell you when Jupiter makes transiting aspects to your *personal important points* begin on page 111. You can fill this information in on your Personal Prediction Charts. Here are things to look for as Jupiter combines with each *personal important point:*

JUPITER—SUN

You almost always feel good, optimistic, and you might think you have really got the hang of life. Maybe you have.

JUPITER—MOON

Your emotions, particularly the positive ones, are expanded and you feel more secure. Avoid sentimentality or attachment.

JUPITER—MERCURY

You may feel an increase of mental activity, communications, and your ability to see how the specifics fit in the overall picture. Avoid talking or thinking too much.

JUPITER — VENUS

These transits are marvelous for relationships, sociability, and appreciation of beauty, but avoid spending too much or eating too many sweets.

JUPITER — MARS

This is a time of much energy and enterprise. Get some physical exercise, but don't overdo or be too assertive.

JUPITER — JUPITER

The transits of Jupiter to itself are marked by increased optimism, self-confidence, and luck, but watch out for over-confidence. The conjunction begins a new twelve-year period of personal growth.

JUPITER — SATURN

You must balance optimism with caution, expansion with practicality. You might have to deal with restlessness.

JUPITER — URANUS

This is a time of unexpected luck and opportunities, as well as new ideas. But don't be too impatient with your limitations.

JUPITER — NEPTUNE

Your ideals and sympathies are strong, but keep in touch with realism.

JUPITER — PLUTO

Your drive for success is particularly strong, and you can make worthwhile changes. Just don't become obsessed with what you are trying to do.

JUPITER — ASCENDANT

In your relationships you will find that the warmth and confidence of your nature are particularly apparent at this time. Don't let your expansive tendencies include gaining unneeded weight.

JUPITER — MIDHEAVEN

This can be a time of expansion and confidence in your profession and your public image. Watch for ego inflation.

Saturn energies ♄

Saturn transits *contract, focus,* and *structure* whatever they contact and also establish a *down-to-earth* connection. This can take many forms, depending upon how realistically you are viewing the areas being affected by the Saturn transit. Saturn first *tests* you. If you pass the test, the transit brings solid accomplishment and security, but only after you get through, not around, anything that may be standing in the way of a truly solid structure, whether on the level of the material world, emotional responses, or ideas and dreams.

Saturn transits can sometimes seem harsh, but only if you cannot face the reality of the situation. This is the reason it has been called a "malefic" planet. Modern astrology, however, is beginning to better understand Saturn's beneficial qualities.

Saturn goes around the zodiac in about twenty-nine years, spending around two and one-half years in a sign. Its retrograde periods are good times for focusing on your inner direction as well as strengthening areas of your life that may be tested when Saturn goes direct again.

Besides the general zodiac influences (beginning on page 10), Saturn can, while it transits each sign, be:

SATURN IN ARIES
A time to learn when to be spontaneous and when to restrict your impulses.

SATURN IN TAURUS
A time to focus on what you really value and what you can do without.

SATURN IN GEMINI
A time to understand when you need variety in experience and when you need to understand something in depth.

SATURN IN CANCER
A period for learning when to go with the flow and when to organize your activities.

SATURN IN LEO
A time for discerning when to follow your own direction and when to be cooperative.

SATURN IN VIRGO
An opportunity to discriminate between when to analyze and when to trust your intuition.

SATURN IN LIBRA
A period to understand when to compromise and when to stand firm.

SATURN IN SCORPIO
A time to understand when to focus your energy and when to let it take the path of least resistance.

SATURN IN SAGITTARIUS
An opportunity to learn when to expand your thoughts and activities and when to contract them.

SATURN IN CAPRICORN
A time to work out when to pursue personal goals and when to focus on larger-than-personal ones.

SATURN IN AQUARIUS
A period for understanding when to try a new direction and when to stick to the tried and true.

SATURN IN PISCES
An opportunity to sense when to be practical and when to dream, as well as when to preserve and when to sacrifice.

Personal predicting with Saturn

Saturn's transits in aspect to your ***personal important points*** mark major cycles in your life. As in all transits, its conjunction with a ***personal important point*** marks the beginning of a new cycle. This is an opportunity to *establish on a realistic basis* the areas of your life to which the ***personal important point*** relates. In any event Saturn will bring you back to reality. If you are not prepared to get at the truth of the matters concerned and take responsibility, you may react negatively (feeling restricted, depressed, etc.). The best use of any Saturn transit is to put things in order and to work on the areas concerned.

A Saturn transit usually lasts eight to fifteen days, but if it is near a stationary position, the transit can go on for about two months. If it makes a transiting aspect, retrogrades over the same position, then crosses it a third time, this series of three transits can take several months. During the whole period in which Saturn is in orb of aspecting a ***personal important point,*** you may feel somewhat serious and perhaps lower in energy. In addition, there may be specific situations which challenge your ability to overcome them during this general period. However, Saturn can also bring achievements.

The charts for Saturn's transiting aspects to your *personal important points* begin on page 111. You can fill this information in on your Personal Prediction Charts. Here is what to look for as Saturn aspects each *personal important point*:

SATURN—SUN

Your energies can be disciplined and your ego drives and basic direction reexamined. Don't be pessimistic or waste energy.

SATURN—MOON

These transits are good for looking deep within yourself and developing discipline, but don't give way to depressive feelings.

SATURN—MERCURY

Concentration and analytical ability is sharpened, but you may have to work through problems in communicating.

SATURN—VENUS

This is a good time for working on the practical and structural elements of creative projects. Your relationships will be tested for their importance and stability.

SATURN—MARS

You can work hard, with discipline and organization, but you may have to deal with ego conflicts and the sense of being bottled up.

SATURN—JUPITER

With these transits you can work and follow through on any opportunities that come your way, but you may have to confront restrictions and restlessness.

SATURN—SATURN

Saturn's twenty-nine-year cycle in connection with its position in your birth chart is one of the most important transit cycles. Here is a chart showing how old you will be (give or take about a year) when Saturn will make its major transiting aspects with respect to its position in your birth horoscope:

First Square	First Trine	Opposition	Last Trine	Last Square	Conjunction
7	9	14	20	22	29
36	38	43	49	51	58
66	68	73	79	81	88

Conjunction begins the cycle. This is a time when you are particularly focused on *establishing a structure* for yourself as an individual. Of course, the first conjunction is at your birth when you are establishing yourself in the world. The second conjunction comes around age twenty-nine, when you are likely to find yourself focusing quite strongly on who you are and where you are going. The third conjunction, about age fifty-eight, is a time of refocusing for your later years, and the conjunction at age eighty-eight is a time of focus on the passage to another life.

FIRST SQUARE challenges your adjustment to the outside world with respect to the focus of the previous conjunction.

FIRST TRINE is a time of smooth flow in your identity.

OPPOSITION is a time of particular challenge to your identity in relationships.

LAST TRINE marks a smooth flow period in your responsibilities and in your concentration.

LAST SQUARE challenges your adjustment to a proper completion of the particular Saturn cycle you are experiencing.

SATURN—URANUS

Saturn transits to Uranus mark a period when you can put to the practical test some of your original and creative ideas. As in all Saturn transits, success will depend on how realistically you can view any specific situation. Try not to feel frustrated by restrictions.

SATURN—NEPTUNE

These transits increase practical creativity, and there is focus on imagination, but there can be disillusionment wherever you have been deceived by yourself or by others.

SATURN—PLUTO

This is a time to delve into and clean up outworn patterns in your life. Don't be obsessive about overcoming frustrations.

The transits of Saturn in connection with the ascendant and midheaven mark another important personal cycle.

SATURN—ASCENDANT

This conjunction begins a period of about seven years in which you are, consciously or unconsciously, incubating a new phase of your particular "statement" as a human being. All Saturn-ascendant aspects can increase responsibilities and test relationships, but they can also bring achievement. You may need to conserve your energy and keep thoughts positive while such a transiting aspect is in orb.

SATURN—MIDHEAVEN

This opposition can mark the beginning of a fourteen-year period that culminates when transiting Saturn conjuncts your midheaven. This period can be a gradual buildup of your "statement" of meaning and its recognition by others. The Saturn-midheaven conjunction is followed by a period of enlarging upon this meaning. All Saturn-midheaven aspects involve work and challenges in connection with your particular "statement."

Uranus energies ⛢

Uranus is the first of the "modern" planets. It was unknown to the ancients, since (unlike the planets closer to the sun) it is not clearly visible to the naked eye. It was discovered in 1781 with the aid of the newly invented telescope.

Uranus is rightly called the planet of the unexpected. Its effects cannot be predicted by any normal reasoning process, and its transits seem to *cut through outworn structures in your life and turn toward new, and often, unexpected directions*. Its actions can be highly beneficial: that flash of insight, that sudden opportunity, that chance meeting that turns out to be very important. However, a Uranus transit can seem highly disruptive if you are clinging to something you should be giving up. On the other hand, Uranus may tempt you to let go of some still valuable patterns. Its transits always *contrast change against the status quo*. Uranus influences (like those of the other outer planets) often seem to come from the more impersonal levels in ourselves, or from the outside environment.

Only once every eighty-four years does Uranus make a circuit around the zodiac; therefore it makes only one transit of all zodiac positions in the average lifetime. It spends around seven years in each sign, revolutionizing the areas of life with which the zodiac sign is connected. Its retrograde periods not only connect with changes in our inner attitudes but also sometimes delay, for that period of time, the outer changes it is making in our lives.

See page 10 for the general influence of each zodiac sign. Here are some more specific characteristics of the transits of Uranus through each sign:

URANUS IN ARIES
March 31, 1927–November 5, 1927
January 12, 1928–June 6, 1934
October 10, 1934–March 27, 1935

Sudden new starts, both in personal directions and in social political, and technological new cycles.

URANUS IN TAURUS
June 6, 1934–October 10, 1934
March 27, 1935–August 7, 1941
October 5, 1941–May 15, 1942

Unexpected losses or discoveries of new resources, both personal, technological, and among the nations; breaks with tradition, practical innovations.

URANUS IN GEMINI
August 7, 1941–October 5, 1941
May 15, 1942–August 30, 1948
November 12, 1948–June 10, 1949

Breakthroughs in communication and ideas, both personally and in social and political organizations.

URANUS IN CANCER
August 30, 1948–November 12, 1948
June 10, 1949–August 24, 1955
January 27, 1956–June 9, 1956

New attitudes toward women and toward the home; new, more independent, emotional patterns.

URANUS IN LEO
August 24, 1955–January 27, 1956
June 9, 1956–November 1, 1961
January 10, 1962–August 9, 1962

Upsets in the power balance, new attitudes toward children, new patterns of creativity.

URANUS IN VIRGO
    November 1, 1961–January 10, 1962
    August 9, 1962–September 28, 1968
    May 20, 1969–June 24, 1969

New directions in health care, employer-employee relationships; new working techniques.

URANUS IN LIBRA
    September 28, 1968–May 20, 1969
    June 24, 1969–November 20, 1974
    May 1, 1975–September 8, 1975

New attitudes toward marriage and other relationships, legal innovations.

URANUS IN SCORPIO
    November 20, 1974–May 1, 1975
    September 8, 1975–February 16, 1981
    March 20, 1981–November 15, 1981

New attitudes toward sex; breakthroughs in understanding the unconscious; new power sources.

URANUS IN SAGITTARIUS
    December 2, 1897–July 4, 1898
    September 10, 1898–December 20, 1904
    February 16, 1981–March 20, 1981
    November 15, 1981–February 14, 1988
    May 26, 1988–December 3, 1988

New attitudes toward both legal systems and universal laws; new means of travel.

URANUS IN CAPRICORN
    December 20, 1904–January 30, 1912
    September 4, 1912–November 12, 1912
    February 14, 1988–May 26, 1988
    December 3, 1988–April 1, 1995
    June 8, 1995–January 12, 1996

New approaches in business, particularly mass marketing; new attitudes toward dealing with crime; new ways to form structures.

URANUS IN AQUARIUS

January 30, 1912–September 4, 1912
November 12, 1912–March 31, 1919
August 17, 1919–January 22, 1920

April 1, 1995–June 8, 1995
January 12, 1996–into the twenty-first century

Emphasis on revolution and new freedoms in many fields—personal, political, technological.

URANUS IN PISCES

March 31, 1919–August 17, 1919
January 22, 1920–March 31, 1927
November 4, 1927–January 13, 1928

New ideals and understanding of suffering; new dreams and fantasies.

Personal predicting with Uranus

A Uranus transit to one of your major *personal important points* is not likely to leave you where it found you. Any principal turning point in your life is likely to be associated with a Uranus transit, usually combined with other major personal transits. Uranus can bring you tremendous release from certain pressures, particularly if you are open to breaking out of self-destructive patterns. However, if you would like things to continue forever exactly as they are, a Uranus transit can come as a great shock, such as a baby bird might feel when it is shoved out of the nest and forced to fly.

If you can flow with the deep changes within yourself, Uranus will bring increased freedom. However, you must always weigh the value of your established patterns against Uranus restlessness. Sometimes Uranus can test your ability to stick with a course you have charted: If the direction is truly worthwhile, a Uranus transit will help you find better ways of doing what you have set out to do; if not, the whole project is likely to get broken up in the process.

Uranus transits can last as little as two months, but they can go on for the better part of a year if the planet retrogrades back over the aspect point and then recrosses it a third time. During the whole period you may feel restless or in need of some kind of change in connection with the *personal important point* being transited, but often the major effect of a Uranus transit is confined to an unexpected event during the period when the transit is in orb.

The Uranus calendars begin on page 111. You can fill the information in on your Personal Prediction Charts. Here are some particular things to look for as Uranus combines with your *personal important points:*

URANUS-SUN

There are changes and challenges in consciousness and the directions in which you are exerting your will.

URANUS-MOON

There are changes in emotional patterns and responses. Repressed feelings can surface.

URANUS-MERCURY

New and exciting ideas and communications challenge your usual way of understanding things.

URANUS-VENUS

There are new patterns in your relationships and your creativity. You must balance your freedom from the people in your life with your closeness to them.

URANUS-MARS

This is a volatile combination. You will be inclined to assert your freedom in a variety of ways in which you have felt restricted. Keep it in balance.

URANUS-JUPITER

Sudden opportunities appear that, in one way or another, can expand your horizons. Check them for soundness, however.

URANUS-SATURN

There are challenges to the structures and routines of your life. Changes can be made in those that are not stable.

URANUS-URANUS

These transits are a major cycle. They come in about the same age span for everyone.

URANUS FIRST SQUARE URANUS, when you are around twenty-one years old, marks a change in your orientation toward adulthood and the world.

URANUS FIRST TRINE URANUS, around twenty-eight, can bring changes in your life toward more self-expression of yourself as an individual.

URANUS OPPOSITION URANUS, at about forty-two, is a time of reassessment of your contributions as an individual.

URANUS LAST TRINE URANUS, around fifty-six, is a time for assessment of your directions as an individual.

URANUS LAST SQUARE URANUS, around sixty-three, can be a change of orientation more toward your inner life.

URANUS CONJUNCT URANUS, around eighty-four, is a time for review and understanding of your general life perspective and orientation toward its deeper meaning.

URANUS-NEPTUNE
Your viewpoint of reality can undergo subtle changes. Idealism is stimulated.

URANUS-PLUTO
There are deep-seated changes in your life, often connected with what others of your generation are undergoing at the same time.

URANUS-ASCENDANT
This is a time for a revolution in your relationships, clearing out what elements no longer enable you to grow.

URANUS-MIDHEAVEN
There are changes in your attitudes toward your public image and your home. You have a need for new freedom that must be tested against reality.

Neptune energies ♆

Neptune is your connection with the realm of *inspiration, dreams, imagination, and fantasy.* Unfortunately, illusion can take over if you forget that the ideal Neptunian dream can never be totally realized in the limited physical world. Neptune's transits always have the potential for broadening your vision and deepening your sense of beauty. However, do not try to possess whatever or whoever is the carrier of the Neptunian quality. If you do, the magic can slip away and leave you painfully disillusioned.

Neptune was discovered in 1846. It takes 165 years to go around the zodiac; therefore it will not make a complete transit of all the signs during your lifetime. It spends around 14 years in a sign.. Its influence is often not immediately obvious, creating something of a behind-the-scenes atmosphere. Retrograde periods of Neptune can reveal subtle deception and false pride.

See page 10 for the general influence of each zodiac sign. Here are more specific characteristics of how Neptune interacts with the signs it travels through during this century.

NEPTUNE IN CANCER
July 19, 1901–December 25, 1901
May 21, 1902–September 23, 1914
December 15, 1914–July 18, 1915
March 20, 1916–May 2, 1916

New appreciation of instinctual and unconscious influences.

NEPTUNE IN LEO
September 23, 1914–December 15, 1914
July 18, 1915–March 20, 1916
May 2, 1916–September 21, 1928
February 19, 1929–July 24, 1929

Awareness of deeper-than-ego centers and increased fantasy in the arts and entertainment.

NEPTUNE IN VIRGO
September 21, 1928–February 19, 1929
July 24, 1929–October 3, 1942
April 17, 1943–August 2, 1943

New interest in spiritual and psychological healing methods and in classifying the unconscious.

NEPTUNE IN LIBRA
October 3, 1942–April 17, 1943
August 2, 1943–December 24, 1955
March 11, 1956–October 19, 1956
June 15, 1957–August 6, 1957

A deepening sense of balance in the arts and in relationships.

NEPTUNE IN SCORPIO
December 24, 1955–March 11, 1956
October 19, 1956–June 15, 1957
August 6, 1957–January 4, 1970
May 2, 1970–November 6, 1970

Increased interest in life in other realms and in the understanding of sexual fantasies.

NEPTUNE IN SAGITTARIUS *January 4, 1970–May 2, 1970*
November 6, 1970–January 18, 1984
June 22, 1984–November 21, 1984
Seeking for ideals in, and uncovering deceptions in, religion and government.

NEPTUNE IN CAPRICORN *January 18, 1984–June 22, 1984*
November 21, 1984–January 28, 1998
August 22, 1998–November 27, 1998
Seeking for perfection in world organizations and in overall structures of scientific understanding.

NEPTUNE IN AQUARIUS *January 28, 1998–August 22, 1998*
November 27, 1998 into the twenty-first century
Ideals of world cooperation and new insights into the nature of the universe.

Personal predicting with Neptune

Neptune exerts a subtle influence when it transits one of your *personal important points*. Whatever area of your life Neptune contacts becomes both idealized and somewhat confused. The dream can be beautiful or grotesque, but it always carries an atmosphere of something greater than everyday reality. During a Neptune transit your creativity will be heightened. You may achieve a long-sought-after ideal, but remember that these connections are not under your conscious control. If, during a Neptune transit, you are not reaching out positively in creative directions, you may experience confusion, vague fears and anxieties, as well as escapist tendencies.

Neptune transits can last from about four months to two years. Its progress is so slow that it usually retrogrades at least once within orb of a transit point.

The Neptune charts begin on page 111. You can fill in the information on your Personal Prediction Charts. Here are some particular Neptunian effects to look for in combination with your *personal important points*:

NEPTUNE-SUN
These transits can bring your ideals more into consciousness but also can confuse your ideas of who you are.

NEPTUNE-MOON
Your sensitivity to your environment and the feelings of others is greatly increased, but you may find yourself in odd and unfamiliar moods.

NEPTUNE-MERCURY
Your imagination is increased and your ideas can be inspired, but watch for confused thinking and deception.

NEPTUNE-VENUS
These transits stimulate your creativity, your appreciation of beauty, and your ability to see the ideal in relationships. Don't lose track of the imperfections.

NEPTUNE-MARS
Your drive is toward goals higher than the purely egotistical ones, but keep in mind the need to use your energies practically as well.

NEPTUNE-JUPITER
Your ideals, expectations and sympathies are greatly expanded, but keep in mind that seeing a goal and reaching it are not the same.

NEPTUNE-SATURN
You can bring some of your ideals to reality now, even though your sense of what reality is may be changing. Don't let this confusion make you lose confidence.

NEPTUNE-URANUS
Your opinions and understanding of the world can undergo great changes. Don't expect your ideas to settle down until the transit is over.

NEPTUNE-NEPTUNE

FIRST SQUARE, when you are around forty-two to forty-five years old, is a time for questioning and changing some of your ideals. Realize that it's not a time when you are going to get all the answers.

FIRST TRINE, around the mid-fifties, is a time of increased compassion and wisdom through reflection.

OPPOSITION, around age eighty-four or so, is a time of potentially broadened consciousness and for understanding the dreamlike qualities of the world and your relationships.

NEPTUNE–PLUTO
You can sense your connections with general cultural changes and even the universe, but you should guard against compulsive traits.

NEPTUNE–ASCENDANT
Under these transits you are particularly likely to see the ideal in yourself and your relationships. Keep in mind that nobody is perfect.

NEPTUNE–MIDHEAVEN
You may be focused on more idealistic goals, which is fine so long as it doesn't confuse you when it comes to practical directions.

Pluto energies ♇ or ♀

Pluto transits indicate possibilities for *fundamental change,* both in direction of events and, even more, as a *basic transformation of personal motivation.* Pluto presides over the cocoon stage, between the caterpillar and the butterfly. Its energies often seem to come, with tremendous power, either from deep layers of the unconscious that are shared by all human beings or else from government or other large organizations.

Pluto is the last planet so far discovered, having been first sighted in 1930. It takes 248 years to circle the zodiac. The orbit of Pluto is very eccentric, causing its speed to vary considerably more than that of the other planets. It can spend as few as 13 years in a sign or as many as 31 and it averages 20 years in a sign. The deep underlying points of view of a whole generation of people born during this time are affected by Pluto energies. As it moves around the zodiac, the collective emphasis changes in many areas. The fashions people relate to, trends in the arts, characteristic patterns of interpersonal relationships, and how people view the universe are all affected. Pluto is connected with natural resources, atomic power, periods of destruction, and the construction that follows. Retrograde periods in Pluto are related to the overthrow of rigid collective patterns that no longer serve the needs of the present.

See page 10 for the general influence of each zodiac sign. Here are more specific characteristics of Pluto's transits through the signs it is in during this century.

PLUTO IN GEMINI   *April 23, 1884–September 21, 1912*
October 4, 1912–July 11, 1913
December 25, 1913–May 28, 1914

Basic changes in methods of communication and in ideas about the deeper levels of human beings.

PLUTO IN CANCER   *September 21, 1912–October 4, 1912*
July 11, 1913–December 25, 1913
May 28, 1914–October 7, 1937
November 23, 1937–August 2, 1938
February 7, 1939–June 13, 1939

Basic changes in collective attitudes toward instinctual patterns, including a deeper psychological understanding of emotions.

PLUTO IN LEO   *October 7, 1937–November 23, 1937*
August 2, 1938–February 7, 1939
June 13, 1939–October 20, 1956
January 16, 1957–August 18, 1957
April 12, 1958–June 9, 1958

Basic changes in the understanding of ego drives, in attitudes toward heads of state, and in the arts, especially entertainment.

PLUTO IN VIRGO   *October 20, 1956–January 16, 1957*
August 18, 1957–April 12, 1958
June 9, 1958–October 4, 1971
April 17, 1972–July 29, 1972

Basic changes in attitudes toward work patterns, social services, health care.

PLUTO IN LIBRA   *October 4, 1971–April 17, 1972*
July 29, 1972–November 5, 1983
May 17, 1984–August 27, 1984

Basic changes in patterns of law, the arts, marriage relationships, and international relations.

PLUTO IN SCORPIO   *November 5, 1983–May 17, 1984*
August 27, 1984–January 16, 1995
April 21, 1995–November 10, 1995

Basic changes in the understanding of individual and collective psychological drives, sex, and life after death.

PLUTO IN SAGITTARIUS   *January 16, 1995–April 21, 1995*
November 10, 1995 into the twenty-first century

Basic changes in patterns of religion and government, as well as travel.

Personal predicting with Pluto

A Pluto transit to one of your **personal important points** has, in one way or another, a transforming effect on an area of your life associated with that particular **personal important point**. This transit can put you in touch with the *basic pattern* of the **personal important point** being aspected, either through events in the outside world or through changes from deep within you. The flow of your life is then brought closer to conforming to this basic pattern. If you have (consciously or unconsciously) been resisting the next stage of your development in connection with the **personal important point** being transited, the changes may seem drastic. However, if you are ready for the next stage, a Pluto transit can bring tremendous release and a new beginning to that area of your life.

Pluto transits can last from about four months to almost three years. Now, and for some time to come, it is in the faster part of its orbit. This means that transits tend to last about four or five months, except when complicated by retrograde periods, when they continue for a year or so. Pluto's orbit is extremely eccentric. About twenty years of its two-and-a-half century trip around the zodiac are spent closer to the sun and moving faster than Neptune. The remaining years are spent beyond the orbit of Neptune. Pluto will be in one of these twenty-year close periods from 1978 to 2000.

The Pluto charts begin on page 111. You can fill in the information on your Personal Prediction Charts. Here are some possible correspondences for Pluto transits to your **personal important points**.

PLUTO–SUN
This is a time for basic changes in your sense of self. Keep your ego drives in proportion.

PLUTO–MOON
Your deeper emotions may be expressed with intensity. Be aware of how much of this intensity you are really feeling.

PLUTO–MERCURY
Your thinking can be deep and your communications intense and significant. Don't be too obsessed with your ideas.

PLUTO-VENUS
This is a time of deep creativity or deep relationship. Be discriminating about whatever is attracting you.

PLUTO-MARS
This is a period of intense energy during which much work can be accomplished if you avoid expressing the energy in ego battles.

PLUTO-JUPITER
You are likely to have both the drive for success and some opportunities, but don't take on more than you can handle.

PLUTO-SATURN
These transits bring changes in the way you structure your life. You may have the ability to work hard. Give up any patterns you no longer need.

PLUTO-URANUS
There should be new insights as well as the possibility of working with others for change. Learn to flow creatively in what needs to be done.

PLUTO-NEPTUNE
These transits mark a transformation in your ideals. Keep an eye to the practical.

PLUTO-PLUTO

PLUTO FIRST SQUARE PLUTO
This comes somewhere between your late forties and your mid-fifties. It marks a regeneration of your deeper power drives. Learn to use this power for something besides ego.

PLUTO FIRST TRINE PLUTO
This comes in your sixties. It relates to a deepening of your perception of wisdom and your spiritual awareness.

PLUTO-ASCENDANT
There are basic changes to your personality and to your relationships. Be careful about giving way to compulsions.

PLUTO-MIDHEAVEN
There are basic changes in your life goals. Keep your energies channeled to your main direction without overriding anyone unnecessarily.

How to make and use a personal prediction chart

1. In the sun transit chart on page 30 you determined the degree of the zodiac for each of your *personal important points.* Transfer this information to the *personal important point* chart below. For each degree of the zodiac where there is a conjunction or other transiting aspect to one of your *personal important points*, fill in both the name of the *personal important point* and the aspect. For example, if Jupiter was at 4° Capricorn when you were born, the first square to it would be 4° Aries. Fill in "♃ 1st □" in the 4° ♈ space. Then check the planet calendars and charts to see when the planets reach these personally important degrees.

(See next page.)

	♈	♉	♊	♋	♌	♍	♎	♏	♐	♑	♒	♓
0												
1												
2												
3												
4												
5												
6												
7												
8												
9												
10												
11												
12												
13												
14												
15												
16												
17												
18												
19												
20												
21												
22												
23												
24												
25												
26												
27												
28												
29												
30												
31												
32												
33												
34												
35												
36												
37												
38												

2. You can now also check the planet calendars and charts for any period for which you wish to find the transits. With these calendars and charts you will be able to determine some of the transiting degrees with accuracy and others approximately. To increase your accuracy you may wish to consult an *ephemeris*, which is an astrological calendar that gives the zodiac degree for each planet once a day. Determining transits with an ephemeris is not difficult. Although most of them are calculated for Greenwich Mean Time, this can easily be converted to your time zone. Calendars which include an astrological ephemeris for the current year are available and it is also possible to purchase ephemeris books which cover both past and future years.

3. Once you have determined what transits are coming up and when to expect them, you can review what you have learned about them. Think about:

   A. The nature of the transiting planet and the sign it is in.

   B. The nature and sign of the *personal important point* being transited.

   C. The effect of the aspect involved.

   D. What this could mean for you personally and how the transit can be most constructively used.

   E. The house positions (if known) of both transiting planet and *personal important point* are also to be considered.

   F. Usually more than one transit is happening during the same time period, so you will wish to consider how all effective transits at one period will combine with each other.

4.   You may be able to get a feel for how transits of the faster-moving planets (sun, moon, Mercury, Venus, Mars) can affect you by checking back to what happened last time each of them made the same transiting aspect that you are now anticipating. You can also do this for Jupiter if you are older than twelve, and Saturn if you are over twenty-nine. The transits of Uranus, Neptune, and Pluto, however, happen only once a lifetime.

   It is important to remember that "a little knowledge is a dangerous thing. In other words, don't jump to the conclusion that an anticipated transit is bound to mean some terrible and unavoidable catastrophe in your life. *Remember that it takes a lot of skill to make specific astrological predictions and the universe has plenty of surprises for all of us.* Also keep in mind that *there are always positive uses for the energies of any transit.*

80

Transits through the houses of your horoscope

If you have had a personal horoscope made for the time and place of your birth, you will be able to determine the *houses* of your horoscope. The First House always begins on the left hand side with the ascendant, which is *the degree of the zodiac that was coming up over the eastern horizon at the time and place you were born.* Going *counterclockwise* around the circle, the Second House begins thirty degrees (more or less) farther on. Except for the equal house system, the number of degrees in each house varies depending on how far away from the equator you were born and what day of the year it was.

Where each house begins (its *cusp*) is a **personal important point**. Also, when a planet is passing through a house, its action is particularly directed (although not exclusively) to the areas of your life under the influence of that house. For example, the expansive influence of a Jupiter transit through your First House can expand your outlook, make you more optimistic, but also perhaps influence you to gain weight. Jupiter transiting through your Second House can expand your personal resources. A Mars transit through your First House would increase your energy and might make you more aggressive, while its transit through your Second House could increase your initiative in going after money.

Here is a diagram of how the houses are placed on a horoscope wheel and what each one means:

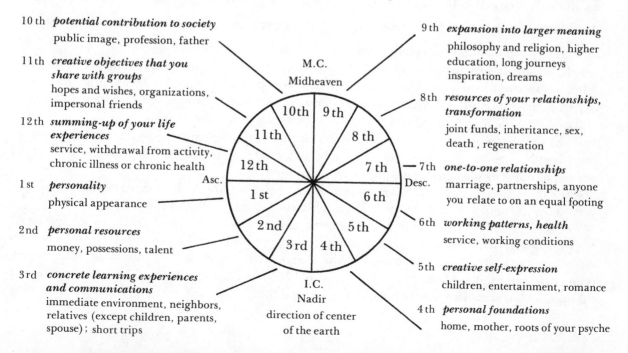

10 th *potential contribution to society*
public image, profession, father

11th *creative objectives that you share with groups*
hopes and wishes, organizations, impersonal friends

12th *summing-up of your life experiences*
service, withdrawal from activity, chronic illness or chronic health

1 st *personality*
physical appearance

2nd *personal resources*
money, possessions, talent

3rd *concrete learning experiences and communications*
immediate environment, neighbors, relatives (except children, parents, spouse); short trips

M.C.
Midheaven

Asc.

I.C.
Nadir
direction of center
of the earth

9 th *expansion into larger meaning*
philosophy and religion, higher education, long journeys inspiration, dreams

8 th *resources of your relationships, transformation*
joint funds, inheritance, sex, death , regeneration

7th *one-to-one relationships*
marriage, partnerships, anyone you relate to on an equal footing

Desc.

6 th *working patterns, health*
service, working conditions

5th *creative self-expression*
children, entertainment, romance

4 th *personal foundations*
home, mother, roots of your psyche

How to find your sunsign, moonsign, and moonphase

With the calendars on pages 85 to 105 you can easily find, for any date between 1911 and 1980, the sunsign, moonsign, and moonphase. These should be determined both for your date of birth and for any date for which you wish to check the transits. (Of course, if you have had an astrological horoscope set up, you will already know your sunsign and moonsign).

Notice that the calendar is divided into two sections, the first from 1911 to 1945 and the second from 1946 to 1980. Look down the left-hand column of the appropriate section until you come to the year in which you are interested, then follow across horizontally until you come to the month and day. Any sunsign, moonsign, or moonphase change that occurred that day, as well as the closest hour to the change, is noted in this square. For example, if the square says ☿/4p it means that the moonsign changed to Taurus at 4 p.m. that day. If the box is in "reverse" (white letters on black) ♒/11p, it indicates a sunsign change. If the sunsign change has a white arrow ◀♒/4a it indicates that the sunsign change occurred on the day represented by a neighboring box. Moonphase changes are also indicated. For example, ◑/8a indicates that the moon went into the first quarter at 8 a.m. on that day. If both a moonsign change and a moonphase change occurred on the same day, then the box is divided in half. For example, ●10a/♒7p indicates that the moon became new at 10 a.m. on that day and the moonsign changed to Aquarius at 7 p.m. on the same day.

Eclipses are indicated by an ⑤ for a solar eclipse and an ⓛ for lunar eclipses. Since solar eclipses must occur when the moon changes to new, the ● will be replaced by an ⑤ if there is an eclipse of the sun that day. Lunar eclipses occur when the moon changes to full and the ○ will be replaced by an ⓛ if there is an eclipse of the moon on that day.

If the square for your date of birth is blank, it means that there were no changes that day. If there is only a moonsign change that day, only that will be indicated, and so forth. There will, of course, be only one sunsign change indicated every month.

For any given change that does not appear in your birth-square, look back along the line of your year to the left until you find the last change. This will still be in effect at the date of your birth.

The time given in this calendar is United States Eastern Standard Time. This is always five hours less than Greenwich Mean Time, which is the "basic" standard time for the world. If you were born on or near the United States east coast (in the Eastern Time zone) you do not need to make any time corrections unless Daylight Saving Time or Wartime Daylight Saving Time was in effect at that particular time. If you were born in the Central Standard Time zone (unless Daylight Saving

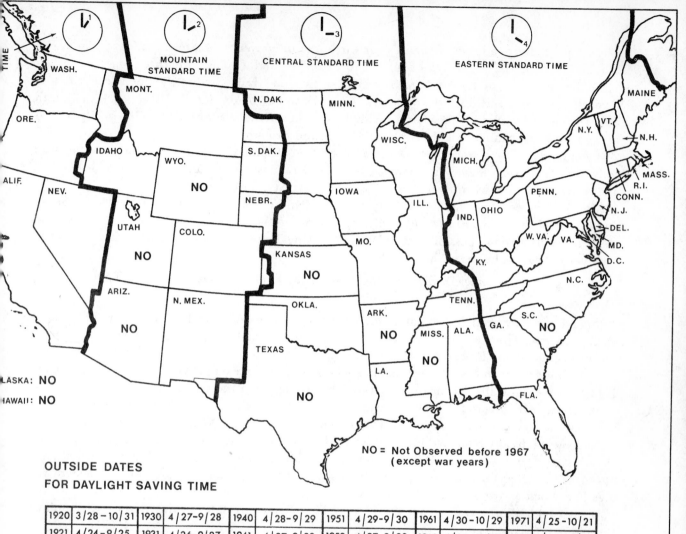

MOUNTAIN STANDARD TIME

CENTRAL STANDARD TIME

EASTERN STANDARD TIME

TIME

WASH.

ORE.

IDAHO

MONT.

N. DAK.

MINN.

WISC.

MICH.

MAINE

N.Y.

VT.

N.H.

CALIF.

NEV.

WYO.

NO

S. DAK.

NEBR.

IOWA

ILL.

IND.

OHIO

PENN.

MASS.

R.I.

CONN.

N.J.

DEL.

MD.

D.C.

UTAH

COLO.

NO

KANSAS

NO

MO.

KY.

W. VA.

VA.

ARIZ.

N. MEX.

NO

OKLA.

ARK.

TENN.

N.C.

S.C.

NO

TEXAS

NO

LA.

MISS.

NO

ALA.

GA.

FLA.

ALASKA: **NO**

HAWAII: **NO**

NO = Not Observed before 1967
(except war years)

OUTSIDE DATES
FOR DAYLIGHT SAVING TIME

1920	3/28 – 10/31	1930	4/27 – 9/28	1940	4/28 – 9/29	1951	4/29 – 9/30	1961	4/30 – 10/29	1971	4/25 – 10/21
1921	4/24 – 9/25	1931	4/26 – 9/27	1941	4/27 – 9/28	1952	4/27 – 9/28	1962	4/29 – 10/28	1972	4/30 – 10/29
1922	4/30 – 9/24	1932	4/24 – 9/25	1942 to 1945	WAR TIME	1953	4/26 – 9/27	1963	4/28 – 10/27	1973	4/29 – 10/28
1923	4/29 – 9/30	1933	4/30 – 9/24			1954	4/25 – 10/31	1964	4/25 – 10/25	1974	1/6 – 10/27
1924	4/27 – 9/28	1934	4/29 – 9/30			1955	4/24 – 10/30	1965	4/25 – 10/31	1975	2/23 – 10/26
1925	4/26 – 9/27	1935	4/28 – 9/29	1946	4/28 – 9/29	1956	4/29 – 10/28	1966	4/24 – 10/30	1976	4/25 – 10/31
1926	4/25 – 9/26	1936	4/26 – 9/27	1947	4/27 – 9/28	1957	4/28 – 10/27	1967	4/30 – 10/29	1977	4/24 – 10/30
1927	4/24 – 9/25	1937	4/25 – 9/26	1948	4/25 – 9/26	1958	4/27 – 10/26	1968	4/28 – 10/27	1978	4/30 – 10/29
1928	4/29 – 9/30	1938	4/24 – 10/2	1949	4/24 – 9/25	1959	4/26 – 10/25	1969	4/27 – 10/26	1979	4/29 – 10/28
1929	4/28 – 9/29	1939	4/30 – 9/24	1950	4/30 – 9/24	1960	4/24 – 10/30	1970	4/26 – 10/25	1980	4/27 – 10/26

Time was in effect) add *one hour* to your birthtime to convert to Eastern Standard Time. For Mountain Standard Time add *two hours* and for Pacific Standard Time add *three hours*.

For Yukon Standard Time add *four hours*. For Central Alaska Standard Time add *five hours*. (Hawaii now uses Central Alaska Standard Time. However, before June 8, 1947, parts of Hawaii used Hawaiian Standard Time. For a birthplace in Hawaiian Standard Time add *five and a half hours*.) For Nome Standard Time (western Alaska) add *six hours*.

If you were born in a place in the world with a different time zone, it may be more convenient to convert to Greenwich Mean Time (since this is the way most world time-conversion charts work) and then subtract five hours to get United States Eastern Standard Time.

After you correct your time for Eastern Standard Time and if you were born in the United States and if your birthtime is *within an hour* of a moonsign, sunsign, or moonphase change, you should check to see if there is a possibility that Daylight Saving Time might have been in effect when you were born. This can be one of three kinds:

1. Summer Daylight Saving Time   3. Fuel crisis Daylight Saving Time
2. Wartime Daylight Saving Time

Although it is a very complex operation to determine whether any given locality did or did not have Daylight Saving Time (within a state different communities might elect, in a given year, to be on or off, or begin and end Daylight Saving Time on different dates), it is relatively simple to eliminate the possibility when and where it was not in effect. Find your state on the map on the opposite page. If there is NO indicated, it means that Daylight Saving Time was not observed anywhere in the state for the years before 1967 (except wartime). If your state does not have a NO, you will have to check with relatives or local records to find out if you need to *subtract one hour* from the time of your birth (already corrected for time zone differences) to conform with Eastern Standard Time. If your state does not have a NO listed, you will still be all right if you were not born within the *outside dates* listed for each year below the map. These are the dates when summer Daylight Savings Time could have started and ended.

During both World War I and World War II, wartime Daylight Saving Time was standard throughout the country during the following times:

1918, 3/31 to 10/27   1942 to 1945, 2/9/42 to 9/30/45
1919, 3/30 to 10/26

Since 1967, automatic nationwide Daylight Saving Time has been in effect from the last Sunday in April to the last Sunday in October. An exception was the fuel crisis Daylight Saving Time in 1974 and 1975 (see dates under map). An entire state (but not a part) can exempt itself. In 1967 Arizona and Hawaii were exempt, and in 1968 Michigan became exempt as well.

Year	5	6	7	8	9	10	11	12	13	14	15	16	17	18	19	20	21	22	23	24	25	26	27	28	29	1	2	3	4	5	6	7	8	9
1911	♉ 6a	☽ 10a	♊ 9a					♌ 2p		♍ 5p		♎ 10p	○ 9p	♏ 8a	♓ 1p	♐ ○ 8a 1a				♑ 9a		♒ 7a		♓ ○ 8a		♈ 8a		♉ ○ 8a 11		♊ 2p	○ 6p	♋ 5p		♐
1912	○ 2½	☽ 12m		♏ 6a	○ 8p	♐ 4p				♑ 4½ 10		♒ 5p			♓ ♈ 1a 4a	○ 7p	2p	11p	10p		♉ 4a		7a	11p	♊ 9a		♋ 9a	○ 6a	♌ 11a		♍ 3p 5p	○		12m
1913	● 12m	♓ 3a		♈ 4p	○ 4a	☽ 3a		♉ 3a			♊ ♋ 4p 1p		♋ 5p	○ 4p	♌ 5p	♓ ♑ 6p 9p			♎ 6p			♏ 8p		♓ ♓ 8a 7p		♈ 9a		♉ 9p		♊ 12m	♋ 7p	♌ 10p		♌ 12
1914	9p	2a	♊ 1a		♌ 1p	○ 3a	♍ 3a		♎ 4a 7a		♏ 5a		● 4 5a	♓ 7a	♑ 2p	♐ 8p 10p						♓ 5a		♈ 8p		♉ 2p		♊ 9p		○ 12m	♋ 7a		♌ 9p	♐ 6a
1915	♏ 7p	☽ 12m 10	♐		♑ ☽ 12m 10		♒ 4a		♎ 10 4a		♋ 6p		♈ 8p	♓ 12n	♉ 5a				♎ 5a		♏ 10p 2p		♐		♑ 11p		♒ 1a		♓ 3a	7a	♈ 6a		♉
1916	♈ 6p 9	☽ 9p 9		♉ 1a	♊ 10p	♋ 12n			♋ 12m		♌ 1p		○ 9p 11	♓ 6p	♑ 7a		♎ 4p	♏ 1p		♐ 5p	☽ 4a		♑ 8p		♒ 5p		♓ 1a 5		♈ 4a		♉		♍ ○	
1917	♌ 10a	○ 10p	♍ 11p			♎ 11a	○ 9p	♏ 9p		○ 9p	♓ 4a		♑ 8a	8a	♐ 10a	♓ 12m	♑ 9a 9a		♒ 11 8		♓ 6p	♈ 12n		♉ 4a		♊ 2p 5			5a	5p	♌ 5p	
1918	♏ 8a	☽ 3p 9		♓ 6p	♐		♒		♓ 5a 6p		♈ 6p	♈ 10a	♉ 7p	○ 11	♊ 6a	♓ ♓ 6a 6a	♑ 3p	♒ 4p			♓ 1a	7p	♈ 9a		♉ 4p		♊ 1p		♋ 12m	♓ ♉ 1 2 4p	♊ 10p	♋ 8p
1919	♉ 7a	○ 2p	♊ 11a		♋ 3p	○ 2a	♌ 8p		♍ 7a	○ 7a	♎ 4a		○ 1p	♏ 5p	♓ 12n	♑ 1a		♓ 2a 9		♓ 1a		♈ 7p	♉ 9a		♊ 12n	6a	♋ 1p		♌ 4p		♍ 10p	♓ ♊ 4 1p
1920	♍ 6a	♎ ○ 11a 5	♏ 8p		♐ 8p		♑ 4p		♒ 8a		♓ 9p		♈ 7p	♉ 8a	♓ ♓ 5p 5p	♑ 11p		♒ 7a		♓ 3a		♈		♉ 4p 4p		♊ 9p		♋		♓ ☽ 1a			♓	● 1p
1921		6a	8p	♓ 6p			♈ ☽ 5 8	♉	♉ 2p		♊ 2 8		♋ 11p	○ 11p	♌ 11p	♓ 12m 11	11p		♍ 5a	♎ 12m		♏ 2p		♐ 1p		♑		♒ 9a			♓ 12m			
1922	● 12m	♊ 3a		♋ 7 6a	♌ 7a		♍ 9a		♎ 8p		♏ 8a		♐ 9a	○ 9	♑ 5a	♓ ♑ 3p 3p	♒ 11p		♓ 11a 10a		♈ 11a		♉ 2p		♊ 12n		♋ 5p 12m		♌		♍ 10a	○ 2p		♎ 4a
1923	♏ 9p		♐ 4a 12m		♑		♒ 12m		♓ 5 6		♈ 12m		♉ 2 10		♊ 9a	♓ ♓ 4p 11a	♑ 10p		♒ 10 7		♓ 8p		♈ 2p		♉ 2a		♊ 4a		♋ 8a 11a		♌ 3p	♍		♓ ○ 2
1924	♓ 11a		♈ ♓ 7 2		♉ 5p	○ 3p	♊ 6a		♋ 6p	○ 5p	♌ 3a		♓ 5p	♐ 10 11		♑ 2p		♒ 11p		♓ 5p		♈ 7p		♉ 8a		♊ 7p 2a		♋ 8a		♌ 11a	○ 3p		♍ 8p
1925		♌ 2a	♓ 5p	♍ 1p		♎ 10p	○ 2p	♏ 5a		○ 11p	♐ 12m	♑ 2p	♓ 3p 9	♑	♒ 5p	♓		♈ 8a		♉ 8a		♊ 7a		♋ 9p		♌ 8a 11a		♍ 3p		○			8p
1926	○ 6p	7p	♐ 11p	♑ 7a			♒ 12m	♓ 12		♈ 11p		♉ 6p	○ 1a		♊ 7a 7p	♑ ♑ 5a 5a	♒ 5p		♓ 8a		♈ 6a		♉ 7p		♊ 7p 12n		♋		♓		♌ 2a	♍ 7a	○ 7a	
1927	♈ ☽ 8 10		♉ 10a 7p	♊ 2p		♋ 9p	○ 12n	♌ 6a			♍ 11 5		♎	♓ 11a	♏ 6a	♐	2p		♑ 6p		♒ 2p		♓ 7p		♈ 6p		♉ 6p		♊ 8p		♋ 7a			♏ 8p
1928	♈ 3p	♓ 5p		♉ 11 2		♊ 2p			♋ 2p		♌ 3a		♍ 2p	♓ 2p	♎ 2p	♑ 10p		♓ 2 2		♈ 4a		♉ 1p		♊ 6a 10		♋ 12n		♌		♓ ♈ 1 6		♎ 6a		♏ 10
1929	♑ ☽ 10 1	☽	♒ 10p		♓ 1p		♈ 7p		♉ 7 11		♊ 2p 7p		♋ ♍		♌ 10p	♓ 2a	♎ 5a 5a		♏ 4a		♍ 6a 10a		♐		♑ 5a 6a		♒ 6p		♓ 1a	♈			♊ 5p	♋
1930	♈ 5a	♓ 12n	♈ 11a		♉ 2p	♊ 2p	♋ 2p				♌ 2p	♍ 11a	♎ 6p	○ 4 1		♏ 4a	♐ 2 4		♑ 1p		♒ 6a		♓ 2p	♈ 9a		♉ 1a		♊ 9a		♋		♌ 5p	11p	♍ 10p
1931	♎ 10p	○ 12m	♏ 12m	♐ 12m		♑ 2p	♒ 7a		♒ 12m		♈ 8 8		♉ 10a	♓ 1a	♊	♋ 1a	12n	♌ 2p		♍ 12 12		♎ 7a		♏ 9a		○ 6a 9a		♐ 6a		♑ 9a			♒ 9p	
1932	3a	● 10p	♓ 11a		♈ 10p	☽ 10a		♉ 11a			♋ ♊ 1 11		♌ 9a	○ 9a	♍ 10a	♓ 3p	○ 3p		♎ 6p		♏ 2a		♐ 10p	1p	♑ 2a		♒ 5 9		♓ 6p		● 3a	♈ 6a		♉
1933	● 11 6		♈ 4p		♉ ♊ 8 11		♊ 5 10		♋ 9a		♌ 9a		○ 9 12	♓ 9p	♍ 2p	♎ 7p 5p		♏ 5a		♐ 10p	♑ 8a		♓ 3 2		♒ 5a		♈ 2a	5a	♉ 3p			♊		
1934	♏ 8p		♐ 4a 1a		♑ 4 3		♒ 4a	♓ ○ 8a 4a		♈ 7a		♉ 6a 7a	♊ 9a		♋ 1a	♌ ♓ 9a			♍ 10a		♎ 5a	♏ 7p		♐		♑ 12 2		♒ 12m		♓		○ 7a		1p
1935		♓ 4p 1		♈ 3p		♉ ♊ 4 10		♊ 7a		♋ 3a	♌ 8p		♍ ♓ 4a 9a	♎ 9p		♏ 9a		♐ 5p		♑ 10p		♒ 5p 12m		♓ 12n		♈ 5p		●		♓ ☽ 12			♉ 12m
1936	♌ 8p		○ 4a	♍ 7a		♎ 6p	♏ 8a		♏ 11 7		♐ 3a	♑ ♓	♒ ♓ 8a 8a	♓ 3a		♈ 9a 7p	9a		♉ 11a		♊ 4a	♋ 5p		○ 11p		♌ 2a		♍ 1p		○			♎ 12m
1937	♑ ☽ 3 3a	☽ 9 3a		♒ 11a		♈ 3 4		♉ 7p	○ 1p	♓ 10p		♎ 11p		♏ 11p	♐ 12n	♓ 8p	♑ 4a	♒ 11a	♓ 9a		♈ 3p 3a		♉ 11p		♊ ○ 11p		♋ 4a		♍ ♌ 11a		♍ 9p		○	♎
1938	♉ 11a	♓ 8p	♈ 3p		♉ 5p	♊ 5a	♋ 7p		♋ 12 8		♌ 11p		♎ 1a	○ 11	♏ 7a	♓ 2a 2a	○ 6 11		♐ 6a		♑ 4a		♒ 1p		♓ 4a 2		♈ 1a		♉ 11a		● 9p			♎ 5 10
1939	♈ 3a	♓ ☽ 3 3a		♉ 7a	♐ 11p	♑ 3p		♒		♓ 3a	♈ 12m		♉ 3p	♓ 2p	♊ 3a	♓ ♓ 8a 4a	♑ 8a		♒ 3p		♓ 4a	♈ 1a		♉		♊ 2p		♋ 1p		♌ 2p	♍ 1p		♓ ● 2p
1940	♒ 2p		● 3a	♓ 2a		♈ 3p	♉ 6a		♊ 4a		♋ ♓ 5 3		♌ 3a	♎	♍ 9p	♐ ♏ 7 11p	11p		♑ 11p	♒ 5a	10p		♓ ♓ 5 2		♈ 2p		♉ 10a		♊ ☽ 7		♋ 3a			♌ 9p
1941	♊ 12n		♋ ○ 10p	♌ 6a		♍ 4a	○ 7p	♎ 7a		○ 9a	♏ 4a		♐ 11a	♓ 1 2p	♑ 8p	♓ ♓ 8p 8p	♒ 3a	♓ 12m		♈ 3a		♉ 4a		♊ ♓ 1 2		♋ 10p		♌ 8p		♍ 3a	♎ 7a		
1942	♏ 1a	♐ 10a	○ 4a		♑ 4a		♒ ♓ 6 7		♓ 8a		♈ 5 12		♉ 6p	♓ 10p	♊ 2a	♓ 2a	♑ 3p	♒ 3a	♓ 3 1		♈ 4a		♉		♊ 1 2		♋ 4a		♌ 10p	♍ 7p		♎ 3a		♐
1943	♓ 6p	♈ 8p	♓ 2a		♉ 1a	♊ 8p			♊ 10a		♋ 10p	♌ 10p		♍ 8a	♏ 11p	♓ 11p		♐ ♑ 9a		♑ 10p		♒ 6p		♓ 1p		♈ 2a		♉ 10p		♊ 4a	♋ 5a		♌ 6a	♍ 7a 11
1944	♌ 9a		♓ 11a	♎ 4a		♏ 10p		♐ 3 7		♑ 1p	♒ 12n		♓ ♈ 2 2		♈ ♓ 7p	♐ 1p	○ 4p	2p		♉ 2p		♊ 2a		♋ 7p		♌ 4a		♍ 4a		○	♎ 5p	♏ 11p	♑ 4
1945	○ 5a	♐ 8a		♑ 4p	☽ 2a	9p	♒ 1p		♓ 11p		♈ 6p		♓ 12m	♓ 7p	○ 3a 4a		♉		♊ 9a	♋ 8p	♌ 5p		♍ 3a	○		♎ 3p		♏ 10p	♐ 4a		♑ 5p	♒ 11p		♓ 2a

	15	16	17	18	19	20	21	22	23	24	25	26	27	28	29	30	MAY 1	2	3	4	5	6	7	8	9	10	11	12	13	14	15	16	17	18	1
1911		♐ 12n	◯ 11a		♑ 1a	♉ 1a	♒ 1p ◑ 2p		♓ 10p		☾ 8a	♈ 3a		♉ 5a Ⓢ 5p		♊ 6a	☽ 11p	♋ 6a		♌ 8a	◐ 8a	♍ 1p		♎ 8p	◯ 1a		♏ 7a		○ 1a ♐ 7p			♑ 7a	◯ 4a	♒ 8p	
1912	♈ 5a		Ⓢ 7a ♉ 12n		♊ 4p	☾ 6p	♋ 7p		♌ 9p	◐ 4a		♍ 12m	◯ 3p	♎ 4a		♏ 10a	○ 5a	♐ 5p			◯ 3a ♑ 4a		♒ 4p		◑ 5a	♓ 4a		♈ 2p	☾ 4a	♉ 9p		● 5p	♊ 1a		[illegible]
1913		♍ 2p	◐ 10a	♎ 3p	♉ 6a	♏ 4p ○ 5p	♉ 12n	♐ 7p		◯ 4a	♑ 1a		♒ 11a	◑ 1a	♓ 11p			☾ 4a ♈ 12n		♉ 11p		● 3a	♊ 7a		♋ 1p ☽ 7p		♌ 5p		◐ 7a ♍ 8p		♎ 11p	◯ 4p		♏ 1a	[illegible]
1914	♑ 3a		◑ 3a ♒ 9a		♓ 8p	♉ 6p	☾ 3a	♈ 8a		♉ 9p	● 6a		♊ 9a		☽ 7a ♋ 8p		♌ 4a		◐ 1a	♍ 9a		♎ 11a ◯ 12n		♏ 11a	○ 5p	♐ 11a		♑ 1p	◯ 12m	♒ 5p		◑ 5p	♓ 3a		[illegible]
1915			♊ 8a	☽ 9a	♋ 9p	♉ 11p		♌ 8a ◐ 11a		♍ 4p		◯ 3a ♎ 8p		♏ 8p	○ 9a	♐ 8p		◯ 2p ♑ 8p		♒ 11p		◑ 12m	♓ 5a		♈ 2p ☾ 9p			♉ 2a	● 11p	♊ 2p			♋ 3a	☽ 1a	[illegible]
1916		♎ 12m		○ 1a ♏ 4a	♉ 5a	♐ 6a	◯ 8a	♑ 8a		♒ 10a ◑ 6p		♓ 2p		☾ 7a ♈ 8p			♉ 3a	● 12m	♊ 12n			♋ 12m ☽ 1a		♌ 1p		◐ 4a	♍ 1a		♎ 9a	◯ 12m	♏ 2p		○ 9a ♐ 3p		[illegible]
1917	♒ 1a		♓ 3a	☾ 12m	♈ 5a	♉ 11a	♉ 8a ● 9a		♊ 12n		☽ 12m ♋ 8p			♌ 8a	◐ 12m	♍ 8p			◯ 3a ♎ 8a		♏ 5p	○ 10p	♐ 11p			♑ 3a ◯ 11a		♒ 6a	◑ 9p	♓ 9a		♈ 12n	☾ 7a	♉ 4p	
1918	♋ 8p		◐ 11p	♌ 4a	♉ 5p	♍ 4p		◐ 1a	♎ 4a		♏ 5p	○ 3a		♐ 3a		◯ 1a ♑ 1p		♒ 5p	◑ 5p	♓ 11p			♈ 1a ☾ 2a		♉ 1a	● 8a	♊ 2a		♋ 6a ☽ 7p		♌ 1p		◐ 3p ♍ 11p		
1919	○ 3a ♏ 3p			♐ 4a	◯ 7a	♑ 4p	♉ 11p		♒ 2a ◑ 6a		♓ 8a	☾ 7p	♈ 11a		♉ 11a	● 12m	♊ 10a		☽ 6a ♋ 11a		♌ 3p	◐ 7a	♍ 10p			♎ 9a ◯ 5p		♏ 9p		○ 8p	♐ 10a		♑ 10p	◯ 10p	
1920	☾ 5a	♈ 5p		● 5p ♉ 7p		♊ 8p	♉ 5a	☽ 12m ♋ 9p			♌ 12m ◐ 8a		♍ 4a	◯ 11p	♎ 11a		♏ 9p	Ⓛ 9p		♐ 8a		♑ 9p ◯ 11p			♒ 9a		◑ 1a ♓ 8p			♈ 2a ☾ 6p		♉ 6p		Ⓢ 1a ♊ 6a	
1921	◐ 5a ♌ 2p		♍ 4p	◯ 3p	♎ 7p	♉ 11a		♏ 12m Ⓛ 3a		♐ 7a	◯ 10p	♑ 4p			♒ 4a ◑ 11p		♓ 5p			☾ 12m ♈ 3a		♉ 11a	● 4p	♊ 3p		♋ 5p	☽ 2a	♌ 7p		◐ 10a ♍ 10p			♎ 2a ◯ 10p		[illegible]
1922	◯ 1a	♑ 2p		◑ 8p ♒ 11p	11p	♉ 5p	♓ 12n	☾ 11p		♈ 1a		♉ 12m	● 12m	♊ 9p		☽ 7p	♋ 4a		♌ 9a	◐ 8a	♍ 12n		♎ 2p ◯ 5p		♏ 4p		○ 1a ♐ 6p		♑ 11p	◯ 2p		♒ 8a		◑ 1p ♓ 7p	
1923		● 1a ♉ 11p			♊ 12m	☽ 12m	♋ 10a		♌ 7p	◐ 12m		♍ 12m	◯ 12n	♎ 2a		♏ 2a ○ 4p		♐ 1a	◯ 10p	♑ 2a		♒ 7a	◑ 1p	♓ 4p			♈ 4a ☾ 3p		♉ 5p		● 6p	♊ 5a		♋ 4p	
1924	♍ 5a	◯ 1a	♎ 9a		○ 9a ♏ 10a	♉ 4a	♐ 10a	◯ 2p	♑ 11a		♒ 2p ◑ 11p		♓ 8p		☾ 6p	♈ 5a		♉ 4p	● 6p		♊ 4a		♋ 4p ☽ 9p			♌ 4a	◐ 9p	♍ 2p		♎ 7p	◯ 11a	♏ 9p		○ 5p ♐ 9p	
1925	◑ 7p	♒ 2a		♓ 6a	☾ 6a	♈ 11a	♉ 10a	♉ 5p ● 9p			♊ 2a	☽ 7p	♋ 1p			♌ 2a ◐ 10p		♍ 2p		◯ 9p ♎ 10p			♏ 3a	○ 9a	♐ 5a		♑ 6a ◯ 4p		♒ 8a		◑ 1a ♓ 11a		♈ 5p	☾ 3p	
1926	♊ 1a ☽ 8p		♋ 9a		◐ 6p ♌ 8p	♉ 4p		♍ 9a	◯ 9p	♎ 9p			♏ 6a ○ 7p		♐ 1p		◯ 11a ♑ 7p		♒ 11p	◑ 10p		♓ 2a		♈ 4a ☾ 7a		♉ 7a	● 6p	♊ 11a		♋ 6p	☽ 11a		♌ 4a		[illegible]
1927		○ 11p	♏ 6a		♐ 6p	◯ 11p	♉ 10p	♑ 4a		♒ 11a ◑ 5p		♓ 3p		☾ 3a ♈ 4p		♉ 3p	● 8a	♊ 4p		☽ 4p ♋ 7p			♌ 2a	◐ 10a	♍ 12n			♎ 12m ◯ 1p		♏ 1p		○ 2p	♐ 12m		
1928	♓ 10p	☾ 6p		♈ 1a		Ⓢ 12m ♉ 1a	♉ 3a	♊ 12m	☽ 5a	♋ 1a		♌ 5a ◐ 5p		♍ 12n		◯ 1p ♎ 11p			♏ 11a	○ 3p		♐ 12m		♑ 12n ◯ 6p		♒ 11p		◑ 4p	♓ 7a		♈ 10a	☾ 3a	♉ 11a		[illegible]
1929		♌ 4a ◐ 9a		♍ 8p	◯ 10p	♉ 9a	♎ 2a		♏ 11a ○ 5p		♐ 9p		◯ 6p	♑ 10a		♒ 10p	◑ 8p		♓ 9a		♈ 4p ☾ 4p		♉ 7p		Ⓢ 1a ♊ 8p		♋ 9p	☽ 7a	♌ 10p		◐ 4p	♍ 2a		♎ 8a	
1930	♐ 8p	◯ 5p		♑ 5a	♉ 3p	♒ 5p ◑ 5p			♓ 5a	☾ 7p	♈ 4p			♉ 12m Ⓢ 2p		♊ 5a		☽ 2a ♋ 9a		♌ 12m	◐ 12n	♍ 2p		♎ 5p ◯ 10p		♏ 10p		○ 12n	♐ 5a		♑ 2p	◯ 9a		♒ 1a	
1931	♈ 2p		Ⓢ 8p	♉ 2a	♉ 9p	♊ 12n	☽ 6p	♋ 8p			♌ 1a ◐ 9a		♍ 4a	◯ 6p	♎ 6a		♏ 7a	○ 12m	♐ 8a		◯ 11a ♑ 1p		♒ 9p		◑ 8a	♓ 8a		♈ 9p	☾ 11a		♉ 9a		● 10a ♊ 6p		
1932		♍ 2p	◯ 11a	♎ 4p	♉ 2a	♏ 4p ○ 4p	♉ 8a	♐ 3p	◯ 9p	♑ 4p		♒ 9p	◑ 10a		♓ 6a		☾ 10a ♈ 6p			♉ 7a	● 1p	♊ 7p			♋ 6a ☽ 2p		♌ 4p		◐ 9a ♍ 10p			♎ 2a ◯ 7p		♏ 2a	
1933	♑ 2a	◑ 11p	♒ 5a		♓ 11a	☾ 3p	♈ 7p			♉ 6a ● 1p		♊ 5p		☽ 4p	♋ 6a		♌ 6p	◐ 6p		♍ 4a		♎ 9a ◯ 10a		♏ 11a	○ 5p	♐ 11a		♑ 10a ◯ 9p		♒ 12n		◑ 8a ♓ 5p			
1934		♊ 3p	☽ 2p		♋ 1a	♉ 2p	♌ 2p ◐ 4p			♍ 2a	◯ 5p	♎ 12n		♏ 5p	○ 8a	♐ 8p		◯ 5p ♑ 10p			♒ 12m	◑ 2a	♓ 3a		♈ 8a ☾ 2p		♉ 2p		● 7a ♊ 11p			♋ 9a	☽ 7a	♌ 10p	
1935		♎ 10a		○ 4p ♏ 8p		♉ 8p	♐ 4a	◯ 10a	♑ 10a		♒ 3p ◑ 11p		♓ 6p		☾ 8a ♈ 7p		♉ 9p	● 5p		♊ 12m		☽ 7a ♋ 7a		♌ 5p		◐ 7a	♍ 5a		♎ 6p	◯ 9a		♏ 4a		○ 5a ♐ 11a	
1936	♒ 2a		♓ 6a	☾ 3a	♈ 6a	♉ 2a	♉ 6a ● 8a		♊ 6a	☽ 2p	♋ 8a		♌ 3p	◐ 4a		♍ 1a		◯ 7a ♎ 2p			♏ 2a	○ 10a	♐ 1p			♑ 12m ◯ 9a		♒ 8a		◑ 1a ♓ 1p		♈ 3p	☾ 10a	♉ 4p	
1937	♋ 4p		◐ 4p ♌ 8p		♉ 7a	♍ 3a	◯ 10a	♎ 1p			♏ 12m ○ 10a		♐ 1p		◯ 2p	♑ 2a		♒ 1p	◑ 2p	♓ 9p			♈ 1a ☾ 3a		♉ 2a	● 8a	♊ 1a		♋ 1a ☽ 1p		♌ 3a		◐ 2a ♍ 9a		
1938	♏ 12m		♐ 10a	◯ 12n	♑ 10p	♉ 1p		♒ 11a ◑ 3p		♓ 10p		☾ 1p	♈ 5a		♉ 9a	Ⓢ 12m	♊ 11a		☽ 8a ♋ 12n		♌ 2p	◐ 4p	♍ 5p		♎ 11p	◯ 7a		♏ 7a		Ⓛ 4a ♐ 6p			♑ 6a	◯ 6a	
1939	☾ 2p		♈ 5a		Ⓢ 12n ♉ 2p	♉ 7p	♊ 8p		☽ 3a	♋ 1a		♌ 4a ◐ 1p		♍ 6a	◯ 11p	♎ 9a		♏ 1p	Ⓛ 10a	♐ 6p			♑ 3a ◯ 4a		♒ 2p		◑ 6a	♓ 2a		♈ 2p	☾ 7a	♉ 10p		● 11p	
1940	◐ 9a ♌ 5p		♍ 8p	◯ 6p	♎ 8p	♉ 1a	♏ 9p	○ 12m	♐ 10p		◯ 8a	♑ 2a		♒ 10a	◑ 3a	♓ 9p			☾ 5a ♈ 10a		♉ 10p		● 7a	♊ 9a		♋ 5p	☽ 3a	♌ 10p		◐ 4p	♍ 2a		♎ 5a	◯ 1a	
1941		♑ 7a		◑ 8a ♒ 12n	♉ 7p	♓ 8p		☾ 5a	♈ 8a		♉ 8p	● 8a		♊ 9a		☽ 11a ♋ 9p		♌ 7a		◐ 8a	♍ 1p		♎ 4p ◯ 8p		♏ 5p		○ 12m ♐ 4p		♑ 4p	◯ 6a	♒ 7p		◑ 8p	♓ 3a	
1942	● 10a ♉ 7p			♊ 7a	☽ 11a	♋ 7a	♉ 1p		♌ 7a ◐ 1p		♍ 5p		◯ 8a ♎ 11p			♏ 1a ○ 5p		♐ 1a	◯ 10p	♑ 1a		♒ 3a	◑ 7a	♓ 8a		♈ 4p	☾ 1a		♉ 2a		● 1a ♊ 1p			♋ 2a	
1943	♍ 3p	◐ 12n		♎ 1a		○ 6a ♏ 7a	♉ 7p	♐ 11a	◯ 5p	♑ 2p		♒ 4p	◑ 3a	♓ 8p		☾ 2p	♈ 12m		♉ 5a	● 5a	♊ 12n		♋ 10p	☽ 2a		♌ 11a		◐ 5a	♍ 11p		♎ 10a	◯ 4a	♏ 4p		
1944		◑ 12m ♒ 7a		♓ 9a	☾ 9a	♈ 11a	♉ 12m	♉ 11a ● 4p		♊ 2p		☽ 3a ♋ 8p			♌ 6a	◐ 1a	♍ 6p			◯ 4a ♎ 7a		♏ 5p		○ 2a	♐ 1a		♑ 8a ◯ 6p		♒ 12n		◑ 6a ♓ 4p		♈ 6p	☾ 3p	
1945	☽ 1p	♋ 10p			◐ 3a ♌ 5a	♉ 6a	♍ 3p		◐ 3a	♎ 3a		♏ 4p	○ 5a		♐ 4a		◯ 6a ♑ 3p		♒ 11p		◑ 3a	♓ 4a		♈ 6a ☾ 11a		♉ 6a	● 3p	♊ 6a		♋ 8a ☽ 11p		♌ 1p		◐ 5p ♍ 10p	

	24	25	26	27	28	29	30	J U L Y 1	2	3	4	5	6	7	8	9	10	11	12	13	14	15	16	17	18	19	20	21	22	23	24	25	26	27	2
1911	♊ 3a		♋ 2a		♌ 2a	♍ 2p	♍ 4a		♎ 9a	⊙ 4a	♏ 6p			⊙ 7a		♐ 8p		♑ 8a	♒ 8a		♓ 6p	⊙ 7a		♈ 3a		⊙ 9a	♉ 12n	♊ 10a	♋ 12n	♌ 7p	♍ 3p			♍ 1p	
1912	⊙ 9a	♐ 7a		♑ 6p	⊙ 9a		♒ 6a		♈ 8a	♉ 12n	♉ 4p		⊙ 9p	♊ 3a	♋ 10p		⊙ 8a	♌ 9p	♍ 1p	♎ 11p			♐ 1a	♑ 4a	♒ 1a	♈ 1p	⊙ 9p		♊ 12m
1913	♊ 4p		♋ 3p		♌ 11a	♊ 12m		♋ 4a	♍ 12m	♌ 7a		♍ 8a		♎ 10a	♏ 5p	♐ 1p		♑ 7p	♒ 6a		♈ 2a	♉ 11a	♉ 7a	♊ 11p	♍ 5a		
1914	♌ 3p		♋ 3a ♍ 9p		♎ 1a	♏ 2a	♏ 3a	⊙ 11p	♐ 5a		♑ 8a	⊙ 9a	♒ 12n		♓ 8p	⊙ 1a	♈ 6a		♊ 7a	♋ 4a ♌ 4p	♍ 1p ♎ 1p	♌ 7p	♍ 3a	♎ 9a	♏ 6a	
1915	♐ 5p	♑ 4a ⊙ 11p	♒ 5p		♉ 7a ♒ 8p			♈ 3a	♉ 1a	♊ 2p		♎ 1a	⊙ 7a	♏ 8a		♐ 12n		♑ 12n	♒ 11a	♓ 2a	♈ 3p	♐ 2a	♐ 12n	♑ 9p
1916	♉ 2p		♋ 4a ♊ 1a		♌ 1p	♍ 6a		♎ 2a	♍ 9a ♏ 9p		♏ 1a	♐ 7a	♑ 8a		♒ 12n ♓ 7p		♈ 7a		♋ 7p	♌ 6a	♍ 7p ♎ 9a	♋ 12m	♌ 7a	♍ 6p	♏ 7p	
1917	♍ 12n	♒ 7a	♏ 11a ♎ 11a		♏ 7p ♐ 3p	♏ 5p		♐ 11p	♑ 3a	♒ 11p		♓ 10p ♈ 11a		♈ 3a	♉ 9p	♊ 6a	♌ 10p	♍ 7p ♎ 6a	♎ 1a	♏ 8a	♍ 7p	
1918	♓ 2a ⊙ 6a		♒ 7a	♓ 6p	♈ 10a		♉ 1p	♊ 4a	♋ 4p ♋ 7a		♌ 12m	♍ 3a	♎ 6a		♏ 3a	♐ 1a ♑ 4a	♑ 1a	♒ 11a ♓ 12m	♓ 5a ♈ 6p	♈ 6p	♉ 12m	♊ 2p	♋ 5p ♌ 4p	♍ 12m
1919	♋ 9a	♊ 7a	♋ 7a ♌ 4a	♌ 9a		♍ 2a	♎ 11p	⊙ 10p	♎ 10a	♏ 10a	♐ 11p	♑ 1a		♒ 11a	♓ 3a ♈ 6p		♈ 8a	♉ 6a ♊ 1a	♊ 2p	♋ 3p	♌ 4p	♍ 7p	♎ 12m
1920	♏ 8a		♐ 1a ♑ 8p		♑ 9a ♒ 4a	♒ 10p		♈ 6p	♈ 12m ♉ 12n		♉ 3a	♊ 11a	♋ 3a	♌ 3p	♍ 3a ♎ 10p	♎ 7a		♏ 2p ♐ 3p	♐ 12m	♑ 3a	♒ 4p	♓ 3p
1921	⊙ 7a	♈ 7a	♈ 8p	♉ 8a		♊ 5a	♋ 1a ♋ 10a		♌ 12n	♍ 9a	♎ 12n	♏ 11p ♐ 1p	♎ 1p	♐ 7p ♑ 2p		♑ 2p	♒ 5a ♓ 6a		♈ 7p	♉ 2a	♊ 2p	♋ 10p ♌ 6a	♍ 3a	
1922	♊ 6p ♋ 11p		♌ 9p	♍ 9a	♍ 12m	♎ 2a ♏ 6a		♏ 5a	♐ 6a ♑ 10a		♒ 4p	♓ 10p		♈ 12m	♉ 11a ♓ 11a		♈ 12m	♉ 10p	♊ 4a	♋ 11a	♍ 6a ♎ 8a	♍ 7a	♍ 2p	♎ 2p
1923	♋ 12m	♋ 12m ♌ 9p		♌ 10p	♍ 8a	♎ 2a	♏ 10p	♐ 8a		♑ 7p ⊙ 9p		♒ 7a	♈ 8p ♓ 11a		♈ 6a	♉ 8p	♊ 1p		♋ 6p	♌ 10a	♍ 10p	♎ 9p	♏ 1a	♐ 5p ♑ 4a	♒ 6a	♓ 7a
1924	♉ 3a	♊ 10p	♋ 4p		♋ 4a	♌ 1a	♍ 4p		♎ 12m ♏ 10a		♐ 5p	♏ 3p	♐ 2a	♑ 2a	♒ 5p		♈ 8p	♉ 4p		♊ 1a	♌ 11p	♍ 11a ♎ 12n	♏ 11p	♐ 2p
1925	♑ 5a	♒ 4a		♓ 3p	♈ 5a	♈ 11p		♉ 6p	♊ 2a	♋ 2a ♌ 12m	♋ 2a		♍ 5a ♎ 2p		♏ 5a ♐ 5p	♑ 11a		♒ 9p	♓ 2p	♈ 9a	♉ 10a ♊ 7p	♌ 9p		
1926	♑ 10a ♒ 4p	♒ 12n		♈ 12m ♓ 1p	♈ 3p	♉ 8a	♉ 7p		♊ 10p ♋ 1a	♋ 9a	♌ 6p	♍ 8p		♎ 4p ♏ 4a	♐ 12m	♑ 2p		♒ 6a	♓ 9a		♈ 10p	♉ 8a	♊ 4p	♌ 8p ♍ 10a	♎ 10p	♏ 10p
1927	♉ 8a	♊ 3p	♋ 10a		♌ 2p	♍ 2a	♍ 8p		♎ 7p	♏ 4a	♐ 4a		♑ 4p ♒ 4p	♒ 12m	♓ 2p		♈ 6a	♉ 9a	♊ 11a		♋ 4p ♎ 1a	♏ 5p	♐ 9p	♑ 10p
1928	♒ 6a ♓ 12m	♏ 11p	⊙ 8p	♈ 12n		♉ 12m ♊ 10p		♋ 11a	♌ 5p	♍ 12m	♎ 7a	♏ 4a		♐ 6a ♑ 4a	♒ 8a		♓ 1p	♈ 12n	♉ 8p		♊ 7a ♋ 10a	♌ 8p
1929	♒ 11a	♒ 2a ♓ 11a		♈ 8a ♉ 11p		♊ 3p	♋ 11a ♋ 5p	♌ 4p	♍ 5p	♍ 5p ♎ 9a		♏ 9p	♐ 11a		♑ 5a	♒ 11a	♓ 5a	♈ 2p		♉ 4a ♌ 5a	♍ 4a	♎ 2p	♏ 2p
1930	♑ 12m	♋ 2a ♑ 9p		♌ 2a	♍ 2p	♎ 2a		♏ 4p ♎ 5a	♐ 6p	♐ 4a	♑ 3p	♒ 3p		♓ 4p ♈ 6a		♈ 4p	♉ 6p	♊ 3a	♌ 10a	♍ 10a ♎ 12m	♏ 10a	♐ 4a ♑ 4p	♒ 12n
1931	♏ 10p	♌ 6a	♍ 1a		♎ 7a ♑ 8p	♒ 2p		♓ 4p ♈ 12m		♈ 4p	♉ 1a		♊ 7p	♋ 1a	♌ 1a ♍ 11p	♎ 5p		♏ 10p ♐ 3p	♑ 3p	♒ 12m	♓ 3p ♌ 12m	♍ 3p	♎ 7a	♏ 1p	♐ 1p
1932		♉ 8a ♊ 4a	♋ 8p		♌ 6p	♍ 9a		♎ 8p	♏ 5p	♐ 3a		♑ 10p ♒ 10p	♒ 2p		♈ 9a ♉ 2p		♊ 8p	♋ 7a	♌ 10p		♍ 4p ♎ 1a	♏ 7a	♐ 8a	♑ 4p ♒ 9p		♓ 4p
1933		♌ 6a ♍ 10p	♎ 3p		♏ 5a ♏ 5a		♐ 9a	♑ 7a	♒ 7a		♈ 3p ♓ 2p	♓ 9a		♈ 3p	♉ 7a	♊ 12n		♋ 12n ♌ 9a	♍ 12m		♎ 3a ♏ 11p	♐ 3a	♑ 9a	♒ 7a
1934	♐ 4p	♑ 4p	♑ 12m ♒ 4p		♈ 5a ♓ 4p		♈ 8p	♉ 3p		♊ 2a	♋ 10a ♋ 11a	♌ 10p		♍ 10a ♎ 12m		♏ 12n	♐ 9p	♑ 2a		♒ 12n ♓ 2a	♈ 9a ♌ 9a	♍ 3a	♎ 4a ♏ 7p	
1935		♉ 11a ♊ 9p	♋ 4p		♌ 11p ♋ 3p	♍ 3p		♎ 7a	♏ 3p ♏ 9p		♐ 10a ♑ 5p	♒ 9p		♈ 5a ♓ 2a	♉ 10p	♊ 12n		♋ 1p ♌ 12m	♍ 12n		♎ 3a ♏ 4a	♐ 3p	♑ 10p	♒ 4a	♈ 6a
1936		♎ 4a ♏ 2a	♏ 5p		♐ 4p	♑ 4a		♒ 2p	♓ 1p	♈ 8p		♉ 12m ♈ 2a		♊ 3a	♋ 11a	♋ 12m		♍ 10a ♎ 6p	♏ 8a		♐ 7a	♑ 6a	♒ 1p		♓ 1a ♈ 7p	
1937		♑ 1a	♒ 4p	♓ 10a		♈ 3p ♓ 8a	♉ 8p		♊ 5p ♋ 10p	♌ 11p		♍ 2a ♎ 9a		♎ 9a	♏ 5p ♐ 8a		♑ 8a	♒ 7a	♓ 9p	♈ 2a ⊙ 7a	♉ 8a ♊ 8a	♌ 3p		
1938	♐ 11a	♊ 7a	♋ 7a ♋ 4a	♌ 7a	♍ 9p	♍ 7a		♎ 11a	♎ 9a ♏ 7p		♐ 3p ♑ 2a	♒ 6p		♈ 6p ♓ 10a	♉ 7a	♊ 5a		♈ 7p ♋ 12n	♌ 5p		♍ 4p	♎ 4p	♏ 6p
1939	⊙ 12m	♍ 1a	♏ 2p	♑ 9a		♐ 6p ♑ 11a	♒ 5a		♈ 5p ♓ 1p	♉ 6a	♊ 3p		♋ 9a ♈ 11p	♌ 9a		♍ 2a ♎ 3a	♏ 2a		♐ 2p ♑ 9p	♒ 8p	♓ 3a	♈ 9a	♉ 3a	♊ 9a		♌ 1a
1940	♓ 1p		♈ 10p ♈ 1p	♉ 2p		♊ 2p ♊ 12n		♋ 4a	♌ 6a	♍ 11a		♎ 2p ♏ 2a	♏ 11p		♐ 8p ♑ 1p	♒ 5a		♓ 4a	♈ 1p		♉ 9p	♊ 8p ♌ 3a	♍ 9a		♎ 10p ♏ 7a
1941	♑ 9a ♒ 2p		♌ 6p	♍ 10a	♎ 1a		♏ 6a ♎ 11p	♏ 10a		♐ 8a ♑ 11a	♑ 12n		♒ 3p ♓ 3p		♈ 8p ♉ 4a	♊ 5a		♋ 5a ♌ 3a	♍ 5a	♎ 6a	♏ 4p	♌ 1a	♍ 7a	♎ 7a
1942		♉ 3a ♊ 10a	♋ 9p	♌ 7a	♍ 9p		♎ 1p ♏ 11a	♐ 2p	♑ 10p		♒ 3p ♈ 1a	♉ 4a		♊ 7a	♋ 2a	♌ 1p ♍ 7a	♎ 2a		♏ 10p	♐ 7a	♑ 4p	♌ 7a	♍ 7a	♎ 9a	♏ 8a
1943	♈ 3a ♓ 11a		♉ 5p		♊ 8a	♋ 12n	♋ 8a		♌ 1a	♍ 7p ♎ 2a		♏ 11a ♏ 11a		♐ 4p	♑ 2a	♒ 5p	♈ 5a ♓ 7a	♓ 5a	♈ 8p	♉ 5a ⊙ 1a	♊ 6p	♋ 12n	♌ 11a ♍ 11a	♎ 12m	♊ 7a	♏ 8p
1944	♋ 10a	♊ 10a		♎ 11p ♍ 12n	♏ 10a	♐ 12n ♑ 11p		♑ 11a	♒ 2a		♈ 4a ♓ 1p	♉ 5a	♊ 1p		♋ 5a ♋ 1p	♌ 8p		♍ 1p	♎ 5a	♏ 8p	♐ 5p	♑ 7p ♒ 2a	♓ 6a	
1945	♑ 3p ⊙ 10a		♒ 11a	♈ 7p ♓ 4p		♈ 1p	♉ 10p		♊ 10p ♊ 12m	♋ 3a	♋ 9a	♌ 8a		♍ 3p ♎ 1a		♎ 1a	♏ 2a	♐ 3a	♑ 11a	♒ 1a	♓ 6p ♈ 9p	♓ 1a		♈ 10p

29	30	31	A U G 1	2	3	G 4	5	6 T	7	8	9	10	11	12	13	14	15	16	17	18	19	20	21	22	23	24	25	26	27	28	S E P 29	30	31	1

	2	3	4	5	6	7	8	9	10	11	12	13	14	15	16	17	18	19	20	21	22	23	24	25	26	27	28	29	30	1 O	2 C	3 T	4	5
1911																																		
1912																																		
1913																																		
1914																																		
1915																																		
1916																																		
1917																																		
1918																																		
1919																																		
1920																																		
1921																																		
1922																																		
1923																																		
1924																																		
1925																																		
1926																																		
1927																																		
1928																																		
1929																																		
1930																																		
1931																																		
1932																																		
1933																																		
1934																																		
1935																																		
1936																																		
1937																																		
1938																																		
1939																																		
1940																																		
1941																																		
1942																																		
1943																																		
1944																																		
1945																																		

	11	12	13	14	15	16	17	18	19	20	21	22	23	24	25	26	27	28	29	30	1 D	2 E	3 C	4 E	5 M	6 B	7 E	8 R	9	10	11	12	13	14
1911	♌ 5p		◑ 2a ♍ 8p			♎ 2a ☾ 6p		♏ 10a		● 4p ♐ 9p		♐ 5a ▶	♑ 9a	☽ 6p	♒ 10p			♓ 10a ◐ 9p		♈ 6p		O 2p	♉ 12m		♊ 1a ○ 10p		♋ 1a		♌ 1a O 2a		♍ 2a	◑ 11p	♎ 8a	
1912		♑ 6a ☽ 4p		♒ 5a		◐ 6p	♓ 5a		♈ 5p	O 7p		♉ 2a	◀ ♐ 11a	♊ 8a ○ 11a		♋ 11a	O 9p	♌ 1p		♍ 3p	◑ 6a	♎ 6p		☾ 7p ♏ 11p			♐ 6a	● 12n	♑ 2p			♒ 1a ☽ 11a		♓ 1p
1913		♉ 1a	○ 6p	♊ 11a		♋ 7p	O 1p		♌ 1a		◑ 3a ♍ 6a	♐ 5p	♎ 8a	☾ 12n	♏ 10a		♐ 12n ● 9p		♑ 3p		☽ 10a ♒ 10p			♓ 8a	◐ 10a	♈ 9p			♉ 9a O 1p		♊ 7p		○ 10a	♋ 2a
1914	♍ 5p		♎ 8p	☾ 6a	♏ 9p		● 11a ♐ 8p		♑ 8p	☽ 5p	♒ 11p	♐ 10p		♓ 6a ◐ 9a		♈ 5p		◐ 10a	♉ 5a		♊ 6p	○ 1p		♋ 5a		O 1p ♌ 3p		♍ 11p		◑ 7a	♎ 4a		♏ 6a ☾ 4p	
1915		♒ 6a	◐ 6p	♓ 11a		♈ 7p	O 12n		♉ 4a		○ 1p ♊ 4p		♐ 4a	♋ 5a	O 4p	♌ 5p			♍ 5a ◑ 5p		♎ 12n		☾ 8a ♏ 4p		♐ 4p	● 1p	♑ 3p		♒ 3p ☽ 6p		♓ 6p		◐ 7a	♈ 1a
1916			♋ 1a O 1p		♌ 2p		◑ 5p	♍ 3a		♎ 1p	☾ 3p	♏ 8p	◀ ♐ 10a	♐ 11p	● 4a		♑ 1a	☽ 11a	♒ 2a		♓ 4a ◐ 9p		♈ 9a		O 11a ♉ 3p		♊ 11p		○ 8a	♋ 9a		♌ 9p	O 10a	
1917		♏ 8p		● 1p	♐ 5a		♑ 11a	☽ 6a	♒ 4p		◐ 5p ♓ 7p	♐ 4p	♈ 10p		O 3a	♉ 12m		♊ 3a ○ 2p		♋ 9a		O 7a ♌ 6p			♍ 5a	◑ 9a	♎ 6p			♏ 5a ☾ 11a		♐ 1p		Ⓢ 4a ♑ 7p
1918	◐ 12n	♓ 8a		♈ 10a O 9p		♉ 10a		○ 3a ♊ 10a		♋ 12n	O 11a	♌ 4p	◀ ♐ 10p		♍ 1a ◑ 5a		♎ 12n		☾ 8a	♏ 1a		♐ 1p	Ⓢ 10a		♑ 12m		☽ 7a ♒ 8a		♓ 2p	◐ 10p	♈ 6p		♉ 8p	O 7a
1919	O 12m	♌ 9p		◑ 11a	♍ 3a		♎ 11a	☾ 7a	♏ 11p			Ⓢ 10a ♐ 12n	♐ 3a		♑ 1a	☽ 2p	♒ 1p		♓ 10p	◐ 12n		♈ 4a		O 12m ♉ 7a		♊ 7a	○ 5a	♋ 6a		♌ 6a O 11a		♍ 10a		◑ 1a ♎ 6p
1920	♐ 10a		♑ 10p	☽ 12n		♒ 11a		◐ 3p ♓ 11p			♈ 8a	O 11a	♉ 1p		♊ 3p ○ 9p		♋ 3p		O 2a ♌ 4p		♍ 6p	◑ 11a	♎ 11p			☾ 5a ♏ 7a		♐ 5p		● 5a	♑ 5a		♒ 6p	☽ 2a
1921	♈ 6a O 1p		♉ 3p		○ 9a ♊ 10p			♋ 2a O 9p		♌ 5a	♐ 9a ↗	◑ 7a ♍ 7a	◀ ♐ 3p	♎ 11a	☾ 6p	♏ 3p		♐ 8p	● 8p		♑ 4a		☽ 5a ♒ 2p			♓ 2a	◐ 8a	♈ 3p			♉ 1a O 8a		♊ 7a	○ 5p
1922		◑ 3a ♍ 11p			♎ 12m ☾ 12n		♏ 1a	● 7p	♐ 2a		♑ 3a	☽ 6a	♒ 11a		♓ 9p	◐ 3a		♈ 9a		O 7a ♉ 10p			♊ 9a	○ 6a	♋ 5p		♌ 11p O 11p			♍ 3a	◑ 12n	♎ 7a		♏ 9a ☾ 10p
1923	♑ 10a ☽ 3p		♒ 1p		◐ 5a ♓ 8p			♈ 6a	O 5a	♉ 7p	♐ 9p ↗	♐ 3a ▶	○ 8a ♊ 8a		♋ 7p		O 9a	♌ 6a		♍ 2p	◑ 5a	♎ 7p		☾ 4p ♏ 9p		♐ 9p	● 9p	♑ 9p		♒ 10p	☽ 4a		♓ 4a	◐ 10p
1924	○ 8a	♊ 6a		♋ 6p	O 10a		♌ 7a		◑ 1p ♍ 6p		♐ 9a ▶	♎ 2a	☾ 6a	♏ 5a		♐ 6a ● 12n		♑ 5a	☽ 5p	♒ 5a		♓ 9a	◐ 4a	♈ 3p			O 12m ♉ 1a		♊ 12n		○ 2a	♋ 12m		♌ 1p
1925		♎ 2a ☾ 11a		♏ 9a		● 2a ♐ 1p		♑ 4p	☽ 11a	♒ 6p	♐ 3p ▶	◐ 9p ♓ 9p			♈ 1a	O 10a	♉ 6a		♊ 1p	○ 3a	♋ 10p			O 4a ♌ 10a		♍ 11p		◑ 7a	♎ 11a		♏ 7p	☾ 4a	♐ 11p	
1926	♒ 8a	◐ 6p	♓ 11a		♈ 1p	O 3a	♉ 3p		♊ 5p ○ 11p		♋ 10p	♐ 8p	O 2a	♌ 6a		♍ 6p	◑ 2a		♎ 6a		☾ 5a ♏ 6p			♐ 3a	● 1a	♑ 9a		♒ 1p ☽ 3p		♓ 5p		◐ 2a ♈ 8p		♉ 10p
1927		♋ 1a O 8a		♌ 6a		◑ 1a ♍ 2p			♎ 2a	☾ 2a	♏ 2p		♐ 2a	♐ 3a ● 5a		♑ 2p		☽ 5a ♒ 11p			♓ 6a ◐ 9p		♈ 9a		O 6a ♉ 11a		♊ 11a	Ⓛ 1p	♋ 12n		♌ 4p O 11p		♍ 10p	
1928		Ⓢ 5a	♐ 1a		♑ 2p	☽ 9a		♒ 3a		◐ 9a ♓ 12n	♐ 8a ▶	♈ 6p	O 10p	♉ 8p		♊ 8p	Ⓛ 4a	♋ 8p		O 9a ♌ 8p			♍ 12m ◑ 10p		♎ 8a		♏ 7p ☾ 8p			♐ 7a		● 12m ♑ 8p		
1929		♈ 10p	O 7a		♉ 2a	○ 7p	♊ 5a		♋ 6a	O 2a	♌ 7a	♐ 2p	♍ 10a ◑ 11a		♎ 2p		☾ 2a ♏ 10p			♐ 7a	● 12m	♑ 6p			☽ 2a ♒ 7a		♓ 7p		◐ 4a	♈ 6a		♉ 1p O 11p		♊ 4p
1930	♌ 9p		◑ 7a	♍ 12m		♎ 2a ☾ 5p		♏ 6a		● 5a ♐ 10a	♐ 8p ▶	♑ 5p	☽ 11p		♒ 2a		♓ 3p	◐ 1a		♈ 3a		O 3a ♉ 2p		♊ 9p	○ 7p		♋ 7a		♌ 3a O 6a		♍ 5a	◑ 3p	♎ 8a	
1931		♑ 6p	☽ 3a	♒ 11p			♓ 10a ◐ 9p		♈ 10p		O 1a	♉ 11a	♐ 1a	♊ 10p	○ 2a		♋ 7a	O 10a	♌ 2p		♍ 7p	◑ 12n	♎ 11p		☾ 9p	♏ 1a		♐ 2a	● 5a	♑ 4a		♒ 9a ☽ 6p		♓ 6p
1932	♉ 9a		○ 2a ♊ 9p			♋ 10a	O 5a	♌ 9p			◑ 1a ♍ 5a	♐ 7a	♎ 10a	☾ 3p	♏ 12n		♐ 11a ● 8p		♑ 10a		☽ 1a ♒ 12n		♓ 5p	◐ 5p		♈ 3a		♉ 3p O 6p			♊ 3a	○ 9p	♋ 3p	
1933	♍ 7a		♎ 3p	☾ 3a	♏ 7p		● 11a ♐ 8p		♑ 7p	☽ 5p	♒ 8p	♐ 1p		♓ 12m ◐ 3a		♈ 6a	O 9p	♉ 3p			♊ 2a ○ 9p		♋ 2p			O 12m ♌ 3a		♍ 3p		◑ 1a	♎ 12m		♏ 5a ☾ 4p	
1934		♒ 10a	◐ 10p	♓ 1p		♈ 4p	O 9a	♉ 9p		○ 11p	♊ 3a	♐ 7p	♋ 11a	O 9p	♌ 11p			♍ 12n	◑ 1a		♎ 12m		☾ 12m ♏ 8a		♐ 1p	● 12n	♑ 3p		♒ 5p ☽ 8p		♓ 7p		◐ 6a ♈ 10p	
1935	♊ 7a		♋ 11a O 9p		♌ 7p		◑ 8p	♍ 6a		♎ 7p	☾ 11p	♐ 1a ▶	♏ 7a		♐ 4p ● 10p		♑ 11p	☽ 2p		♒ 5a		♓ 9a	◐ 2a	♈ 12n		O 12n ♉ 2p		♊ 5p	○ 10p	♋ 9p			♌ 4a O 3p	
1936		♏ 4a		Ⓢ 12m ♐ 5p			♑ 4a	☽ 1a	♒ 2p		◐ 8p ♓ 9p	♐ 6a		♈ 1a	O 6a	♉ 1a		♊ 1a ○ 11a		♋ 2a	O 7p	♌ 5a		♍ 12n	◑ 1p	♎ 10p			♏ 10a ☾ 4p		♐ 11p		● 6p	♑ 10a
1937	◐ 5a	♓ 2a		♈ 8a O 8p		♉ 10a		Ⓛ 3a ♊ 10a		♋ 10a	O 8a	♌ 11a	◀ ♐ 12n	♍ 3p ◑ 7p		♎ 10p		☾ 3p	♏ 9a		♐ 9p	Ⓢ 6p		♑ 10a		☽ 10p ♒ 11p			♓ 9a	◐ 8p	♈ 5p		♉ 9p	O 9a
1938	O 2a		♌ 11p	◑ 11a	♍ 2a		♎ 6a	☾ 12m	♏ 12n		Ⓢ 7p	♐ 9p	◀ ♐ 5p	♑ 8a	☽ 8p		♒ 8a		♓ 8a ◐ 11p		♈ 7p		O 7p	♉ 2a		♊ 5a	○ 5a	♋ 6a		♌ 6a O 11a		♍ 7a	◑ 8p	♎ 11a
1939	● 3a	♐ 12m		♑ 6a ☽ 6p		♒ 3p		◐ 6p	♓ 3a		♈ 4p	O 9p	♐ 12m	♉ 2a		♊ 10a ○ 5p		♋ 3p		O 6a ♌ 7p		♍ 9p	◑ 4p		♎ 12m		☾ 3a ♏ 4a		♐ 9a	● 5p	♑ 3p			♒ 12m ☽ 1p
1940			♉ 12m	○ 9p	♊ 12n		♋ 10p	O 8p		♌ 6a	♐ 6a ▶	♍ 11a ◑ 12n	12n ↙	♎ 2p	☾ 9p	♏ 4p		♐ 4p	● 4a	♑ 6p		☽ 2p ♒ 10p			♓ 7a	◐ 11a	♈ 6p			♉ 7a O 3p		♊ 7p		○ 3p
1941		◑ 12m ♍ 7p			♎ 12m ☾ 2p		♏ 2a	● 7p	♐ 1a		♑ 12m	☽ 12m	♒ 2a		♓ 7a ◐ 1p		♈ 4p		O 12n	♉ 4a		♊ 5p	○ 4p		♋ 5a		♌ 5p O 6p			♍ 2a	◑ 2p	♎ 9a		♏ 12n
1942	♑ 10a ☽ 5p		♒ 12n		◐ 2a ♓ 4p		♈ 10p	O 6p		♉ 6a		○ 3p ♊ 4p	◀ ♐ 5p ↙	11p	♋ 3a	O 6p	♌ 4p			♍ 4a ◑ 9p		♎ 2p		☾ 2p ♏ 7p		♐ 8p	● 9p	♑ 8p		♒ 10p	☽ 2a	♓ 10p		◐ 1p
1943	○ 8p	♊ 5p			♋ 12m O 3p		♌ 11a		◑ 6p	♍ 12m		♎ 12n	☾ 7p	♏ 9p			♐ 3a ● 10a		♑ 6a	☽ 8p	♒ 8a		♓ 11a	◐ 6a	♈ 2p		O 6p ♉ 7p			♊ 1a	○ 11a	♋ 9a		♌ 8p
1944	♎ 8a ☾ 5p		♏ 8p		● 5p	♐ 6a		♑ 2p	☽ 1p	♒ 9p	11a ↘	♐ 5a	♓ 1a ◐ 3a		♈ 4a	O 12n	♉ 5a		♊ 7a ○ 8p		♋ 10a		O 10a ♌ 5p			♍ 3a	◑ 10a	♎ 3p			♏ 4a ☾ 1p		♐ 2p	
1945	♒ 5a	◐ 6p	♓ 12n		♈ 3p	O 6a	♉ 4p		○ 10a ♊ 3p		♋ 3p	O 5p	♌ 6p			♍ 1a ◑ 8a		♎ 11a		☾ 10a	♏ 12m		♐ 12n	● 1p		♑ 12m		♒ 11a ☽ 1p		♓ 6p		◐ 6a ♈ 11p		

16	17	18	19	20	21	22	23	24	25	26	27	28	29	30	31
☾ 9a		♐ 3a		● 11a / ♑ 3p		♑ 6p	♒ 4a	☽ 2p	♓ 4p			♈ 3a / ◐ 2p		♉ 9a	
◐ 3p	♈ 2a		♉ 12n	◔ 1p	♊ 6p	♑ 12m	♋ 8p / ○ 11p		♌ 9p		◔ 6a / ♍ 9p			♎ 12m / ◑ 3p	
♌ 7a	◔ 12m	♍ 11a		◑ 11a / ♎ 2p	♑ 5a ▶	♏ 5p	☾ 10p	♐ 8p			♑ 1a / ● 10a		♒ 7a		☽ 5a / ♓ 5p
● 0p	♑ 7a		♒ 9a	☽ 7a	♓ 2p	◀ ♑ 11p		♈ 12m / ◐ 3a		♉ 12n		◔ 7a	♊ 1a		♋ 12n
♉ 0a	◔ 5a	♊ 10p		11p ↘	○ 8a / ♋ 11a	♑ 5p	♌ 11p		◔ 11a	♍ 11a		♎ 8p	◑ 8a		♏ 1a
	◑ 1p / ♎ 10p			♏ 6a	☾ 7a	♐ 10a		♑ 11a / ⓢ 4p		♒ 11a	☽ 9p	♓ 12n		♈ 2p	◐ 7a
♒ 0p	☽ 3p		♓ 1a		◐ 1a / ♈ 3a	◀ ♑ 5a	♉ 6a	◔ 1p	♊ 11a		♋ 5p	◷ 5a		♌ 2a	
	○ 2p / ♋ 11p			♌ 2a	◔ 3a	♍ 10a	◀ ♑ 11a	♎ 8p	◑ 2a		♏ 9a		☾ 5a / ♐ 9p		
	♏ 5a	☾ 2a	♐ 6p			● 6a / ♑ 7a	♑ 4p	♒ 6p		☽ 6a	♓ 5a		♈ 11a	◐ 12m	♉ 2p
♓ 6a		♈ 4a / ◐ 10a		♉ 11p	♑ 10p	◔ 1a	♊ 2a		♋ 2a / ○ 8a		♌ 1a	◔ 12n	♍ 2a		♎ 5a
	♌ 12n	◔ 6a	♍ 1p		◑ 3p / ♎ 4p	♑ 4a	♏ 9p		☾ 5a	♐ 3a		♑ 11a	● 1a	♒ 10p	
♐ 1a		● 7a / ♑ 3p		♒ 8p	☽ 11p	♑ 10a	♓ 5a		♈ 5p	◐ 1a		♉ 6a		◐ 3a / ♊ 5p	
		♉ 1a	◔ 12m	♊ 2p		♑ 4p	♋ 2a / ○ 3a		♌ 12n		◔ 12m / ♍ 8p			♎ 2a / ◑ 4p	
	♍ 1a		◑ 5a / ♎ 10a	♑ 10p ▶	♏ 3p	☾ 6p	♐ 5p		♑ 4p / ● 11p		♒ 4p		☽ 4a / ♓ 5p		♈ 10p
♑ 1a		♒ 2a / ☽ 9p		♓ 3a	♑ 4a ▶	◐ 4a / ♈ 6a		♉ 11a	◔ 10p	♊ 7p			♋ 5p / ○ 9p		♌ 5p
	♊ 2a		○ 1a / ♋ 7a		♌ 3p	◔ 9p	◀ ♑ 10a	♍ 2a		♎ 3p	◑ 12m		♏ 2a		☾ 12m / ♐ 12n
♎ a		♏ 10p	☾ 10p		♐ 10a	♑ 3p	♑ 9p / ⓢ 11p			♒ 5a	☽ 6p	♓ 11a		♈ 3p	◐ 6a
☽ a	♓ 7p		◐ 11p	♈ 2a	♑ 9p	♉ 6a	◔ 10a	♊ 8a		♋ 7a / ○ 3p		♌ 7a	◔ 10p	♍ 9a	
♋ 4p		♌ 4p	◔ 11a	♍ 4p		♎ 8p / ◑ 9p	◀ ♑ 3a		♏ 3a	☾ 5p	♐ 1p			♑ 1a / ● 7p	
☾ a	♐ 6p		● 8p	♑ 1a	♑ 9a ▶	♒ 11a	☽ 7p	♓ 11p			♈ 11a / ◐ 11p		♉ 11p		◔ 9p
◐ p	♈ 6a		♉ 7p	◔ 9p		♊ 6a	◀ ♑ 2p	♋ 2p / ○ 5p		♌ 8p		◔ 9a	♍ 1a		♎ 4a / ◑ 8p
◔ 9p		♍ 11a		◑ 3p / ♎ 5p	♑ 8p	♏ 9p		☾ 1a / ♐ 10p		♑ 10p	● 6a	♒ 10p		☽ 4p	♓ 2a
● p	♑ 6a		♒ 6a	☽ 3a	♓ 6p	♑ 2a	♈ 12n / ◐ 3p		♉ 9p		◔ 1p	♊ 8a		♋ 8p	○ 4p
◔ 8p		♊ 10a		○ 4p / ♋ 7p		♑ 8a	♌ 7a	◔ 4p	♍ 8p			♎ 8a / ◑ 9p		♏ 6p	
	◑ 5p	♎ 3a		♏ 3p	☾ 7p	♑ 2p	♐ 1a		♑ 7a / ⓢ 1p		♒ 12n		☽ 1a / ♓ 3p		♈ 5p
♒ p	☽ 4p		♓ 3a		◐ 6a / ♈ 7a	◀ ♑ 7p	♉ 10a	◔ 4p	♊ 11a		♋ 12n / ○ 11p		♌ 3p		◔ 11a / ♍ 9p
	○ 2p / ♋ 9p		♌ 9p	◔ 7p	♍ 11p	♑ 1a		♎ 5a / ◑ 9a		♏ 3p		☾ 10a	♐ 3a		♑ 4p
♏ p	☾ 1p		♐ 4a		● 1p / ♑ 3p	◀ ♑ 7a	♑ 1p ↙	♒ 3a	☽ 4p	♓ 4p			♈ 5a / ◐ 6p		♉ 12n
♓ a		◐ 4p	♈ 12m		♉ 12n	◔ 4p	♊ 8p			♋ 12m / ○ 6a		♌ 2a	◔ 3p	♍ 3a	
	♌ 11a	◔ 8a	♍ 5p	♑ 7p ▶	◑ 9p / ♎ 9p		♏ 11p		☾ 7a	♐ 2a		♑ 4a / ● 4p		♒ 8a	
♐ n		● 5a / ♑ 11a		♒ 12n	☽ 12n	♓ 4p	◀ ♑ 1a	♈ 11p	◐ 6a		♉ 11a		◔ 8a / ♊ 11p		
	♉ 11a	◔ 9a	♊ 10p			○ 10a / ♋ 10a	◀ ♑ 7a	♌ 11p		◔ 2p	♍ 11a		♎ 10p	◑ 2p	
	♍ 8a		◑ 3p / ♎ 9p		♑ 12n ▶	♏ 7a	☾ 12n	♐ 1p		♑ 3p / ● 11p		♒ 4p		☽ 6a / ♓ 5p	
		♒ 3a	☽ 12m	♓ 7a	♑ 6p	♈ 10a / ◐ 11a	12m ↙	♉ 12n	◔ 9p	♊ 3p		♋ 8p	○ 10a		♌ 2a
	♊ 2a	◷ 9p	♋ 2a		♌ 5a	◔ 7a	♍ 10a		♎ 7p	◑ 3a		♏ 7a		☾ 6a / ♐ 7p	

	1 J	2 A	3 N	4 U	5 A	6 R	7 Y	8	9	10	11	12	13	14	15	16
1946		♑ 7a	ⓢ 7a	♒ 5p			♓ 12m / ☽ 2a		♈ 5a	◐ 3p	♉ 8a		♊ 11a	◔ 1a	♋ 1p	
1947	♉ 8p		◔ 7p / ♊ 10p		♋ 10p		○ 12m / ♌ 10p		♍ 11p	◔ 6a		♎ 3a	◑ 10p	♏ 11a		♐ 11p
1948		♎ 10a	◑ 6a	♏ 3p			♐ 12m / ☾ 1a		♑ 11a		● 3a / ♒ 11p			♓ 12n	☽ 6a	
1949			☽ 3a / ♓ 8a		♈ 9p		◐ 7a	♉ 9a		♊ 6p	◔ 5a		♋ 12m	○ 5p	♌ 2a	
1950			♋ 2a	○ 3a	♌ 9a		♍ 2p / ◔ 6p		♎ 6p		◑ 5a / ♏ 9p			♐ 12m / ☾ 4p		♑ 3a
1951	◑ 12m	♏ 11a		☾ 10a / ♐ 1p		♑ 1p	● 3p	♒ 1p		♓ 3p	☽ 12m	♈ 8p			◐ 7a / ♉ 7a	
1952			♈ 1a	◐ 12m	♉ 8a		♊ 6p / ◔ 9p			♋ 6a		○ 12m / ♌ 6p			♍ 7a	◔ 3a
1953	♌ 4p			◔ 2a / ♍ 5a		♎ 6p		◑ 5a	♏ 5a		♐ 12n	☾ 12m	♑ 4p		● 9a / ♒ 5p	
1954	☾ 3a / ♐ 12n		♑ 8p	ⓢ 9p		♒ 1a		♓ 5a / ☽ 9a		♈ 7a	◐ 7p	♉ 10a		♊ 2p	◔ 6a	♋ 6p
1955	◐ 3p		♉ 12m		◔ 1a / ♊ 2a		♋ 3a	○ 8a	♌ 5a		♍ 9a / ◔ 8p		♎ 4p		◑ 5p	♏ 3a
1956	◔ 4a / ♍ 1p		♎ 5p	◑ 6p		♏ 1a		♐ 1p / ☾ 6p			♑ 2a	● 10p	♒ 2p			♓ 2a / ☽ 11p
1957		♒ 12n			☽ 12m / ♓ 1a		♈ 1p		◐ 2a / ♉ 11p			♊ 6a / ◔ 7p		♋ 8a		○ 1a / ♌ 8a
1958		◔ 12m / ♊ 7a		♋ 1p	○ 3p	♌ 4p		♍ 6p	◔ 12m	♎ 8p		◑ 9a / ♏ 11p			♐ 4a / ☾ 11p	
1959	♎ 10a	◑ 6a	♏ 2p		♐ 4p / ☾ 4p		♑ 6p		● 2a / ♒ 9p			♓ 3a / ☽ 4p		♈ 12n		◐ 4p
1960	☽ 9p	♓ 4a		♈ 10a	◐ 2p	♉ 8p			♊ 9a / ◔ 4p		♋ 10p		○ 7p	♌ 9a		♍ 7p
1961	○ 6p		♌ 8a		♍ 9p / ◔ 10p			♎ 9a	◑ 10p	♏ 5p		♐ 10p	☾ 11a	♑ 11p		● 5p / ♒ 10p
1962		☾ 8p	♐ 1a		♑ 5a	● 8a	♒ 7a		☽ 3p / ♓ 7p		♈ 9a		◐ 12m / ♉ 1p		♊ 7p	◔ 3p
1963		♈ 12m / ◐ 8p		♉ 3a		♊ 5a / ◔ 6a		♋ 9a	◷ 6p	♌ 2p		♍ 10p	◔ 1p		♎ 9a	
1964		◔ 4p / ♍ 10p			♎ 5a	◑ 11a	♏ 4p			♐ 5a / ☾ 2p		♑ 5p		ⓢ 4p	♒ 4a	
1965	♑ 3p	● 4p		♒ 4a		♓ 4p / ☽ 7p			♈ 2a	◐ 4p	♉ 9a		♊ 1p	◔ 4a	♋ 2p	
1966	♉ 1p		◔ 3p / ♊ 7p	♊ 7a	♋ 10p		○ 12m / ♌ 10p		♍ 10p	◔ 5a	♎ 11p		◑ 3p	♏ 3a		♐ 9a
1967		♎ 12n	◑ 9a	♏ 3p		♐ 8p / ☾ 9p			♑ 1a	● 1p	♒ 8a		♓ 6p	☽ 11a		♈ 6a
1968	♒ 10a		☽ 11a / ♓ 4p			♈ 1a	◐ 10a	♉ 1p			♊ 2a / ◔ 1p		♋ 1p		○ 11a / ♌ 10p	
1969		♋ 11a	○ 1p	♌ 11p			♍ 10a / ◔ 2p		♎ 6p		◑ 9a	♏ 12m		♐ 3a / ☾ 7p		♑ 4a
1970		♏ 7a		☾ 10a / ♐ 11a		♑ 12n	● 4p	♒ 12n		♓ 12n / ☽ 8p		♈ 2p		◐ 8a / ♉ 7p		
1971			♈ 1a	◐ 12m	♉ 5a		♊ 10a / ◔ 1p		♋ 5p		○ 8a	♌ 2a		♍ 2p	◔ 10a	
1972		♌ 3a		◔ 8a / ♍ 11a		♎ 10p		◑ 9a	♏ 10a		♐ 10p	☾ 11a		♑ 7a		ⓢ 6a / ♒ 2p
1973			♑ 7a	ⓢ 11a	♒ 6p			♓ 3a / ☽ 9a		♈ 10a		♉ 12m / ◐ 2p		♊ 5p	◔ 10a	♋ 6p
1974	◐ 1p		♉ 12m		◔ 2a / ♊ 2a		♋ 3a	○ 8a	♌ 3a		♍ 3a / ◔ 1p		♎ 5a		◑ 2a / ♏ 12n	
1975	◔ 5a / ♍ 1p		♎ 2p	◑ 2p	♏ 7p			♐ 2a / ☾ 6a		♑ 11a	● 5p	♒ 10p			♓ 10a / ☽ 8p	
1976	● 10a	♒ 10p			☽ 5a / ♓ 7a		♈ 6p		◐ 8a	♉ 7a		♊ 6p	◔ 9a		♋ 2a	
1977	◔ 7a / ♊ 3p			♋ 2a	○ 7p	♌ 11a		♍ 6p	◔ 1a		♎ 12m	◑ 3p	♏ 4a		♐ 6a	☾ 1a
1978	♎ 10a	◑ 7p	♏ 4p		♐ 6p / ☾ 7p		♑ 6p	● 11p	♒ 5p		♓ 6p	☽ 5a	♈ 10p		◐ 10p	♉ 7a
1979	♓ 8p	☽ 2a		♈ 5a	◐ 6a	♉ 10a		♊ 7p	◔ 1a		♋ 5a		○ 2a / ♌ 5p			♍ 6a
1980	♋ 7a	○ 4a	♌ 4p			◔ 3a / ♍ 3a		♎ 4p		◑ 7a	♏ 4a		♐ 1p	☾ 5a	♑ 7p	

	17	18	19	20	21	22	23	24	25	26	27	28	29	30	31	F 1	E 2	B 3	R 4	U 5	A 6	R 7	Y 8	9	10	11	12	13	14	15	16	17	18	19
1946	10a	8p	11a	12m	4a		3p	12m		3a				12m	2a	7a	11a	1p		2p		1p	5p	8p	10a		12m		12m	1p	1a	7p		
1947		12m	12n	4p		1a 4a		11a		2a 8p		7p	7a		5a 9a		9a	11a	10a		9p			8p		5p	5a		7p	9p		8a	7a	
1948	12m		7a 10p	10p	4p	9p	6p		6p	2a	5p		10p	8p		5a		5p 7p			5a	10p	6p		6a	12m	4p		9p	12m	1p		
1949	3a	12m	4a	4a	1a 7a		12n		1a 7a			4a			3p		12n 4a		5p		3a	4a		10a 9p		1p		1p	9a	2p		6p		
1950	3a		10a			12n		12n	12m		1a			1a 11a		5a	5p	10p			3a	2p	6a		10a	2a	3p		12m			8a	
1951	8p	10p		4p	10p	12m		4a	8p	12n		6p	10a	8p		10a	12m	11p		2a	2a		7a 5p		4p		4p	3a		4p	7p		3a	
1952	6p		11p	1 3a		7a	1p	8a	8a 5p		8a		12n 10a		3p	3p		12m		12n 4p				1a		7p	1p			9a		1p		
1953	5p	3a	6p	3a	9p	1a		3a	8a	12n	11p	7p		12n	11p	1a		12n	11p	9p	3a 2p			4a	8p	4a		4a	1a	5a		
1954	10p	12m	9a	9a	7p	9p			9a 10p		10p		9p	5a		11a	1p		2 7p		4p		4a 6p		12m		8a			2 5p	12m		
1955	4p	9p	10p	4a			2 8p		9p		12n	2a		6a	12m	9a		10a 12	2p	9p	7p	2a	1p		12n		3p	12m	1p	5p	10p		
1956	11a	6a	9p	9p		4 11a		11p	10a	11p		5p	4a		9a	11a	7p	9p		4a 2p		5p	8a		5p	1p		12m		4 8p		
1957	7a	6a	8a	3a	2 5p		8p	2p	7a			7p	4p		7a			7a	6p	2p		7p	7a	7p		6p	9a		6p	5p	8p	5a	
1958	10a	6 5p	9a		5a	5p		6a 9p	5p		3 4a		6p	12m	3a	3a	3a	3 9a		5a	7p	9a		4p	12n		1a	11p	11a		2p	
1959	1a		1p	2p 2p	12m		7a 3a		12n		3 4a		7p	2p	10p			4a	9a	4p	5a 1p		12n		9p			9a	6a	2p	6 2p	
1960	5p	3a		8p	9 10a		12n	7p	1p		1p	1a	3p	12 8a			4a	9a	4p		5a 1p		4p		12n	2a		9a	6a	2p		
1961	10p	10p	2a	2a	5 11a			11p		10a			2p	2p		3a	2 4p		12m	12n	6a		6p 10a			9a			10a	11a	1p	
1962	3a		1 0p	8a	1p		1a	4p	2p	3 8p			11a	12 4a		6p	7p	6p		6p	12m	8p		10a	12m		8a	6a	7p	4a	10p	
1963	4 10p		2p	9a	4p	6p		12 7a		4a	7p	6a		8a	4a	11a		4 4p			10p		10a	7a		5p	10a		6a		1p 4a	
1964	12n	11a	6p	8p	10p	12m			1a	10a	3a	5 5a		8a		8 3a		8a		1a	2p		12n		7p			2p	1p	4a		
1965	9 4a	1 6a		1p	3p	4p 10p		6a		9a		4 8a			10a	12m	10p		8 11a		3p			4 9p	11p	2p		12m	7p	12m	3p	2a	
1966	10a	9p		7a	9 11a		9p		2p	10a		9p		5a		6 3a		9a	11a	8a			8 3a		10a		4 5a			2a	3a	2p	
1967	3p 7p		1p	6a	2p	1p		4p	2a	6p		9 7p		9p	6p		1a		7 4a		3p		6a	1a		1p	8a			2a	3a	
1968	3a	3a	8a	7p	1 3p		2p			1 5p		8p	12m	1a		3 5a		9p		7a	10a		10p	9a		6a	2 11a		2p	1p	5p	
1969	12 3a	3 1a		4a	8a	9a		6p	3a		5a		6 4a		5a	8a	4p		2 4a		7a	8p	10a		2a	4a	2p		11 4a	2p	7p	
1970	2a	5a	6a			4a 1a		5p		11a	5a		3p	10a	9p		11a 10a		4p	11p	3a			3a	11p	11a			9p		12m	10a
1971	3a	3a 1p		12n		8a	6a		6 8a		8a			7a 9a		11a	10a	4p		11p	3a		9a				10a	10a	6a	10p		
1972	6p	6p	10p	6p		12n 4a		3a	3p	7a			12n	6a	8p		3 6a		6p		6a	7a		5p	6a		12m	7p	3a	5a	3a	6
1973	4 0p	7 7a		9p	12m	4a	2a		1p		5p		12n 6a			1a	9a		8p		2 7p		4a			3 7p		2p	2a	
1974	10p		2a	11a 6a		12m 6a		12n	7 11a		7a	3a	12n		1 2 2a		2p	6p	2p		3p	2a	8p		7p	5a		5p	10p	8p	
1975	11p		6 10a	5p	6p		3 10a		11p		10a	10a		6 10p		5p	1a	1a	7a		5a 10a		4a		12 5p		5a	4a	5p		3 3a
1976	12 6a	8a	9a	10a		1 6a			5p		7 12 5p				6a	1a	3p		1 2a		3p		5a		12n	12 6a	2a	5p			6 6p
1977	8a	9 10a		11p 3p		12 10a			10a	12m	11p			3 10a		7p	11p		1a		6 12 6a		9a	11p	12m		3p	10a	7p		11p	12m
1978		6p	5a	12m	7a		7p	3a		6a			2 3a		10p	7p		2a	4 4a		10a	5a				3p			5p	2p	
1979	6a	4 7p		11a	5a	11a	8p	2p		1p	1a	12n	7 3a		5p	8p		1a		11 6a		11p		10p	12n		1a	12n	11a	7a	
1980	4p	9p	11p	5p	12m 12m			3a 9a		7p			12m		11p	9p		10a		11p 12m		12n		3 6a 10p			8a		4a	

21	22	23	24	25	26	27	28	29	1 M	2 A	3 R	4	5 H	6	7	8	9	10	11	12	13	14	15	16	17	18	19	20	21	22	23	24	25	26
	♐ 12n ○ 10p				♑ 12m	☽ 10p	≈ 9a			♓ 3p	●	♈ 6p		♉ 8p ○ 10p	☽		Ⅱ 10p		⊙ 7a	⊙ 2a		♌ 6a ○ 8p	⊙ 1p		○ 2p ⊙ 9p	♎		♏ 7a	○ 2p	◀ ♈ 1a	⊗ 8p		♑ 8a ○ 5p	
	♈ 2a	☽ 3p	♉ 8a		⊙	♑ 1p	Ⅱ 4a	≈ 1p		⊙ 1p	○ 2p ○ 6p			♏ 8p	≈ 10p	≈ 11p		♏ 5a 1a		○ 3p		○ 1p	☽ 3a		≈ 4p	○ 4p		♓ 2a	○ 6a ○ 10p 12n					☽ 1p ⊙
⊙ 8a	♌ 5a		⊙ 4a 12n		○ 4a	○ 7p	♏ 6a		♐ 12n	○ 11p	♑		♓ 12m	♈ 4p	♈ 12n			♌ 11p	⊙ 9a			♏ 12m	○ 2p		Ⅱ 6a			○ 6p	♌ 2p	○ 4p	○ 3p		♓ 4p	♏ 5p
♌ 1a	☽ 3p	≈ 10a		♓ 10p ● 4p		♈ 10a			○ 8p	♉ 12m		☽ 2p	⊙ 8p		♌ 11p	○ 9a			♏ 12m		♓ 4p	○ 2p	♌ 12n			● 2a	♉ 6p		♉ 4a	♈ 1p	○ 4p			
⊙ 8p		Ⅱ 9a	○ 9p		⊙ 8p			⊙ 6p	♌ 3a		○ 7a	○ 6a	○ 9a		♏ 12n	○ 10p		⊙ 9a		♈ 1p	○ 5a		♓ 12m		♈ 4a		♉ 1p							⊙ 5a
♌ 12n			♍ 9p 7p	♏		♐ 6p		♑		Ⅱ		○ 12n		⊙ 3p	♈ 11a	♉ 4p		♈ 6a		♏ 2p	♐ 8a	♐ 8p		♌ 12n	♈ 11a	♏ 3a				≈ 6a			○ 6a	○ 4p
⊙ 11p	☽ 7p		♓ 7p	♈ 4a	♉ 8p		○ 2p 12m		♐ 8a	Ⅱ 9a	○ 7p		♓ 11p	⊙ 4p	○ 4p		♏ 3p	○ 1a	♓ 6a			○ 3p	Ⅱ 6a		♏ 2p	○ 8a	○ 8p		♈ 3a	♓ 7a	♉ 5a			♈ 9p
♏ 6p			♌ 11a 5a	○ 6p	♍ 2p	○ 7a		⊙ 5p 7p		♈ 4a	○ 1p	♐ 11a		♏ 3p	○ 1a	♏ 3p		♌ 1p	○ 7a	♌ 11p		♏ 8a			♍ 12m 8p	♏ 5p				♏ 11a				⊙ 5a
⊙ 4p	♏ 5p		☽ 5a 6p	⊙ 3p	♈			○ 7p 9p	♌ 1p		●	♓ 11p	♈ 10p			♉ 12m			♌ 6a	♏ 5a		♏ 11p		○ 8a	♏ 12m	♏ 12n		♏ 11a	♌ 11a		○ 12n			♑ 11p
♌ 5 11a			♈ 9a	☽ 10p	♉		Ⅱ 12n	⊙ 2p	⊙ 6p		○ 7a 8p	♈ 3a	♉ 11a				♏ 8p	♌ 8p		○ 8a		○		♓ 3p	○ 6a	♏ 8a				♏ 3p	♏ 6a			♉ 8p
⊙ 8a	⊙ 2p	♌ 9a	♍ 10p 9p		○ 8p 6p			♐ 3a	⊙ 7a	♑ 4p		○		♏ 3p				○ 9p 11p	⊙ 6a			☽ 6a	♏ 12m	♌ 9a			♈ 2a	♏ 10a	♓ 4p	○ 10p	♍ 7p		♎ 4a	○ 8a
♏ 7a 12n		♑ 12n	☽ 8a	≈ 1a		♓ 1p		♈ 1a		♌ 12m 9p		Ⅱ 9p			○ 7a	⊙ 7a		♌ 5a 5p	⊙ 6a			♏ 5a	♈ 9p	♉ 5a			♏ 6a	♏ 4p	♏ 8p	12m				♉ 7a
♈ 2m	♉ 2p 1p	☽ 1p		Ⅱ 1a 4p	⊙ 4a 9a		♌ 9a		♍ 2p 2p		○ 1p	≈ 2p		⊙ 6a 10p			⊙ 4p	○		♌ 6a	♏ 2a	♏ 6p		○ 10p	♏ 4a			♌ 4a	♏ 5a		♉ 8a	♏ 7a			
♍ 9p	○ 4a	♎ 11p		○ 1p	♏ 1a	♏ 1a			♏ 4 10p 7a	♐ 7a		♓ 7p		●	⊙ 6a	♉ 5a		♈ 5p	⊙ 7a		Ⅱ 6a			♏ 9p 4p	○ 5a 4a		♌ 5a 5a	⊙ 7a	♏ 3p			☽	Ⅱ 7a	
♑ 9a	☽ 4 11a 1p		♈	♉ 6a		♈			☽ 3 1p	♉ 6a	Ⅱ 12m			○ 4a 4a		♏ 1p		○ 12 8 m a	♏	♏ 10a				○ 3 4 a	♏ 4p			♏ 5a 12n	♏ 10a	♌ 2a			♏ 9a	♌ 10a
Ⅱ 9p	⊙ 4a		♌ 8a		♍ 6p 9p	○ 1p	♍ 1a		♍ 3 10 a a	Ⅱ 12m		○ 5p	⊙ 9a		♏ 1p	♏	♌ 9a 9a	♌ 8p		♌ 4a		♏ 1a 9a		♌ 6p 2p	♏ 7p		♏ 7p		♈ 3 6 a	♏ 5a		○ 5a		♌ 4a 1a
♏ 9p		♏ 12n	♍ 10a 8p	♏ 7p	♐ 11a		♑ 1a	♈ 2p		♈ 6a		○ 4 4 a a	♍ 2p			♉ 3a 1a		♏ 1p	♏ 5a		♏ 1a		♈ 8p	○ 7 1 p a	♏ 1a 12n	♏ 12n		♏ 9a	♉ 3 10 a a		♏ 12m 12n		♈ 1 7 a	♏ 10a
♏ 10a	♏ 7p	♌ 1p		♍ 6p	♍ 8a		♍ 1a		♎		♓ 2p	☽ 3 1p	♈ 6a			♉ 5p 12n		♍ 9a	♌ 1p		♏ 1a			♏ 6a	♌ 12n	♍ 12n		○ 8p		♏ 7p		♏ 5a	♏ 1a	
♐ 4p	⊙ 1a	♑ 4a	♈ 4 5 a a	≈		♓ 9p		♈ 5a	♉ 2p		○		Ⅱ 11p 9a		♏ 2a	♏ 1p			♌ 4a		♏ 11a		○	♏ 5p	♏ 9p	♏ 10p 12m		♏ 9a	○ 9a		♌ 5a	♏ 1a	☽ 9p	Ⅱ 6p
♏ 3p	☽ 8a	♏ 3a	Ⅱ 12n	⊙ 5a		♍ 6p		♍ 11p	♏ 8p		○ 9p	♏ 3a		♏ 8a	♍ 11p	♍ 7p		♍ 8a				♈ 9p		♏ 9a	♏ 3a	♌ 9p		♈ 9a	♏ 11p	♏		♌ 9a		♏ 6p
♌ 3a	♍ 4 1p	☽ 12m		♍ 4a	○ 4a	♏ 4a	○ 10a	♈		Ⅱ 6p		○ 4a 6a		♌ 3p		♍		♌ 2a 9p		♏ 12 4 p		○ 4p		♏ 8a	♏ 11p		♌ 1p	♏ 5p	♌ 3p			○ 3 10 a		
♐ 4p 1p	♍ 10a		≈ 4a	♍ 4 5 a a		♓ 11p	♍ 9p			♏ 8a		♏ 5a	♏ 5a	♉ 2p		♍ 11p		♍ 2a 1p	○ 6a			♏ 7p		♍ 5p	♌ 9p		○ 9p	♏ 12m	♏ 2a			○ 5p	♏ 2a	♏ 5a
♈ 3p	☽ 8a	♏ 3a	Ⅱ 12n		⊙ 6p		♍ 5a	♍ 9a		Ⅱ 10p		♏ 8p	♍ 9p	♏ 7p		♍ 8p		♍ 3a		♍ 5a		♈ 11a		♏ 2p	♏ 2p	♌ 9p		♈ 1p	♏ 6a	♓		♌ 1a	♏ 3p	♌ 10a
≈ 7p	♓ 7p	⊙ 5a	♈ 7p		Ⅱ 10p		⊙		♍ 5a	○		♏ 5a				♍ 3a 10p		♏ 5a	♍ 12n		♏ 5a		♍ 5a	♍ 12m	♍ 2a	♏ 9p 12m	♏ 2a		♉ 6 2 a	♏ 4a	♌ 9a	♏ 6a		♌ 2a
♏ 1p	⊙	♏ 2 7 p	♈ 10p		○	♍ 2p	♍		♍ 9p 10p		♓ 6p	♏ 7p	♈			♉ 2p 5a		♌ 2p				♏ 2p	♍ 12n		♏ 7 3 a		♌ 1a	♏ 7a	♌ 10a		♌ 1a 3p	♏ 10a		♍ 10a
♌ 1a	●	♈ 4a	☽ 12n	Ⅱ 6p	♌ 1p		○ 10p	♍		♌ 10p 12m		♏ 1a	♏		♌			♏ 2p	♏ 1a		○ 2p	♈ 1a		♏ 2p	♈ 8p		♏			♏ 6p			♏ 6p	
♈ 4p	♌ 10a	♏ 3a			♍ 9a		♏ 1a 10 a		♎	○ 2p 3p		♏ 12m		♏ 10a 3a		♏ 11a		♈ 11p	♏ 7p		♈ 7p		♏ 2a 1a		♏ 8p	♏ 1a		♏ 9a	♌ 8p		♉		≈		♏ 8p
♍ 3a	♏	♑ 4a	♏ 8p	12n		♓ 10p	●		♈ 9a			♏ 4 8 a	♍ 11a			♏ 3 12 a m		♉ 5a 10p	♌ 5a			♌ 4a 3a		♍ 6a	♏ 7a		♈ 4a 3a	♏ 6a	♏ 7a 1a			♏ 5p		♏ 10a
♉ 6p		Ⅱ 7 10 a	♌ 7p		♍ 10p 4a		♍ 10a 12n	♈ 9a		♍ 6p 4a		○	♏ 2p	♍ 2p		♍ 4 9 a a		♏ 6p		♍ 1a			♏ 6a	♍ 5a	♏ 3a		♏		♏ 1p		♏ 5p			♏ 10a
♏ 1 7 p a			♌ 9p	♏ 3a	♏ 3a		♏ 7p		♍ 12m		♓ 3p	●	♈ 12n			Ⅱ 6 9 p a		♈ 7p 2a	☽	♉ 8a		♈ 4p		♌ 5p	♏ 3p		♏ 1a	♌ 4p 9p	♏ 9a	♏ 9p		♍ 9a	♓ 4p	♏ 10a
♏ 7a 12m	☽	♓ ⊙ 12 12 n n	♈ 12m			♓		♌ 2a		Ⅱ 7a		♏ 2a	♌			♍ 7p 7p		♏ 4p	♌ 6a	♏ 5p			♌ 5p	♏ 3p		♉	♏ 12m 6a	♏ 6a	♍ 6 4 a			♏ 9a	♏ 4p	♏ 10a
♏ 8p		♏ 2p	♉ 5a	♏ 4p		♈ 6a		♏ 5p 4p	♏ 4p		♏ 6a	♍ 2p	○		♍ 10a 12n		♏ 3a	♉ 7p		♏ 6a		♍ 4a 6a		♌ 5p	♏ 3a		♏ 1a				♏ 5p	♏ 7p	♍ 9p 9p	♏ 11a

	27	28	29	30	31	A P R I L 1	2	3	4	5	6	7	8	9	10	11	12	13	14	15	16	17	18	19	20	21	22	23	24	25	26	27	28	29
1946		2p	1a	4a	1a	5a		5a			7a	3p	12n		6p	7a			3a		6a			2a	9a	3p			3a		11a			2p
1947		9p	11a	12m	10p	4a		8a	10a	11a		11p	7a		11a		9a	12m		9a	9a	6p	6p	11	12n		1a	8a	3a		6a	5p		9a
1948	9a	10		7a	5a	3p		7a	8a	6p		4a	4a		11a	2a	5p		3p		10p	11p	11	12m		3a	3a	8a		12	3p		
1949	5p	5p		5a		12	5p		2a	8a	8a		10 6p		11a		12m	11a	6a	3p		11 11	5a		10a		12 11			12n	3a	11p
1950	1p		6p	8p	4p	8p	8 p	9 p	8p	8p		7a	2a		11a	2a	10p			3a		11p	11a	7p	11a			9p	6a		3a	7p	6a
1951	8a		10a	1a	1p	1p	6p	12m	6a	9a		8p	5a		8a		8 8p	6a	5a	12n	5p	3 4p		4p	11a	4p			7p	7a	11p
1952	10a	5a	5p	3a	4a	3p	4 7a		2p	4p		2 6p		6a		4 8p	10p	12n	2p	3p		7p	2a		2a	9p	11a
1953	12m		1p	8a	12m	7 10a		5p	12 10m	1 a	1a	3p	2a		3a	12m	9a	4a	6 8p			7a	11p	8p		7 a	12m
1954	11a	7a		11a	7a	10a	2 10a		10 12a	1p		1a		12 7p	5 10p		10a	6p		3a	5a		2p	12n	7p	11 a
1955	9p	11p	3p	3a		6 10a	6p		2a	4a	4p	4a		6 4p		12m	12m	4p			5a	1p	6a		9a	11
1956	3a		1 12 2n	12m	3a	12n		4m	8a	10p	1p		4p	9a	7p		10p	1a	6a	6a		12 9p		8p		7p	4a
1957	3a	8a		8a	4a	6p	1 2a		7a	7a	4p	2p	12n	2p	12m	3p	7 4a	9p	8p		4a	4a	3 6p		3a	9p	3a
1958	5p	6a	11p		6p	1a	1 2a		12m		5a	7p	1p		12 7p		12n	10p	9a	11p	11p		10a
1959	9p	11a		1p	6a	6p	11p	3a		12n	10p	12m		12n	2a	1a	3 11p	5p	6p	8p	3p	9p	12m	8p	12
1960	3a	10p		12 9n		9p	2a	9a		7p	1a		2a	5a		7 11p	8a	8 8p	9p	3p	9p	9p		6 5p		4p	
1961		1 4p			3a	1a	12n		10p		5a	1a	4 3a	6a	1 9a		3p	4p	12n	3a	12 5n		12m	7p	12n
1962	9 11a	2p		10 4a	4p	3p	2p	5 10a		10a	4p	9a	8p	5p	5 8p	9a 2p	6a	5p	2p		8p	8a
1963	12m	12n	12m	3 10a	10a	6 7p		7a	8p	7p	8 a	11 a	7p		10p	5a	10a	11a		10a	8p	12n	5p
1964	8 10a		9p	5a	6p	1a	6a	2 2p	9 p		8 8p	2p	9p		11p	12m	8p	6a	3p	2a	12 1		12n
1965	1a	11p	12n	9p	7p	3a		8 9a		11a	8p	2p	5p	6a	9p		6p	2a	10a	8p	12n	9a	9p	4p	6a
1966		12 6n	4a	1 5a		6a	5a	6a	10 4a	5p	1p	4a	4p	3p	12m	1 4	11p	10a	6a	10 11	1a	1
1967	2p	3 7p	7p	6p	3p	2 2p		2a	5p	3p	3 8	2p	2p	9	1a	2a	2p	1a	3p	4a
1968	2 6p	1p	8p	2a	2p	10p	12m	7 4a	10a	12 11	10a	5a	11a	8p	3 3p	10p	9a	8a	7p	10a	8a
1969	10p	9p	8a	3p	7p	10p	12m	3a	12 7a	12n	1 8p	5a	12n	5p	6 3p	5p	3p	12n	5p
1970	9a	2p	6a	5p	3 7p	9p	11p	11p	4 12	1p	11a	12m	1p	2p	1a	7a 9 11	3p	2 7p	11p	12n
1971	5a	8p	7a	12n	11a	9p	9 12	10p	3p	10a	9p	3p	6a	8 12 1p	3p	6p	4p	4 11	5p	8
1972	9p	3p		9a	6 9	9a	7p	7p	12 10	2a	4p	1a	2a	7p	7 9	3p	5a	3a	3p	8a
1973	6p	6p	3a	8a	7a	10a	1 1a	1p	11p	5p	10p	2p	5a	9 a	1a	1a	10a	2p	2 a	12n
1974	9a 12m	4 9	7a	9 a	11a	4p	9a	9a	10a	12n	7p	6a	6a	6a	5p	6a	5p	12n
1975	6a 8p	1 11	6a	7a	5p	5 10	6p	12n	5a	2p	9a	9p	12 2 12n	5a	8a	6a	7 3	9a
1976	4a	4p	12n	5a	2 5	4a	2p	12n	3p	4p	7 3	12n	6p	6p	9a	12 9a	2 10	9a	10a
1977	3 5	2p	8p	12 11	1a		1 3	2a	2p	6p	1p	7a	10p	6 9 12m	10p	9a	10a	10p	6a
1978	12 2m	4p	10a	7p	10 6	3a	9a	9a	6p	7a	6a	9 7 6a	9a	2p	6a	9p	12
1979	11 10	1p	9p	1 12	1a	5a	1p	8 2	2p	6a	1a	11a	2 3 12n	6p	11p	10p	8a	3a 1
1980	7 11	12n	10a	12m	12 12	9p	7p	3a	6 6a	7a	11p	6a	7a	5a	10a	5p	6	5a

May 1	2	3	4	5	6	7	8	9	10	11	12	13	14	15	16	17	18	19	20	21	22	23	24	25	26	27	28	29	30	31	June 1	2	3	4
● 8a	♊ 3p		☽ 1p / ♋ 4p		♌ 6p		◐ 12m	♍ 12m		♎ 9a / ◯ 8p		♏ 8p		○ 10p	♐ 9a		♑ 10p		◯ 1a	♒ 9a	**♊ 12n**	♓ 6p / ◑ 11p			♈ 12m	☾ 11a	♉ 2a		♊ 2a / Ⓢ 4p		♋ 2a	☽ 9p	♌ 3a	
◯ 6a / ♎ 2p		♏ 10p		○ 12m	♐ 7a		♑ 7p	◯ 12m		♒ 8a		◑ 3a / ♓ 7p			♈ 4a / ☾ 11p		♉ 9a		Ⓢ 9a / ♊ 11a	**♊ 5p**	♋ 11a	☽ 3p	♌ 12n		♍ 3p	◐ 12m	♎ 8p		◯ 4p	♏ 4a		♐ 2p	Ⓛ 2p	
◑ 12m	♓ 3p			☾ 2a / ♈ 2a		♉ 12n	Ⓢ 9p	♊ 6p		♋ 11p	☽ 10a		♌ 2a	◐ 8p	♍ 4a		♎ 7a	◯ 6a	♏ 11a	**♊ 11p**	♐ 1p / ○ 8p			♑ 12m	◯ 4p	♒ 11a		♓ 11p	◑ 6p		♈ 11a		☾ 5p / ♉ 9p	
	☽ 1a / ♋ 8a		♌ 2p	◐ 5p	♍ 6p		♎ 8p	◯ 1a	♏ 9p		○ 8a / ♐ 10p			♑ 1a / ◯ 6p		♒ 7a		◑ 2p / ♓ 5p		**♊ 5a**	♈ 6a	☾ 5p	♉ 7p			♊ 5a / ● 5p		♋ 2p		☽ 10a / ♌ 8p			♍ 12m / ◐ 10p	
♏ 7a	○ 12m	♐ 6a		◯ 5a / ♑ 6a		♒ 9a	◑ 6p	♓ 5p			♈ 4a / ☾ 4p		♉ 4p		● 8p	♊ 5a		♋ 5p	☽ 9p	**♊ 10a**	♌ 3a		♍ 11a / ◐ 5p		♎ 3p		◯ 3a / ♏ 5p		♐ 5p	○ 8a	♑ 4p		◯ 2p / ♒ 6p	
☾ 11p	♈ 6a		♉ 4p	● 9p		♊ 3a		♋ 2p / ☽ 11p			♌ 4a		◐ 12m / ♍ 3p		♎ 10p	◯ 6p		♏ 1a		○ 1a / ♐ 2a	**♊ 4p**	♑ 1a	◯ 5a	♒ 2a		♓ 5a / ◑ 3p		♈ 12n		☾ 11a / ♉ 10p			♊ 9a	● 12n
◐ 11p		♍ 12m		♎ 11p	◯ 12m		♏ 6a	○ 3p	♐ 10a		♑ 12n	◯ 12m	♒ 2p		◑ 10a / ♓ 5p		♈ 9p	☾ 10p	**♊ 10p**	♉ 2a		♊ 10a / ● 2p		♋ 7p		☽ 2p	♌ 7a		♍ 8p	◐ 5p		♎ 7a		◯ 2p / ♏ 3p
	◯ 6p / ♑ 11p			♒ 4a	◑ 7a	♓ 8a		♈ 10a / ☾ 4p		♉ 11a		● 12m / ♊ 1p		♋ 6p	☽ 2p		♌ 3a		◐ 1p / ♍ 3p	**♊ 4a**	**♊ 9a**	♎ 3a	◯ 4p	♏ 3p		♐ 11p	○ 12n		♑ 5a		◯ 2a / ♒ 10a		♓ 1p	◑ 1p
♉ 9p	● 8p	♊ 3p		♋ 10p / ☽ 10p			♌ 3a	◐ 1p	♍ 11a		♎ 11p	◯ 2p		♏ 12n		○ 5p	♐ 12m		♑ 11a	◯ 4p	♒ 8p			♓ 2a / ◑ 9a		♈ 6a	☾ 6p	♉ 7a		♊ 7a / ● 11p		♋ 8a		☽ 9a / ♌ 12n
	◯ 5p / ♎ 11p			♏ 10a	○ 5p	♐ 10p			♑ 11a / ◯ 9p		♒ 11p		◑ 9p	♓ 9a		♈ 2p	☾ 10a	♉ 4p	**♊ 3p**	♊ 4p / ● 4p		♋ 4p	☽ 9p	♌ 5p		♍ 9p	◐ 9a		♎ 5a		◯ 6a / ♏ 4p			♐ 4a
♒ 8p	◑ 10p	♓ 8a			♈ 5p / ☾ 8p		♉ 10p		● 8a	♊ 1a		♋ 2a / ☽ 4p		♌ 4a		◐ 12m / ♍ 7a		♎ 11a	◯ 2p	♏ 6p			♐ 4a / Ⓛ 10a		♑ 3p		◯ 12n	♒ 4a		♓ 4p	◑ 2p		♈ 2a	
♊ 9a		☽ 10a / ♋ 2p		♌ 6p	◐ 9p	♍ 9p		♎ 11p	◯ 7a		♏ 2a	Ⓛ 6p	♐ 6a		♑ 1p	◯ 11a	♒ 11p	**♊ 9p**	**♊ 3a**	♓ 11a / ◑ 12n			♈ 12m	☾ 1p	♉ 10a		♊ 5p	● 7a	♋ 9p		☽ 5p	♌ 12m		♍ 2a
	♏ 11a	Ⓛ 7a	♐ 12n		♑ 2p / ◯ 4p		♒ 9p		◑ 10a	♓ 6a		♈ 7p	☾ 12n		♉ 8a		● 2p / ♊ 7p		**♊ 9a**	♋ 4a	☽ 10a	♌ 11a		♍ 4p	◐ 12m	♎ 7p		◯ 8a / ♏ 9p		♐ 10p	○ 4p		♑ 2a	
♓ 7a		☾ 12n / ♈ 5p			♉ 6a	● 3p	♊ 7p			♋ 7a / ☽ 6p		♌ 6p		◐ 3p	♍ 2a		♎ 6a	◯ 3a	♏ 7a	**♊ 3p**	♐ 7a / ○ 8a		♑ 6a	◯ 1p	♒ 8a		♓ 2p	◑ 3a	♈ 11p			☾ 4a / ♉ 12n		
	♌ 5p	◐ 8p		♍ 4a		♎ 11a / ◯ 4p		♏ 3p		○ 1a / ♐ 4p		♑ 4p	◯ 6a	♒ 5p		◑ 3p / ♓ 8p		**♊ 9p**	♈ 3p	☾ 8a	♉ 12n		♊ 11p	● 7a		♋ 11a		☽ 10a	♌ 12m		♍ 12n	◐ 11a	♎ 8p	
	♐ 12m		◯ 1a / ♑ 4a		♒ 6a	◑ 11a	♓ 9a		♈ 1p / ☾ 10p		♉ 5p		● 12n	♊ 12m		♋ 8a	☽ 8a	♌ 8p		**♊ 2a**	♍ 9a / ◐ 11a		♎ 8p		◯ 11a	♏ 5a		♐ 9a	○ 12m	♑ 11a		◯ 7a / ♒ 1p		♓ 3p
♈ 1a		♉ 2a / ● 11p		♊ 3a		♋ 7a / ☽ 10a		♌ 4p		◐ 8a	♍ 3a		♎ 4p	◯ 11a		♏ 4a		○ 10a / ♐ 11a		♑ 8p	**♊ 8a**	◯ 2a	♒ 1a		♓ 5a / ◑ 2p		♈ 8a	☾ 11p		♉ 10a		● 8a / ♊ 1p		♋ 5p
	♍ 1a		◯ 10a / ♎ 1p			♏ 1a	○ 12n	♐ 2p			♑ 1a / ◯ 2p		♒ 11a		◑ 9a / ♓ 5p		♈ 9p	☾ 7p	♉ 9p	**♊ 9p**	♊ 9p / ● 11p		♋ 10p		☽ 7a	♌ 1a		♍ 8a	◐ 12m	♎ 7p			◯ 2a / ♏ 8a	
♑ 1a		♒ 1p	◑ 5p	♓ 11p			♈ 4a / ☾ 9a		♉ 6a	● 4p	♊ 6a		♋ 6a / ☽ 9p		♌ 8a		◐ 8a / ♍ 12n		♎ 8p	**♊ 8p**	◯ 3a	♏ 6a		♐ 6p	○ 4a		♑ 7a		◯ 8a / ♒ 7p			♓ 6a	◑ 6a	♈ 1p
● 7a	♊ 3p		☽ 4p / ♋ 6p		♌ 8p		◐ 1a / ♍ 11p			♎ 3a / ◯ 1p		♏ 9a		○ 7a / ♐ 6p			♑ 4a	◯ 7a	♒ 5p	**♊ 2a**		♓ 5a / ◑ 10a		♈ 3p		☾ 6a / ♉ 10p			♊ 1a / Ⓢ 4p		♋ 2a	☽ 10p	♌ 3a	
◯ 7a / ♎ 3p		♏ 4p	Ⓛ 4p		♐ 8a		♑ 2a / ◯ 7a		♒ 12n		◑ 6a	♓ 12m		♈ 12n	☾ 8a	♉ 11p			Ⓢ 5a / ♊ 7a	**♊ 7a**	♋ 12n	☽ 6p	♌ 4p		♍ 6p	◐ 3a	♎ 9p		◯ 2p	♏ 12m		♐ 5a	○ 3a	♑ 11a
◑ 6a	♓ 8p			☾ 7a / ♈ 8a		♉ 9p		Ⓢ 10a	♊ 9a		♋ 7p	☽ 9a		♌ 3a		◐ 12m / ♍ 8a		♎ 11a	◯ 9a	♏ 11a	**♊ 1p**	♐ 12m / ○ 3p		♑ 2p		◯ 1a / ♒ 6p			♓ 3a / ◑ 9p		♈ 3p			☾ 12m / ♉ 4a
☽ 2p / ♋ 9p			♌ 8a	◐ 1p	♍ 4p		♎ 8p	◯ 3a	♏ 9p		○ 8a / ♐ 9p		♑ 9p	◯ 1p	♒ 10p			◑ 1a / ♓ 4a	**♊ 7p**	♈ 1p	☾ 11p		♉ 1a		♊ 2p	● 2a		♋ 3a		☽ 4a / ♌ 2p		♍ 11p		◐ 12m
♏ 4a	○ 12m	♐ 6a		◯ 7a / ♑ 7a		♒ 8a	◑ 3p	♓ 12n		♈ 6p	☾ 7a		♉ 2a		● 3a / ♊ 1p			♋ 1a	☽ 5a	♌ 1p	**♊ 12m**		♍ 1a / ◐ 7a		♎ 10a		◯ 1a / ♏ 3p		♐ 4p	○ 8a	♑ 4p		◯ 1p / ♒ 4p	
☾ 10p	♈ 5a		♉ 8a	● 10a	♊ 1p		♋ 9p	☽ 4a		♌ 8a		◐ 5a / ♍ 9p			♎ 9a	◯ 7a	♏ 6p		♐ 11p / ○ 11p	**♊ 7a**	**♊ 12n**	♑ 2a	◯ 8a	♒ 4a		♓ 7a / ◑ 5p		♈ 10a		☾ 5a / ♉ 3p		♊ 9p	● 9p	
♌ 5a	◐ 3a	♍ 4p			♎ 5a / ◯ 6a		♏ 5p		○ 6a	♐ 3a		♑ 11a	◯ 1a	♒ 5p		◑ 3p / ♓ 10p			♈ 12m	☾ 12m	♉ 2a		♊ 3a / ● 8a		♋ 6a	☽ 9p	♌ 1p			♍ 12m / ◐ 8p		♎ 12n		◯ 10p
	◯ 10a / ♑ 3p			♒ 2a	◑ 7a	♓ 8a		♈ 12n / ☾ 7p		♉ 12n	● 11p	♊ 11a		♋ 11a	☽ 5a	♌ 3p		◐ 8p / ♍ 10p	**♊ 6p**		♎ 9a	◯ 9p	♏ 9p			♐ 10a / ○ 11p		♑ 9p		◯ 11p	♒ 7a		♓ 3p	◑ 4p
♉ 8p	● 4p	♊ 8p		♋ 9p / ☽ 9p		♌ 11p		◐ 7a	♍ 3a		♎ 11a	◯ 12m	♏ 8p			○ 12m / ♐ 8a		♑ 8p	**♊ 12m**	◯ 3a	♒ 9a		♓ 8p	◑ 4a		♈ 3a	☾ 6p	♉ 6a		♊ 7a	● 12m	♋ 5a		☽ 5a / ♌ 7a
	◯ 1p / ♎ 7p			♏ 12m	○ 4a	♐ 7a		♑ 5p	◯ 2a		♒ 6a		◑ 4a / ♓ 6p			♈ 4a	☾ 3a	♉ 11a	**♊ 6a**	♊ 3p / ● 4p	**♊ 11a**	♋ 5p	☽ 11p	♌ 6p		♍ 8p	◐ 8a		♎ 12m	◯ 9p	♏ 6a		♐ 2p	Ⓛ 5p
	♒ 1a	◑ 1a	♓ 1p			♈ 1a / ☾ 3a		♉ 12n		Ⓢ 2a / ♊ 9p			♋ 3a / ☽ 6p		♌ 8a		◐ 5a / ♍ 11a		♎ 1p	◯ 2p	♏ 3p		♐ 7a	Ⓛ 1a		♑ 1a	◯ 6p	♒ 9a		♓ 9p	◑ 6p		♈ 9a	
		☽ 6a / ♋ 10a		♌ 6p		◐ 12m	♍ 12m		♎ 2a / ◯ 10a		♏ 2a	Ⓛ 3p	♐ 2a		♑ 4a / ◯ 11p		♒ 8a		♓ 4p / ◑ 4p	**♊ 5p**		♈ 4a	☾ 7p	♉ 5p			♊ 5a / ● 9p		♋ 4p		☽ 5p	♌ 12m		♍ 5a
	♏ 11a	○ 8a	♐ 11a		♑ 11a / ◯ 1p		♒ 1p	◑ 11p	♓ 6p			♈ 3a / ☾ 7p		♉ 3p		● 10p	♊ 4a		♋ 5p	**♊ 11p**	☽ 1a	♌ 4a		♍ 2p / ◐ 10p		♎ 7p		◯ 11a / ♏ 10p		♐ 10p	○ 4p	♑ 9p		◯ 9p / ♒ 10p
♓ 4a		☾ 5a / ♈ 9a		♉ 5p		● 12m	♊ 2a		♋ 2p	☽ 12m		♌ 2a		◐ 3a / ♍ 2p		♎ 11p	◯ 11p		♏ 5a	**♊ 5a**	♐ 7a / ○ 8a		♑ 7a	◯ 2p	♒ 7a		♓ 10a / ◑ 11p		♈ 3p		☾ 3p / ♉ 11p			♊ 9a
	♌ 9p	◐ 11p		♍ 10a		♎ 10p	◯ 2a		♏ 7a	○ 9p	♐ 1p		♑ 5p	◯ 9a	♒ 8p		◑ 7p / ♓ 11p		**♊ 11a**	♈ 3a	☾ 6a	♉ 6a		♊ 11a / ● 7p		♋ 7p		☽ 3p	♌ 5a		♍ 6p	◐ 6p		♎ 6a
♐ 5p			◯ 12m / ♑ 2a		♒ 9a	◑ 4p	♓ 2a		♈ 4p	☾ 1a	♉ 4p		● 7a / ♊ 5p		♋ 8p	☽ 5p		♌ 2a	**♊ 5p**	♍ 1p / ◐ 2p			♎ 1a	◯ 5p	♏ 2p			♐ 12m / ○ 4p		♑ 8a		◯ 9a / ♒ 2p		♓ 7p

Ephemeris grid (Moon sign and time positions). Columns are days of the month; the letters spanning days 2–5 spell "JULY". Rows are years 1946–1980.

Day	5	6	7	8	9	10	11	12	13	14	15	16	17	18	19	20	21	22	23	24	25	26	27	28	29	30	1	2	3	4	5	6	7	8
1946																																		
1947																																		
1948																																		
1949																																		
1950																																		
1951																																		
1952																																		
1953																																		
1954																																		
1955																																		
1956																																		
1957																																		
1958																																		
1959																																		
1960																																		
1961																																		
1962																																		
1963																																		
1964																																		
1965																																		
1966																																		
1967																																		
1968																																		
1969																																		
1970																																		
1971																																		
1972																																		
1973																																		
1974																																		
1975																																		
1976																																		
1977																																		
1978																																		
1979																																		
1980																																		

10	11	12	13	14	15	16	17	18	19	20	21	22	23	24	25	26	27	28	29	30	31	1 A	2 U	3 G	4 U	5 S	6 T	7	8	9	10	11	12	13
◑ 2a		♑ 10a		○ 4a ♒ 9p			♓ 5a	◑ 1a	♈ 1p		◐ 3p ♉ 5p		♊ 8p	◀ ♌ 7a	☾ 12m ♋ 11p		♌ 11p	● 7a		♍ 2a	☽ 6p	♎ 7a		♏ 4p	◐ 4p		♐ 5a		♑ 5p ◑ 7p			♒ 4a	○ 5p	♓ 1p
	◐ 6a	♉ 3a		♊ 7a ☾ 6p		♋ 8a	● 11p	♌ 8a		♍ 7a	☽ 4a	♎ 10a	♌ 12n	♏ 4p ◐ 6p			♐ 2a	◑ 6p	♑ 2p			♒ 3a ○ 9p		♓ 3p		◑ 9p	♈ 1a		♉ 11a	◐ 3p	♊ 3p		♋ 6p	☾ 1a
	♎ 6p		◐ 6a ♏ 11p			♐ 5a ◑ 11p		♑ 2p		○ 10p	♒ 1a	♌ 6p	♓ 1p		◑ 12m	♈ 2a		♉ 1p	◐ 1a	♊ 10p		☾ 5p	♋ 2a		♌ 3a ● 11p		♍ 2a		♎ 3a ☽ 4a		♏ 5a	◐ 3p	♐ 11a	
○ 3a	♒ 1a		♓ 10a ◑ 10p		♈ 10p			◐ 1a ♉ 11a		♊ 10p		☾ 1a	♋ 6a	◀ ♌ 12m	♌ 10a ● 2p		♍ 1p	☽ 11p	♎ 2p		♏ 5p	◐ 8a	♐ 8p		◑ 9p	♑ 2a		♒ 9a	○ 3p	♓ 6p			♈ 5a ◑ 3p	
♊ 6p	☾ 1a		♋ 6a		● 12m ♌ 3p		♍ 10p	☽ 5p		♎ 4a		◐ 6a ♏ 7a	♌ 6a	♐ 10a	◑ 3p	♑ 12n		♒ 2p ○ 11p		♓ 6p		◑ 3p	♈ 2a		♉ 1p	◐ 3p		♊ 2a		♋ 2p ☾ 5p		♌ 11p		● 12n
♎ 1p		◐ 12m ♏ 7p		♐ 10p	◑ 10a	♑ 10p		○ 2p ♒ 10p		♓ 11p	◑ 9p	♌ 11a ▶	♈ 2a		♉ 10a ◐ 2p		♊ 9p		☾ 3p	♋ 10a		♌ 10p	● 6p		♍ 9a		☽ 4p ♎ 6p			♏ 1a	◐ 7a	♐ 5a		♑ 7a ◑ 4p
♓ 7a ◑ 12n		♈ 9a	◐ 11p	♉ 2p		♊ 10p	☾ 5p		♋ 8a		● 6p ♌ 8p	♌ 5p	↙ ♌ 11p	♍ 9a	☽ 10p	♎ 10p			♏ 8a ◐ 9p		♐ 3p		◑ 10a ♑ 5p		♒ 6p	Ⓛ 3p	♓ 5p		♈ 6p ◑ 8p		♉ 9p		◐ 8a	♊ 4a
Ⓢ 9p	♌ 7p			♍ 6p ☽ 9p		♎ 7p			◐ 12m ♏ 7a		♐ 5p	◑ 8p	♑ 11p			♒ 2a Ⓛ 7a		♓ 3a	◑ 2p	♈ 4a		♉ 6a ◐ 10p		♊ 10a		☾ 1p ♋ 5p			♌ 2a	Ⓢ 11a	♍ 2p			♎ 2a ☽ 2p
	♐ 2p ◑ 11p			♑ 1a	Ⓛ 7p	♒ 8a		♓ 2p	◑ 9a	♈ 5p		◐ 7p ♉ 8p	♌ 5a	♊ 11p		☾ 5a	♋ 2a		♌ 6a ● 5p		♍ 1p		☽ 12n ♎ 10p			♏ 10a	◐ 2p	♐ 11p			♑ 9a ◑ 2p		♒ 5p	
	♈ 5a	◐ 3p	♉ 9a		♊ 12n	☾ 1a	♋ 12n		● 7a ♌ 1p		♍ 3p	☽ 4p	♎ 8p	◀ ♌ 10a		♏ 5a ◐ 11a		♐ 5p		◑ 2p	♑ 6a		♒ 6p	○ 2p		♓ 3a		◑ 9a ♈ 10a		♉ 3p	◐ 10p	♊ 7p		♋ 9p
♍ 10p	☽ 4a		♎ 12m	◐ 4p	♏ 6a		♐ 4p	◑ 2p		♑ 4a	♌ 4p ▶	♒ 4p ○ 4p			♓ 5a	◑ 6p	♈ 4p			♉ 1a ◑ 2p		♊ 6a		☾ 2a ♋ 9a		♌ 8a	● 6a	♍ 8a		♎ 9a ☽ 12n		♏ 1p		◐ 4a ♐ 10p
♑ 5a	○ 6p	♒ 3p			♓ 4a ◑ 7p		♈ 3p		◐ 9p	♉ 3a	♌ 10p ▶	♊ 10a	☾ 3p	♋ 4p		♌ 5p ● 11p		♍ 5p		☽ 4a ♎ 5p		♏ 8p	◐ 2p		♐ 2a		◑ 8a ♑ 10a		♒ 9p		○ 8a	♓ 9a		♈ 10p
		♊ 11a ☾ 9p		♋ 7p		● 2p	♌ 12m		♍ 4a	☽ 12m	♎ 6a	♌ 4a ▶	◐ 9a ♏ 9a	↙ ♌ 10a	♐ 12n	◑ 9p	♑ 5p		♒ 11p	○ 12n		♓ 7a		◑ 10a ♈ 5p			♉ 7a	◐ 1p	♊ 7p			♋ 4a ☾ 11a		♌ 10a
	♎ 7p		◐ 7a	♏ 12m		♐ 2a ◑ 4p		♑ 3a	○ 11p	♒ 4a		♓ 8a	◑ 11a	♈ 3p			♉ 2a ◐ 9a		♊ 2p		☾ 12n	♋ 2a		♌ 12n	● 10a	♍ 7p			♎ 1a ☽ 1a		♏ 5a	◐ 12n	♐ 8a	
	♓ 12n ◑ 8p		♈ 4p		◐ 11a	♉ 12m		♊ 11a	☾ 11a	♋ 11p		♌ 4p	♌ 12n ● 2p		♍ 11p		☽ 2p	♎ 10a		♏ 5p	◐ 8a	♐ 9p		◑ 5p ♑ 10p		♒ 10p	○ 10p	♓ 11p			♈ 1a ◑ 6a		♉ 8a	
♋ 10p		● 2p	♌ 10a		♍ 11p	☽ 5p		♎ 12n		◐ 6p ♏ 10p		♌ 9p	♐ 5a	◑ 9a	♑ 7a		♒ 8a ○ 3p		♓ 7a	◑ 8p	♈ 8a		♉ 12n	◐ 7a	♊ 6p			☾ 3a ♋ 4a		♌ 4p		Ⓢ 6a	♍ 5a	
♏ 8p			♐ 6a ◑ 5p		♑ 12n		♒ 4p Ⓛ 7p		♓ 6p	◑ 3p	♈ 8p	♌ 3a ▶	♉ 10p ◐ 11p			♊ 2a	☾ 12n	♋ 8a		♌ 4p	Ⓢ 7a		♍ 3a		☽ 9a ♎ 3p			♏ 4a	◐ 11a	♐ 3p		♑ 10p	◑ 6a	
♓ 5a ◑ 10a		♈ 9a	◐ 9p	♉ 12n		♊ 2p	☾ 6a	♋ 5p		Ⓢ 4p ♌ 8p		♌ 10a	♍ 2a	☽ 8a	♎ 11a		♏ 11p	◐ 8a		♐ 11a		◑ 10a ♑ 10p			♒ 8a	○ 5a	♓ 12n		♈ 3p ◑ 4p		♉ 6p		◐ 1a ♊ 8p	
♌ 3a		♍ 5a ☽ 2p		♎ 10a		◐ 7a ♏ 7p			♐ 6a	◑ 9a	♑ 7p	♌ 3p		♒ 8a ○ 11a		♓ 6p		◑ 8a	♈ 1a		♉ 7a ◐ 10p		♊ 10a		☾ 8a ♋ 12n		♌ 1p	● 2p	♍ 3p		♎ 7p	☽ 1a		♏ 3a
	♑ 6p		○ 12n	♒ 6a		♓ 7p	◑ 3p		♈ 6a		◐ 1p ♉ 3p	♌ 9p	♊ 9p		☾ 2a ♋ 11p		♌ 11p	● 7a	♍ 10p		☽ 12n ♎ 11p			♏ 3a	◐ 1a	♐ 12n		♑ 11p	◑ 12m		♒ 12n		○ 3a	♓ 1a
◐ 5p	♉ 4p			♊ 1a ☾ 1p		♋ 6a		● 12m ♌ 8a		♍ 8a	☽ 5a	♎ 9a	♌ 2a	♏ 12n ◐ 2p		♐ 5p		◑ 6a	♑ 1a		♒ 11a	○ 4a	♓ 11p			◑ 6a ♈ 11a			♉ 12m	◐ 8a	♊ 9a		♋ 4p	☾ 12m
♍ 7p	☽ 1a	♎ 10p		◐ 11a	♏ 1a		♐ 4a ◑ 9p		♑ 8a		○ 10a ♒ 1p	♌ 8a ▶	♓ 9p		◑ 5a	♈ 7a		♉ 8p	◐ 7a		♊ 8a		☾ 7a ♋ 5p		♌ 11p	● 10p		♍ 3a		♎ 5a ☽ 7a		♏ 7a	◐ 4p	♐ 10a
♒ 6p		♓ 9p	◑ 8a		♈ 4a		◐ 4a ♉ 3p			♊ 3a	☾ 7a	♋ 3p	◀ ♌ 2p		♌ 2a ● 7a		♍ 10a		☽ 1a ♎ 5p		♏ 9p	◐ 12n		♐ 12m	◑ 10p	♑ 2a		♒ 4a	○ 6a	♓ 7a		♈ 1p ◑ 9p		♉ 11p
♊ 1a ☾ 6a		♋ 1p		● 9a	♌ 1a		♍ 2p	☽ 11a		♎ 12m		♏ 8a ◐ 7p	◀ ♌ 8p	♐ 12n	◑ 5p	♑ 1p		♒ 1p ○ 10p		♓ 1p		◑ 4a ♈ 3p		♉ 9p	◐ 10p		♊ 7a		♋ 7p ☾ 10p			♌ 8a		● 12m ♍ 8p
♎ 1a	◐ 3p	♏ 12n		♐ 6a	◑	♑ 9p		○ 3p ♒ 10p		♓ 10p	◑ 8p	♈ 11p	♌ 2a		♉ 2a ◑ 6a		♊ 9a		☾ 12m ♋ 6p			♌ 6a	● 1a	♍ 7p			☽ 5a ♎ 8a		♏ 7p		◐ 4a	♐ 3a		♑ 7a ◑ 5p
	♓ 9a ◑ 4p		♈ 12n		◐ 1a ♉ 2p		♊ 6p	☾ 12n	♋ 11p		♌ 1p ↘	● 4a ♌ 6a	♌ 7a	♍ 4p		☽ 3a	♎ 5a		♏ 5p	◐ 6a		♐ 4a		◑ 3a ♑ 12n		♒ 4p	Ⓛ 3p	♓ 6p		♈ 6p ◑ 9p		♉ 8p		◐ 6a ♊ 11p
Ⓢ 3p	♌ 10a		♍ 3p	☽ 4a		♎ 12m		◐ 3a ♏ 11a			♐ 12m	◑ 5a	♑ 11a		♒ 8p	Ⓛ 2a		♓ 2a	◑ 5p	♈ 7a		♉ 10a	◑ 3a	♊ 1p		☾ 1p ♋ 3p		♌ 7p		● 1a	♍ 12m		♎ 8a ☽ 7p	
♐ 8p	◑ 4a		♑ 9a		Ⓛ 7a ♒ 9p			♓ 8a	◑ 6a	♈ 5p	♌ 7p ▶	♉ 11p ◐ 11p			♊ 2a	☾ 8a	♋ 3a		♌ 3a ● 2p		♍ 5a	☽ 11p	♎ 8a		♏ 4p	◐ 5p		♐ 3a		♑ 3p ◑ 8p			♒ 4a	○ 9p
♈ 8p		◐ 11a	♉ 5a		♊ 11a	☾ 1a	♋ 1p		● 7a ♌ 1p		♍ 12n	☽ 12n	♎ 1p	◀ ♌ 1a	♏ 6p ◐ 11p			♐ 2a	◑ 8p	♑ 1p			♒ 2a ○ 11p		♓ 2p			◑ 1a ♈ 2a		♉ 12n	◐ 10p	♊ 7p		♋ 11p
	♍ 11p	☽ 6a		♎ 12m	◐ 3p	♏ 3a		♐ 8a	◑ 5a	♑ 4p		♌ 6a ▶	○ 12m ♒ 1a		♓ 12n		◑ 1a	♈ 12m		♉ 1p	◐ 4a	♊ 11p		☾ 11p	♋ 5a		♌ 8a	● 7a	♍ 8a		♎ 8a ☽ 12n		♏ 10a	◐ 9p
	○ 8a	♒ 3a		♓ 10a	◑ 12m	♈ 8p			◐ 1a ♉ 8a		♊ 9p	♌ 12n	☾ 3a	♋ 7a		♌ 1p ● 9p		♍ 5p		☽ 7a ♎ 8p		♏ 11p	◐ 5p		♐ 2a		◑ 4a ♑ 6a		♒ 11a	○ 7p	♓ 6p			♈ 4a ◑ 4p
	♊ 4p	☾ 2a		♋ 5a		● 4a ♌ 4p			♍ 1a	☽ 12m	♎ 8a	♌ 6p	♏ 1p ◐ 3p	↙ ♌	♐ 4p	◑ 11p	♑ 5p		♒ 6p	○ 6a	♓ 8p		◑ 6p	♈ 2a		♉ 11a	◐ 4p	♊ 11p			♋ 12n ☾ 6p		♌ 11p	
	♎ 3p		◐ 6a ♏ 11p			♐ 3a ◑ 6p		♑ 4a	○ 10p	♒ 3a		♓ 2a	◑ 3a	♈ 5a		♉ 11a ◐ 6p		♊ 9p		☾ 5p	♋ 8a		♌ 9p	● 8p		♍ 9a		♎ 8p ☽ 9p			♏ 5a	◐ 3p	♐ 11a	
♒ 12n		♓ 12n ◑ 9p		♈ 1p		◐ 6a ♉ 6p			♊ 12m ☾ 10p		♋ 9a	♌ 6a ▶	♌ 8p ● 9p			♍ 8a		☽ 12m ♎ 9p			♏ 9a	◐ 1a	♐ 5p		◑ 4p ♑ 9p		♒ 10p	○ 10p	♓ 10p		♈ 10p	◑ 3a		♉ 12m
♋ 2p		● 2a ♌ 8p			♍ 5a ☽ 10p		♎ 5p			◐ 1a ♏ 6a		♐ 5p	◀ ♌ 12n	◑ 12m	♑ 1a		♒ 6a ○ 2p		♓ 8a	◑ 10p	♈ 10a		♉ 12n	◐ 7a	♊ 3p		☾ 8p ♋ 8p			♌ 3a	Ⓢ 2p	♍ 1p		

	14	15	16	17	18	19	20	21	22	23	24	25	26	27	28	29	30	31	S 1	E 2	P 3	T 4	E 5	M 6	B 7	E 8	R 9	10	11	12	13	14	15	16
1946		♈ 7a	◯ 9a	♉ 11p		◑ 8p	♊ 2a		♋ 5a	☾ 6a	♌ 8a		♍ 11a / ● 4p		♎ 5p		☽ 9a	♏ 1a		♐ 1p	◐ 10a		♑ 1a		◯ 12n / ♒ 1p		♓ 9p		○ 5a	♈ 2a		♉ 5a / ◯ 4p		♊ 8a
1947	♌ 6p		● 6a / ♍ 6p		♎ 7p	☽ 2p		♏ 12m	♍ 1p	◐ 8a / ♐ 9a	♍ 7p	♑ 9p		◯ 10a	♒ 9a		♓ 9p	○ 12n		♈ 7a		◯ 8a / ♉ 3p		♊ 9p	◑ 11p		♋ 1a		♌ 3a / ☾ 8a		♍ 4a	● 3p	♎ 5a	
1948	♑ 8p	◯ 11a		♒ 7a		○ 1p / ♓ 7p			♈ 8a	◯ 3p	♉ 8p			♊ 6a / ◑ 2p		♋ 11a		☾ 2a / ♌ 1p		♍ 1p	● 6a	♎ 1p		☽ 12n / ♏ 2p		♐ 6p		◐ 2a	♑ 2a		♒ 1p	◯ 2a		♓ 1a
1949	♉ 6p		◑ 6p	♊ 6a		♋ 3p	☾ 1p	♌ 8p	♍ 1a	♍ 10p / ● 11p	♍ 7a	♎ 11p		☽ 5a / ♏ 11p			♐ 2a / ◐ 2p		♑ 7a		☾ 6a / ♒ 3p			♓ 12m	○ 5a	♈ 12n			♉ 1a / ◯ 8a		♊ 2p		◑ 9a	♋ 12m
1950	♍ 5a		♎ 9a	☽ 1a	♏ 1p		◐ 11a / ♐ 4p		♑ 6p	◯ 9p	♒ 10p			♓ 3a / ○ 10a		♈ 11a		◯ 6a / ♉ 9p			♊ 10a	◑ 9a	♋ 10p			☾ 8a / ♌ 8a		♍ 2p	Ⓢ 10p	♎ 5p		♏ 7p	☽ 7a	♐ 9p
1951		♒ 8a	○ 10p	♓ 9a		♈ 12n	◯ 9a	♉ 7p	♍ 12n	♍ 6p	♊ 4a / ◑ 5a		♋ 5p		☾ 8a	♌ 5a		♍ 4p	Ⓢ 8a		♎ 12m		☽ 1a / ♏ 7a		♐ 11a	◐ 1p	♑ 2p		♒ 4p / ◯ 10p		♓ 6p		○ 8a / ♈ 10p	
1952		♋ 2p	☾ 7a		♌ 2a		Ⓢ 10a / ♍ 3p		♍ 12m	♎ 4a	☽ 12n	♏ 2p		♐ 10p	◐ 7a		♑ 2a	◯ 5p	♒ 4a		♓ 4a / ○ 10p		♈ 4a		◯ 5a / ♉ 6a		♊ 11a	◑ 9p	♋ 8p			♌ 9a / ☾ 11p		♍ 10p
1953		♏ 3p		◐ 3p	♐ 1a		♑ 9a	◯ 8a	♒ 12n	♍ 6a	♓ 1p / ○ 3p		♈ 1p	◯ 9p	♉ 1p		♊ 4p	◑ 6a	♋ 11p			☾ 1a / ♌ 8a		♍ 8p		● 3a	♎ 8a		♏ 9p	☽ 6a		♐ 9a		◐ 5a / ♑ 5p
1954	○ 6a / ♓ 9p			♈ 12m / ◯ 3p		♉ 1a		◑ 12m / ♊ 4a	♍ 11a	♋ 8a	☾ 12n	♌ 12n		♍ 9p	● 5a		♎ 6a		☽ 5a / ♏ 6p			♐ 7a	◐ 7a	♑ 6p			♒ 2a / ◯ 5a		♓ 7a	○ 3p	♈ 8a		♉ 9a / ◯ 9p	
1955	☾ 7a	♌ 11p		● 3p	♍ 3a		♎ 6a	☽ 5a	♏ 2p	♍ 5p		♐ 1a / ◐ 4a		♑ 2p		◯ 7a	♒ 2a		♓ 10a	○ 3a	♈ 4p		◯ 4p / ♉ 9p			♊ 12m	◑ 3a	♋ 3a		♌ 6a / ☾ 1p		♍ 10a		● 1a / ♎ 3p
1956			♑ 10a	◯ 5a	♒ 11p			○ 8a / ♓ 11a	♍ 11p	♈ 9p		◯ 6a	♉ 6a		♊ 1p / ◑ 11p		♋ 5p		☾ 9a / ♌ 6p		♍ 6p	● 2p	♎ 7p		♏ 11p / ☽ 11p			♐ 6a	◐ 7p	♑ 5p			♒ 5a / ◯ 10p	
1957	◯ 11a		♉ 10a		◑ 11a / ♊ 8p			♋ 2a	☾ 1a	♌ 4a	♍ 5a	♍ 4a / ● 7a		♎ 3a	☽ 12m	♏ 4a		♐ 8a	◐ 12m	♑ 4p		◯ 9p	♒ 3a		♓ 3p		○ 12m	♈ 4a		♉ 4p	◯ 2a		♊ 2a	◑ 11p
1958	● 11p	♍ 12n		♎ 1p	☽ 6a	♏ 3p		◐ 3p / ♐ 6p		♍ 11a	♑ 11p	◯ 5a	♒ 6a		♓ 2p	○ 1a		♈ 2a		◯ 3a / ♉ 2p			♊ 3a	◑ 5a	♋ 1p		♌ 8p / ☾ 11p		♍ 10p		● 7a / ♎ 11p		♏ 11p	☽ 12n
1959	♑ 10a / ◯ 9p		♒ 1p		○ 8a / ♓ 5p			♈ 12m	◯ 2a	♉ 10a	♍ 5p	♊ 10p	◑ 3a		♋ 11a		☾ 4a / ♌ 8p			♍ 3a / ● 9p		♎ 8a		☽ 8a / ♏ 11a		♐ 1p	◐ 5p	♑ 4p		♒ 8p	◯ 4a		♓ 1a	○ 8p
1960	◑ 1a / ♊ 6p			♋ 6a	☾ 3a	♌ 6p			● 4a / ♍ 6a	♍ 11p	♎ 3p		☽ 1a / ♏ 10p			♐ 3a / ◐ 2p		♑ 6a	◯ 11p	♒ 8a		♓ 9a	Ⓛ 6a	♈ 11a		♉ 4p / ◯ 7p			♊ 2a	◑ 5p	♋ 1p			♌ 2a / ☾ 8p
1961	♎ 6p	☽ 9a		♏ 5a		◐ 6a / ♐ 1p		♑ 5p	◯ 5p	♒ 6p	♍ 4a	♓ 6p / Ⓛ 10p		♈ 6p		◯ 4a / ♉ 8p			♉ 1a / ◑ 6p		♋ 10a		☾ 6p / ♌ 10p			♍ 11a	● 10p		♎ 12m		♏ 10a / ☽ 10p		♐ 7p	
1962	♒ 2a	Ⓛ 3p	♓ 3a		♈ 3a / ◯ 9p		♉ 4a		◑ 5a / ♊ 12n	♍ 10a	♋ 2p	☾ 10p	♌ 11p			♍ 10a	● 1a	♎ 10p			☽ 1a / ♏ 11a		♐ 10p		◐ 2a	♑ 7a		♒ 12n / ◯ 5p		♓ 2p	○ 11p	♈ 2p		♉ 1p
1963		♋ 12m / ☾ 12n		♌ 4a		● 3a / ♍ 11a		♎ 7p	☽ 11p	♍ 4p	♏ 7a		♐ 7p	◐ 2a		♑ 7a		◯ 1a / ♒ 4p		♓ 9p	○ 3p	♈ 11p		◯ 10p	♉ 12m		♊ 2a	◑ 7a	♋ 5a		♌ 11a / ☾ 9p		♍ 6p	
1964		♐ 2p / ◐ 10p			♑ 3a	◯ 1a	♒ 3p		♍ 10p	♓ 12m / ○ 12m	♍ 2a	♈ 7p	◯ 4p	♉ 12m		♊ 4p	◑ 4a	♋ 7p		☾ 2p / ♌ 10p			♍ 12m	● 12m	♎ 4a		♏ 11a / ☽ 3p		♐ 10p		◐ 4p	♑ 11a		♒ 11p
1965		♈ 12n	◯ 4a	♉ 9p		◑ 11p	♊ 4a		♋ 8a	☾ 9a	♌ 9a		♍ 9a / ● 2p		♎ 9a	☽ 9p	♏ 12n		♐ 7p	◐ 3p		♑ 6a		◯ 5p / ♒ 7p			♓ 7a	○ 6p	♈ 6p			♉ 3a / ◯ 4p		♊ 10a
1966	♌ 6p		● 7a / ♍ 6p		♎ 5p	☽ 11a	♏ 6p		◐ 10p / ♐ 11p	♍ 9a		♑ 7a	◯ 6p	♒ 5p			♓ 5a / ○ 7p		♈ 5p		◯ 10p	♉ 6a		♊ 5p	◑ 9p		♋ 12m		♌ 4a / ☾ 10a		♍ 4a	● 2p	♎ 4a	
1967		♑ 2p	◯ 4p	♒ 8p		○ 9p	♓ 4a		♈ 3p	◯ 9p	♍ 3p	♉ 3a		♊ 4p	◑ 1a		♋ 3a	☾ 9p	♌ 9a		♍ 12n	● 7a	♎ 1p		☽ 1p / ♏ 2p		♐ 4p	◐ 10p	♑ 8p			♒ 2a / ◯ 2p		♓ 11a
1968		◑ 9p	♊ 11a		♋ 11p	☾ 11p		♌ 10a	♍ 9p	♍ 5p / ● 7p		♎ 11p		☽ 8a	♏ 3a		♐ 6a / ◐ 7p		♑ 8a		◯ 4a / ♒ 11a		♓ 4p	○ 5p	♈ 10p			♉ 7a / ◯ 1p		♊ 7p		◑ 3p	♋ 7a	
1969			♎ 6a / ☽ 11p		♏ 2p		◐ 3p / ♐ 7p		♑ 10p	♍ 3a	◯ 12m / ♒ 11p		♓ 11p	Ⓛ 6a		♈ 1a	◯ 4p	♉ 6a		♊ 2p	◑ 12n		♋ 2a		♌ 3p / ☽ 3p			♍ 2a	Ⓢ 3p	♎ 12n		♏ 7p	☽ 9a	
1970		♒ 9a	Ⓛ 10p	♓ 8a		♈ 8a	◯ 3a	♉ 10a		♊ 3p / ◑ 4p	♍ 9a		♋ 12m	☾ 2p	♌ 12n			♍ 1a / Ⓢ 5p		♎ 1p		☽ 7p	♏ 1a		♐ 10a	◐ 3p	♑ 4p		♒ 7p	◯ 1a	♓ 7p		○ 6a / ♈ 7p	
1971			♋ 5a / ☾ 9p		♌ 1p		Ⓢ 6p / ♍ 11p		♍ 2p	♎ 11a	☽ 8p		♏ 12m		♐ 12n / ◐ 10p		♑ 9p		◯ 3p	♒ 2a		♓ 4a / ○ 11p		♈ 4a		◯ 4a / ♉ 4a		♊ 5a	◑ 1p	♋ 10a		♌ 7p	☾ 8a	
1972	♏ 7p		♐ 8p / ◐ 8p			♑ 8p	◯ 9p	♒ 8p	♍ 8p		♓ 10a / ○ 1p		♈ 2p	◯ 11p	♉ 4p		♊ 6p	◑ 8a	♋ 9p		☾ 8p	♌ 2a		♍ 8a	● 12n	♎ 5p			♏ 3a / ☽ 11a		♐ 4p		◐ 2p	♑ 4a
1973	♓ 2p		♈ 10p	◯ 4p		♉ 4a		◑ 5a / ♊ 8a	♍ 2a	♋ 11a	☾ 2p	♌ 12n		♍ 3p / ● 10p		♎ 6p		☽ 11a	♏ 12m		♐ 10a	◐ 10a	♑ 11p			♒ 11a / ◯ 1p		♓ 10p		○ 10a	♈ 5a		♉ 10a	◯ 12m
1974	☾ 9a	♌ 11p		● 2p / ♍ 11p		♎ 11p	☽ 8p		♏ 2a	♍ 7a	♐ 9a / ◐ 11a		♑ 7p		◯ 12n	♒ 8a		♓ 8p	○ 2p		♈ 8a		◯ 2p / ♉ 6p			♊ 2a	◑ 7a	♋ 7a		♌ 9a / ☾ 5p		♍ 9a	● 10p	♎ 9a
1975	♐ 2p		♑ 9p	◯ 3p		♒ 7a		○ 3p / ♓ 7p		♍ 1p	♈ 7a	◯ 6p	♉ 8p			♊ 7a / ◑ 6p		♋ 3p		☾ 9a / ♌ 6p		♍ 6p	● 2p	♎ 6p		♏ 6p / ☽ 7p		♐ 9p		◐ 7a	♑ 3a		♒ 1p	◯ 4a
1976		♉ 4p		◑ 7p	♊ 5a		♋ 4p	☾ 6p	♌ 10p	♍ 7p		♍ 2a / ● 6a		♎ 4a	☽ 1p	♏ 5a		♐ 7a / ◐ 11p		♑ 12n		◯ 1p / ♒ 5p			♓ 1a	○ 8a	♈ 11a			◯ 12m / ♉ 10a		♊ 1p		◑ 12n
1977	● 5p	♍ 7a		♎ 2p	☽ 8a	♏ 7p		◑ 8p / ♐ 10p		♍ 1a	♑ 1a	◯ 5a	♒ 3a		♓ 6a / ○ 3p		♈ 11a		◯ 8a / ♉ 8p			♊ 7a	◑ 10a	♋ 8p			♌ 7a / ☾ 11a		♍ 4p		● 4a / ♎ 9p			♏ 1a / ☽ 4p
1978	♑ 1p	◯ 1a	♒ 1p		○ 5a / ♓ 1p		♈ 2p	◯ 1p	♉ 9p	♍ 7a		♊ 4a / ◑ 7p		♋ 3p		☾ 9a	♌ 4a		♍ 4p	● 11a		♎ 2a		☽ 8a / ♏ 11a		♐ 5p	◐ 11p	♑ 8p		♒ 10p	◯ 7a	♓ 11p		Ⓛ 2p
1979	◑ 2p	♊ 6a		♋ 2p	☾ 10a		♌ 1a	♍ 7p	Ⓢ 12n / ♍ 2p	♍ 1p		♎ 3a	☽ 3p	♏ 3p			♐ 1a	◐ 1p	♑ 7a		◯ 1a / ♒ 9a		♓ 9a	Ⓛ 6a	♈ 8a		♉ 9a / ◯ 12n		♊ 1p		◑ 1a / ♋ 8p			♌ 7a
1980	♎ 1a / ☽ 3p		♏ 1p		◐ 5p	♐ 1a		♑ 10a	◯ 1p	♒ 4p		♓ 6p / ○ 11p		♈ 6p		◯ 4a / ♉ 7p		♊ 9p	◑ 1p		♋ 2a		☾ 6a / ♌ 9a		♍ 8p		● 5a	♎ 7a		♏ 8p	☽ 8a		♐ 8a	

	23	24	25	26	27	28	29	30	31	1	2	3	4	5	6	7	8	9	10	11	12	13	14	15	16	17	18	19	20	21	22	23	24	25
1946																																		
1947																																		
1948																																		
1949																																		
1950																																		
1951																																		
1952																																		
1953																																		
1954																																		
1955																																		
1956																																		
1957																																		
1958																																		
1959																																		
1960																																		
1961																																		
1962																																		
1963																																		
1964																																		
1965																																		
1966																																		
1967																																		
1968																																		
1969																																		
1970																																		
1971																																		
1972																																		
1973																																		
1974																																		
1975																																		
1976																																		
1977																																		
1978																																		
1979																																		
1980																																		

Chart for finding degree of moonsign

To find approximate degree of moonsign for a specific hour:

1. Count number of hours from *moonsign time before event* to *time of event* (expressed in *Eastern Standard Time*). (See page 82 for converting other times to Eastern Standard Time.)
2. Look down MOONSIGN CHANGE TIME *BEFORE* EVENT column on left until you find the time indicated in the box.
3. Follow this line to the right until you find the time corresponding with MOONSIGN CHANGE TIME *AFTER* EVENT.
4. Follow this column down until you find the figure in the MULTIPLY BY line.
5. Multiply this figure by the number of hours obtained in no.1 above. The result is the approximate degree of the moonsign. (Moonsign is indicated in box giving moonsign time *before* event.)

Example: To find degree of moonsign for an event that took place on January 5, 1911 at 5 p.m. Eastern Standard Time:

1. At the top of the page follow the 1911 line across until you are under January 5. As there is nothing in the corresponding box, look to the left and you will see, under January 4 ⊞. The left side of the box refers to the last moon*phase* change, but we are interested in the moon*sign* change to the right, which tells us that the moon entered Pisces (♓) at 1 p.m. on January 4 Eastern Standard Time. From that time to 5 p.m. January 5 is 28 hours.
2. Look down MOONSIGN CHANGE TIME *BEFORE* EVENT column on left until you come to 1p.
3. Follow this line to the right until you come to 8p, which is the moonsign time change after the event indicated by this box ⊞ on January 6.
4. Follow this column down until you find the figure "0.55" in the MULTIPLY BY line.
5. Multiplying 0.55 by 28 hours equals 15.40. This means that the moon was in approximately 15 degrees of Pisces (♓) on January 5 at 5 p.m. Eastern Standard Time.

MOONSIGN CHANGE TIME *AFTER* EVENT
(two to two-and-a-half days later)

MOONSIGN CHANGE TIME *BEFORE* EVENT														
12m	12m	1a	2a	3a	4a	5a	6a	7a	8a	9a	10a	11a	12n	1p
1a	1a	2a	3a	4a	5a	6a	7a	8a	9a	10a	11a	12n	1p	2p
2a	2a	3a	4a	5a	6a	7a	8a	9a	10a	11a	12n	1p	2p	3p
3a	3a	4a	5a	6a	7a	8a	9a	10a	11a	12n	1p	2p	3p	4p
4a	4a	5a	6a	7a	8a	9a	10a	11a	12n	1p	2p	3p	4p	5p
5a	5a	6a	7a	8a	9a	10a	11a	12n	1p	2p	3p	4p	5p	6p
6a	6a	7a	8a	9a	10a	11a	12n	1p	2p	3p	4p	5p	6p	7p
7a	7a	8a	9a	10a	11a	12n	1p	2p	3p	4p	5p	6p	7p	8p
8a	8a	9a	10a	11a	12n	1p	2p	3p	4p	5p	6p	7p	8p	9p
9a	9a	10a	11a	12n	1p	2p	3p	4p	5p	6p	7p	8p	9p	10p
10a	10a	11a	12n	1p	2p	3p	4p	5p	6p	7p	8p	9p	10p	11p
11a	11a	12n	1p	2p	3p	4p	5p	6p	7p	8p	9p	10p	11p	12m
12n	12n	1p	2p	3p	4p	5p	6p	7p	8p	9p	10p	11p	12m	1a
1p	1p	2p	3p	4p	5p	6p	7p	8p	9p	10p	11p	12m	1a	2a
2p	2p	3p	4p	5p	6p	7p	8p	9p	10p	11p	12m	1a	2a	3a
3p	3p	4p	5p	6p	7p	8p	9p	10p	11p	12m	1a	2a	3a	4a
4p	4p	5p	6p	7p	8p	9p	10p	11p	12m	1a	2a	3a	4a	5a
5p	5p	6p	7p	8p	9p	10p	11p	12m	1a	2a	3a	4a	5a	6a
6p	6p	7p	8p	9p	10p	11p	12m	1a	2a	3a	4a	5a	6a	7a
7p	7p	8p	9p	10p	11p	12m	1a	2a	3a	4a	5a	6a	7a	8a
8p	8p	9p	10p	11p	12m	1a	2a	3a	4a	5a	6a	7a	8a	9a
9p	9p	10p	11p	12m	1a	2a	3a	4a	5a	6a	7a	8a	9a	10a
10p	10p	11p	12m	1a	2a	3a	4a	5a	6a	7a	8a	9a	10a	11a
11p	11p	12m	1a	2a	3a	4a	5a	6a	7a	8a	9a	10a	11a	12m
MULTIPLY BY:	0.62	0.61	0.6	0.59	0.58	0.57	0.56	0.55	0.54	0.53	0.52	0.51	0.5	0.49

Aspect chart

If you have a *personal important point* in	□ First Square is in	△ First Trine is in	☍ Opposition is in	△ Last Trine is in	□ Last Square is in
♈ Aries	♋ Cancer	♌ Leo	♎ Libra	♐ Sagittarius	♑ Capricorn
♉ Taurus	♌ Leo	♍ Virgo	♏ Scorpio	♑ Capricorn	♒ Aquarius
♊ Gemini	♍ Virgo	♎ Libra	♐ Sagittarius	♒ Aquarius	♓ Pisces
♋ Cancer	♎ Libra	♏ Scorpio	♑ Capricorn	♓ Pisces	♈ Aries
♌ Leo	♏ Scorpio	♐ Sagittarius	♒ Aquarius	♈ Aries	♉ Taurus
♍ Virgo	♐ Sagittarius	♑ Capricorn	♓ Pisces	♉ Taurus	♊ Gemini
♎ Libra	♑ Capricorn	♒ Aquarius	♈ Aries	♊ Gemini	♋ Cancer
♏ Scorpio	♒ Aquarius	♓ Pisces	♉ Taurus	♋ Cancer	♌ Leo
♐ Sagittarius	♓ Pisces	♈ Aries	♊ Gemini	♌ Leo	♍ Virgo
♑ Capricorn	♈ Aries	♉ Taurus	♋ Cancer	♍ Virgo	♎ Libra
♒ Aquarius	♉ Taurus	♊ Gemini	♌ Leo	♎ Libra	♏ Scorpio
♓ Pisces	♊ Gemini	♋ Cancer	♍ Virgo	♏ Scorpio	♐ Sagittarius

Mercury and Venus charts

The charts on the following pages show graphically the zodiac positions of Mercury and Venus from 1978 through 1981. Both of these planets are nearer the sun than earth is. Therefore, from our viewpoint they never stray very far from each other's zodiac position (or that of the sun).

Wherever the planet lines cross, a Mercury-Venus conjunction is indicated. Retrograde periods are shown where the planet line angles down. Degrees of each sign are indicated along the side of the chart so you can find the approximate zodiac degree of the planets at any given time.

(see also page 111)

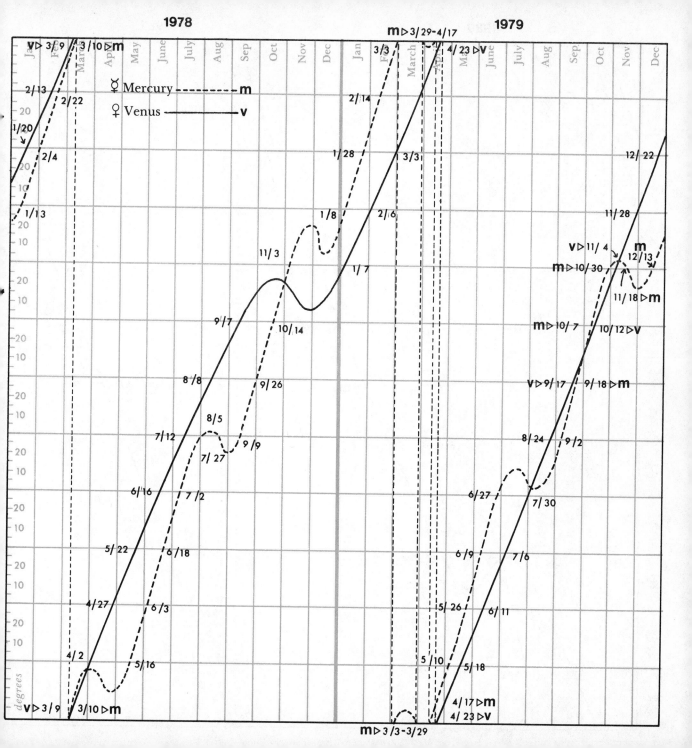

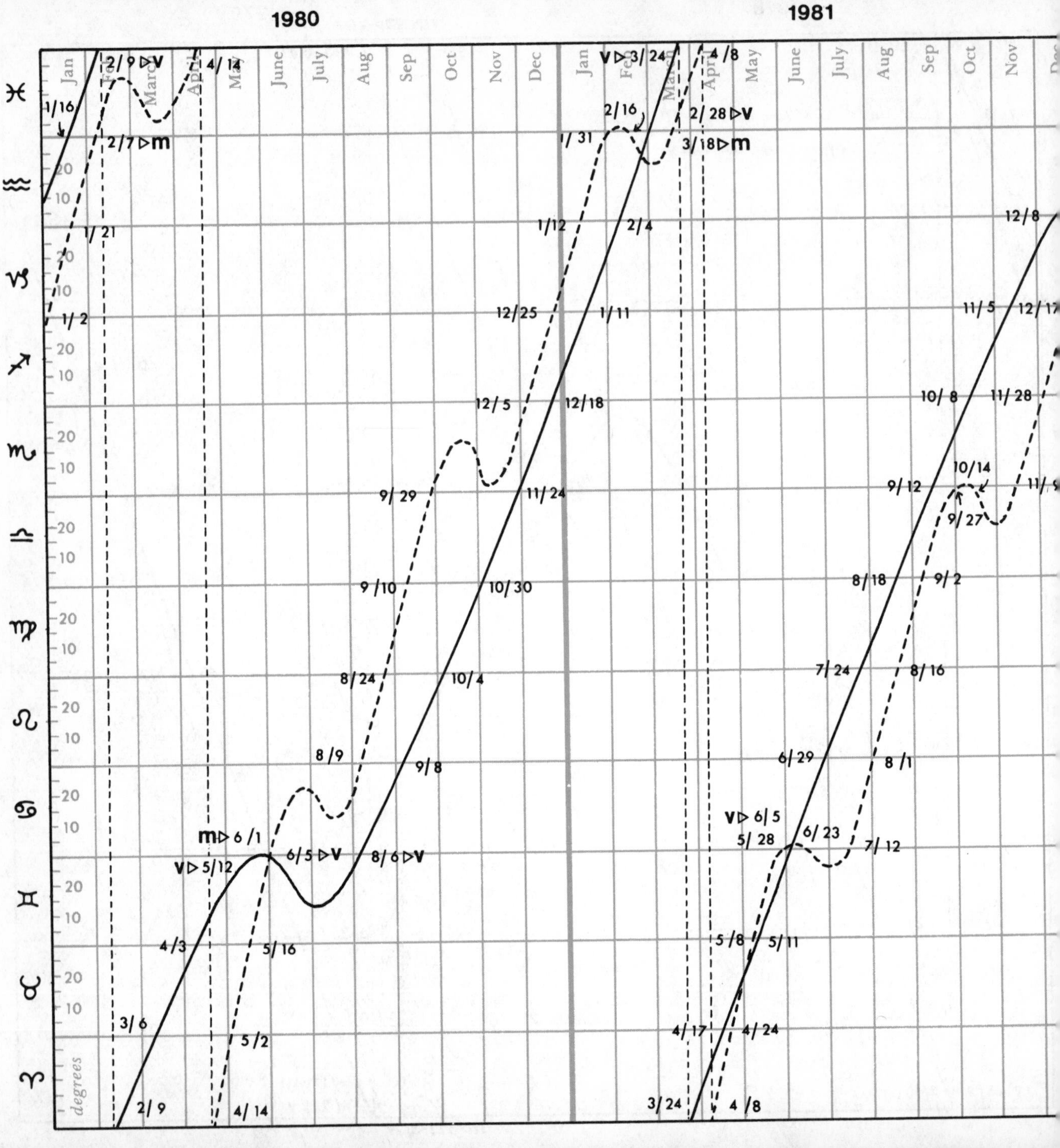

1980
1981
Jan
Feb
March
April
May
June
July
Aug
Sep
Oct
Nov
Dec
Jan
Feb
March
April
May
June
July
Aug
Sep
Oct
Nov
Dec
degrees
20
10
1/16
2/9 ▷V
4/14
2/7 ▷m
1/21
1/2
V▷3/24
4/8
2/16
2/28 ▷V
1/31
3/18▷m
1/12
2/4
12/8
12/25
1/11
11/5
12/17
12/5
12/18
10/8
11/28
10/14
9/12
9/29
11/24
9/27
9/10
10/30
8/18
9/2
8/24
10/4
7/24
8/16
8/9
9/8
6/29
8/1
V▷6/5
m▷6/1
5/28
6/23
7/12
V▷5/12
6/5 ▷V
8/6 ▷V
4/3
5/16
5/8
5/11
3/6
5/2
4/17
4/24
2/9
4/14
3/24
4/8

Outer planet charts

The charts on the following pages show graphically the zodiac positions and interrelations of the outer planets from 1901 through 2000. Across the top run the years, divided into three month periods beginning January, April, July, and October.

The planet lines are marked at intervals, but you will quickly learn to recognize each planet's characteristics: the steep line of Mars, which goes through the zodiac once every two years, with its retrograde period when the line dips down; the wavy advance (alternately direct and retrograde) of Jupiter's twelve-year cycle; Saturn's somewhat flatter wavy line; the line of Uranus, flatter still; and finally the almost horizontal lines of Neptune and Pluto.

A conjunction is indicated wherever two planet lines cross. You can find other aspects between the planets by tracing the aspect ruler on the side of this page and placing your traced ruler vertically on the chart with its base point on one planet line. Accuracy within a few degrees is possible with the scale of these charts, but for more precision an astrological ephemeris must be consulted.

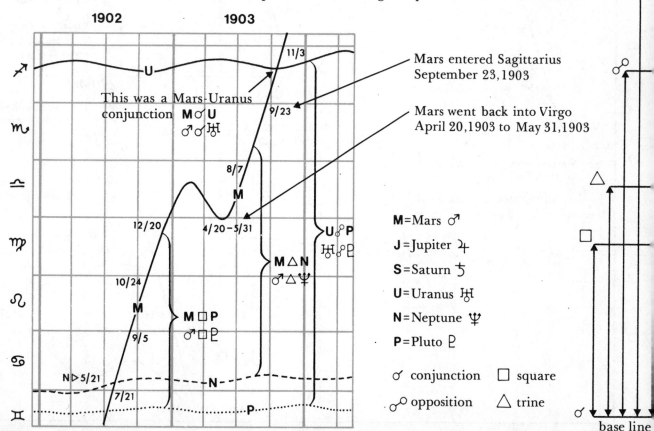

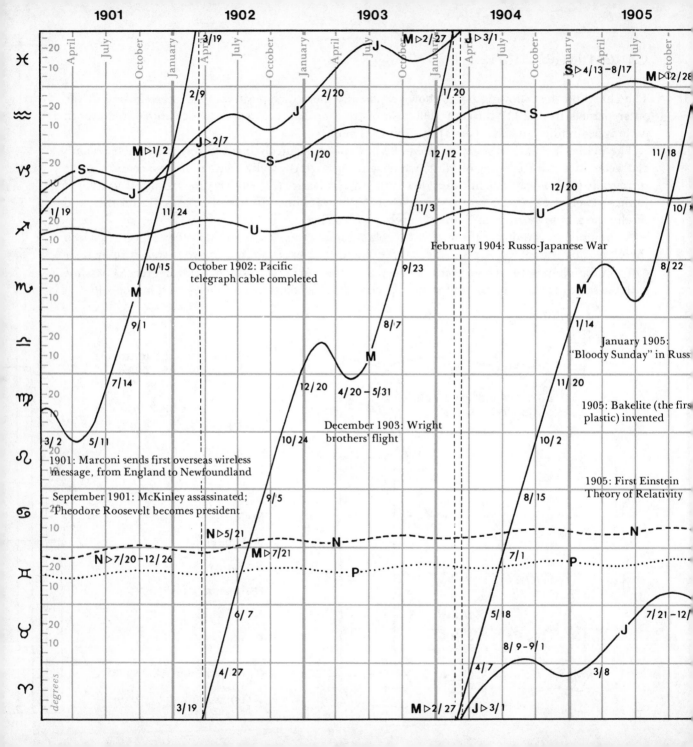

1901 1902 1903 1904 1905

October 1902: Pacific telegraph cable completed

February 1904: Russo-Japanese War

December 1903: Wright brothers' flight

January 1905: "Bloody Sunday" in Russ

1905: Bakelite (the firs plastic) invented

1901: Marconi sends first overseas wireless message, from England to Newfoundland

September 1901: McKinley assassinated; Theodore Roosevelt becomes president

1905: First Einstein Theory of Relativity

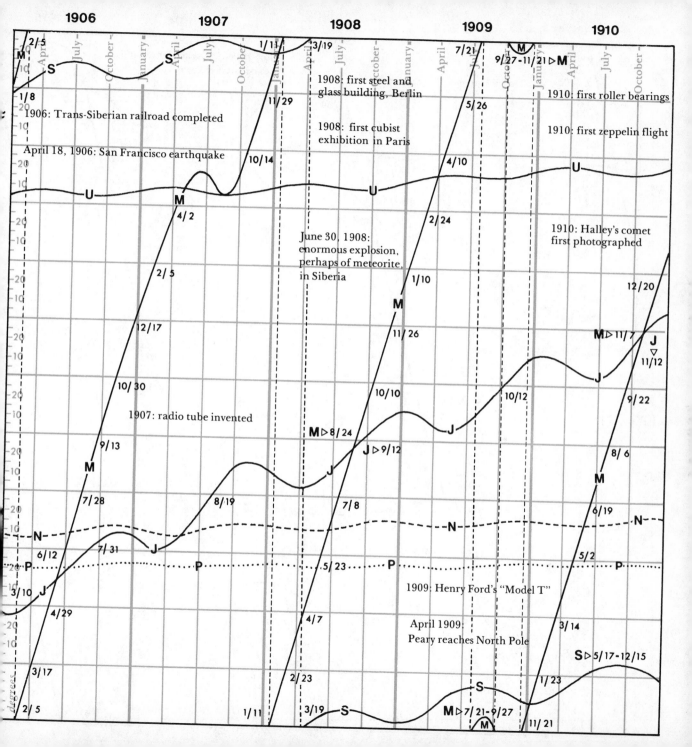

1906   1907   1908   1909   1910

2/5
M
S   S
1/8

1906: Trans-Siberian railroad completed

April 18, 1906: San Francisco earthquake

1/11
3/19

1908: first steel and glass building, Berlin

1908: first cubist exhibition in Paris

7/21
9/27-11/21 ▷ M

1910: first roller bearings

1910: first zeppelin flight

11/29
10/14
5/26

U   U   U
4/10

M
4/2

2/5   2/24

June 30, 1908: enormous explosion, perhaps of meteorite, in Siberia

1910: Halley's comet first photographed

12/17   1/10   12/20

M

10/30   11/26   M▷11/7   J
                                          ▽
                                          11/12

1907: radio tube invented   10/10   10/12   J   9/22

9/13   J   8/6

7/28   M▷8/24   7/8   M

8/19   J▷9/12   6/19   6/19
J
N   N   N   N

7/31
6/12   J   5/2
N
P   P   5/23   P   P
3/10   J

1909: Henry Ford's "Model T"

4/29   4/7

April 1909: Peary reaches North Pole   3/14

S▷5/17-12/15

3/17   2/23   1/23

S

2/5   1/11   3/19   S   M▷7/21-9/27   11/21
                                          M

degrees

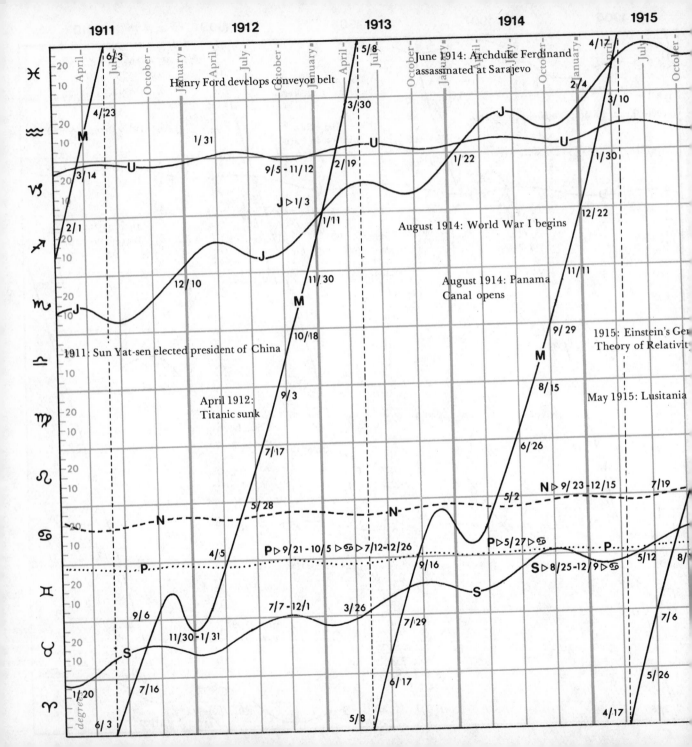

1911 1912 1913 1914 1915

Henry Ford develops conveyor belt

June 1914: Archduke Ferdinand
assassinated at Sarajevo

August 1914: World War I begins

August 1914: Panama
Canal opens

1915: Einstein's General
Theory of Relativity

1911: Sun Yat-sen elected president of China

April 1912:
Titanic sunk

May 1915: Lusitania

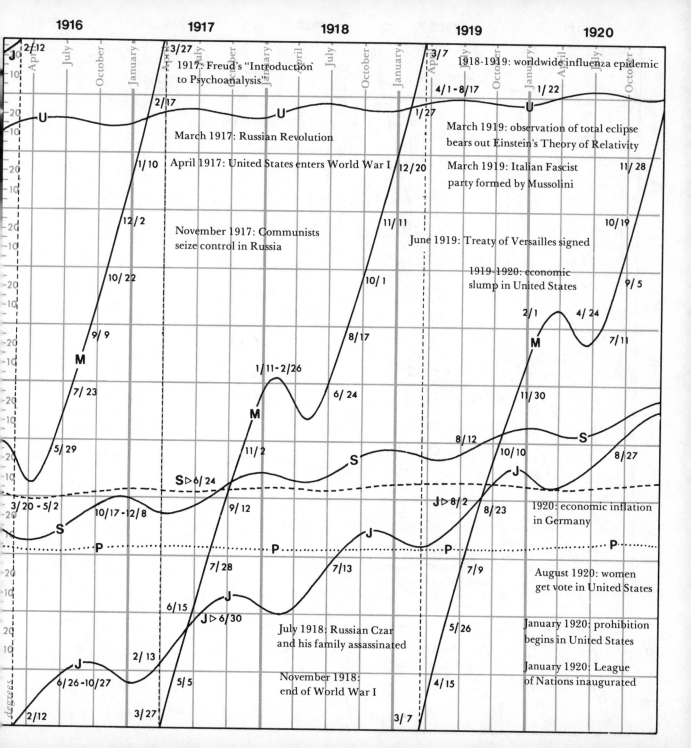

1916   1917   1918   1919   1920

1917: Freud's "Introduction to Psychoanalysis"

1918-1919: worldwide influenza epidemic

March 1917: Russian Revolution

March 1919: observation of total eclipse bears out Einstein's Theory of Relativity

April 1917: United States enters World War I

March 1919: Italian Fascist party formed by Mussolini

November 1917: Communists seize control in Russia

June 1919: Treaty of Versailles signed

1919-1920: economic slump in United States

July 1918: Russian Czar and his family assassinated

1920: economic inflation in Germany

August 1920: women get vote in United States

January 1920: prohibition begins in United States

November 1918: end of World War I

January 1920: League of Nations inaugurated

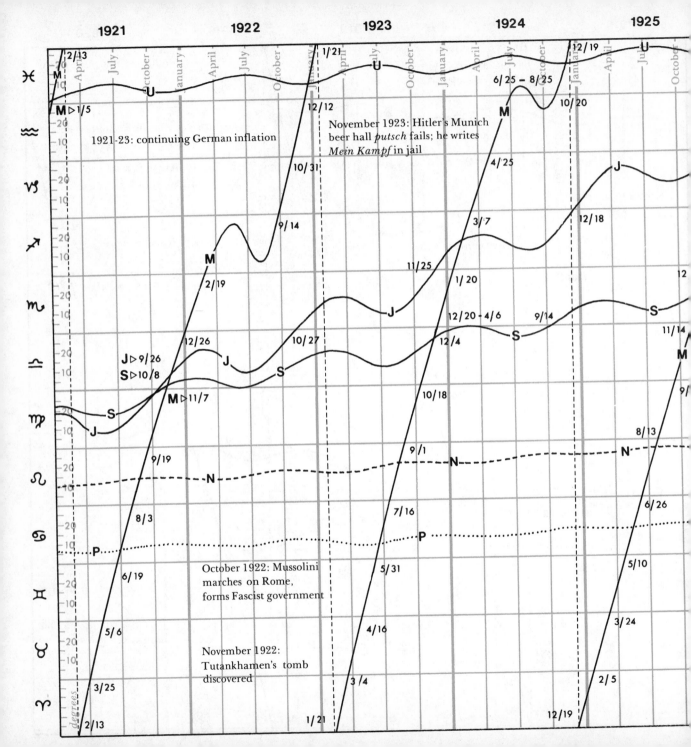

1921　1922　1923　1924　1925

1921-23: continuing German inflation

November 1923: Hitler's Munich beer hall *putsch* fails; he writes *Mein Kampf* in jail

October 1922: Mussolini marches on Rome, forms Fascist government

November 1922: Tutankhamen's tomb discovered

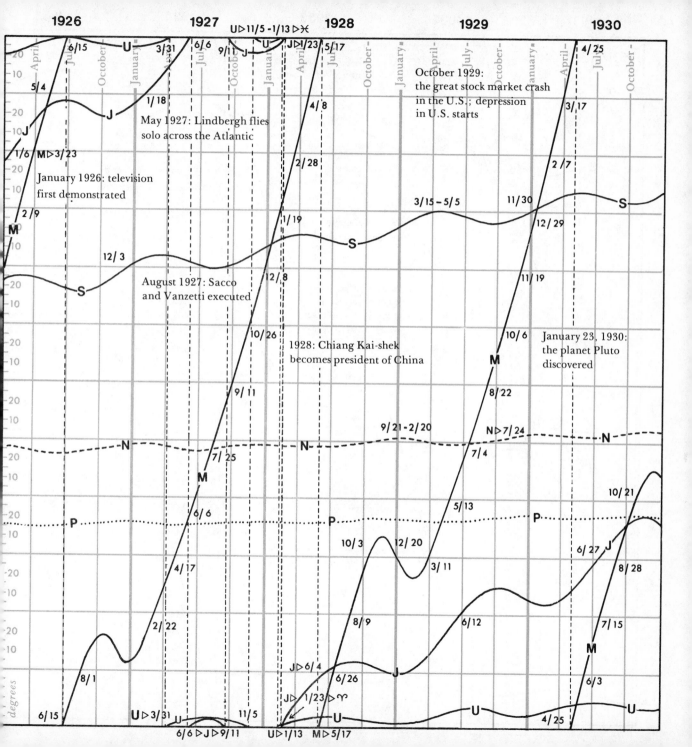

1926   1927   U▷11/5 -1/13 ▷⊬   1928   1929   1930

6/15   U   3/31   6/6   9/11 J   U   J▷1/23 5/17   4/25

5/4   1/18   4/8   3/17

J   2/28   2/7

1/6   M▷3/23   October 1929: the great stock market crash in the U.S.; depression in U.S. starts

May 1927: Lindbergh flies solo across the Atlantic

January 1926: television first demonstrated   3/15 – 5/5   11/30   S

2/9   1/19   12/29

M   12/8   11/19

12/3   August 1927: Sacco and Vanzetti executed

S   10/26   1928: Chiang Kai-shek becomes president of China   10/6   January 23, 1930: the planet Pluto discovered

9/11   M

8/22

9/21-2/20   N▷7/24

N   7/25   N   7/4   N

M   5/13   10/21

6/6   P   P   P

10/3   12/20   6/27 J

4/17   3/11   8/28

2/22   8/9   6/12   7/15

J▷6/4   M

8/1   6/26   J   6/3

J▷ 1/23 ▷♈   7/15

degrees   U   U   4/25   U

6/15   U▷3/31 J   11/5   U▷1/13 M▷5/17

6/6 ▷J▷9/11

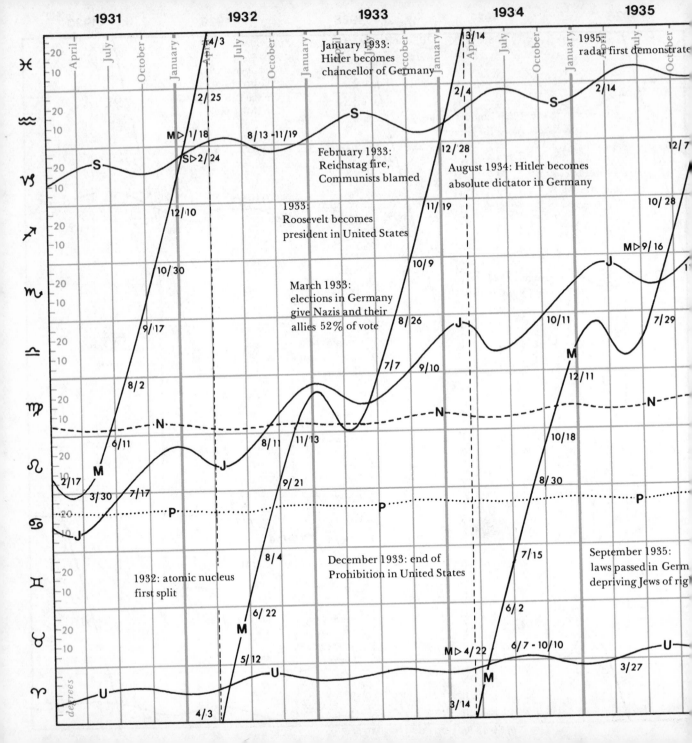

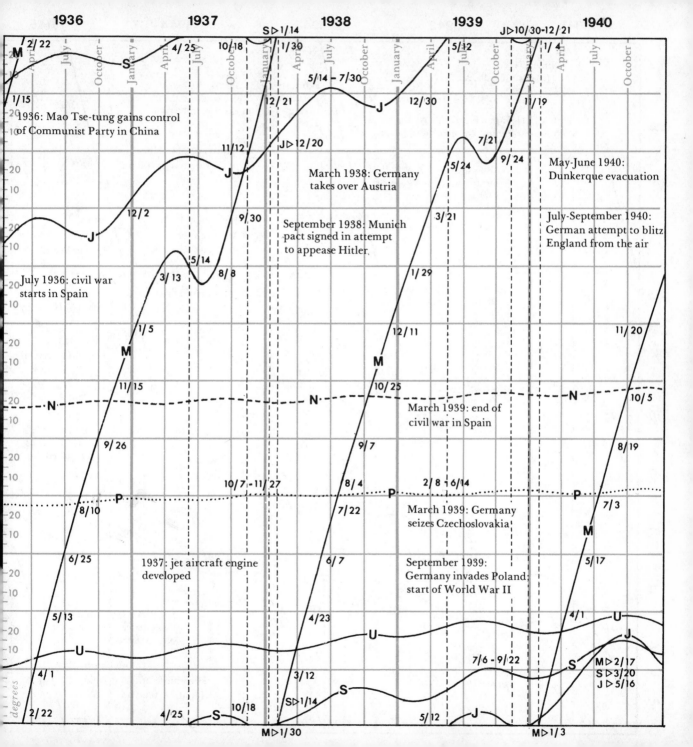

1936: Mao Tse-tung gains control of Communist Party in China

March 1938: Germany takes over Austria

September 1938: Munich pact signed in attempt to appease Hitler

July 1936: civil war starts in Spain

March 1939: end of civil war in Spain

1937: jet aircraft engine developed

March 1939: Germany seizes Czechoslovakia

September 1939: Germany invades Poland; start of World War II

May-June 1940: Dunkerque evacuation

July-September 1940: German attempt to blitz England from the air

degrees

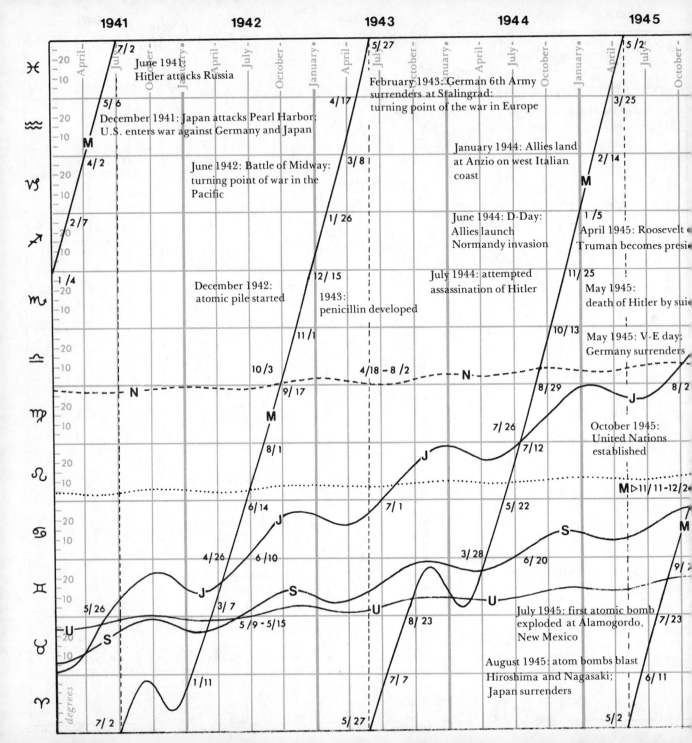

1941 1942 1943 1944 1945

June 1941:
Hitler attacks Russia

February 1943: German 6th Army
surrenders at Stalingrad;
turning point of the war in Europe

December 1941: Japan attacks Pearl Harbor;
U.S. enters war against Germany and Japan

January 1944: Allies land
at Anzio on west Italian
coast

June 1942: Battle of Midway:
turning point of war in the
Pacific

June 1944: D-Day:
Allies launch
Normandy invasion

April 1945: Roosevelt
Truman becomes presi

December 1942:
atomic pile started

1943:
penicillin developed

July 1944: attempted
assassination of Hitler

May 1945:
death of Hitler by sui

May 1945: V-E day;
Germany surrenders

October 1945:
United Nations
established

July 1945: first atomic bomb
exploded at Alamogordo,
New Mexico

August 1945: atom bombs blast
Hiroshima and Nagasaki;
Japan surrenders

degrees

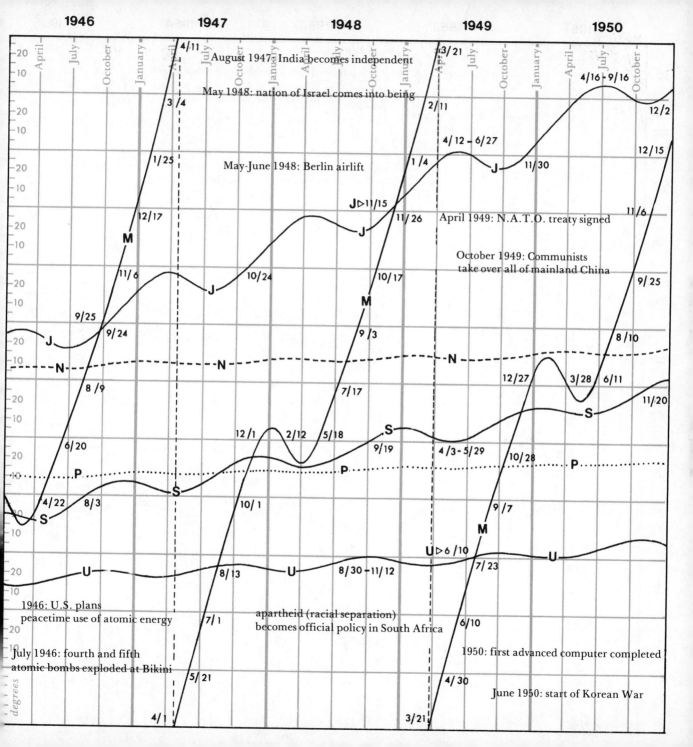

1946   1947   1948   1949   1950

August 1947: India becomes independent

May 1948: nation of Israel comes into being

May-June 1948: Berlin airlift

April 1949: N.A.T.O. treaty signed

October 1949: Communists
take over all of mainland China

1946: U.S. plans
peacetime use of atomic energy

apartheid (racial separation)
becomes official policy in South Africa

1950: first advanced computer completed

July 1946: fourth and fifth
atomic bombs exploded at Bikini

June 1950: start of Korean War

degrees

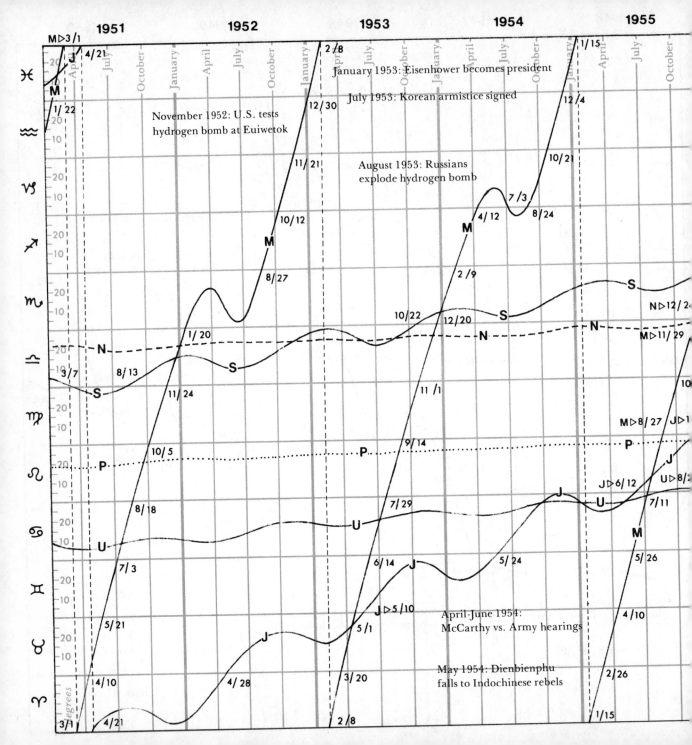

January 1953: Eisenhower becomes president

July 1953: Korean armistice signed

November 1952: U.S. tests
hydrogen bomb at Euiwetok

August 1953: Russians
explode hydrogen bomb

April-June 1954:
McCarthy vs. Army hearings

May 1954: Dienbienphu
falls to Indochinese rebels

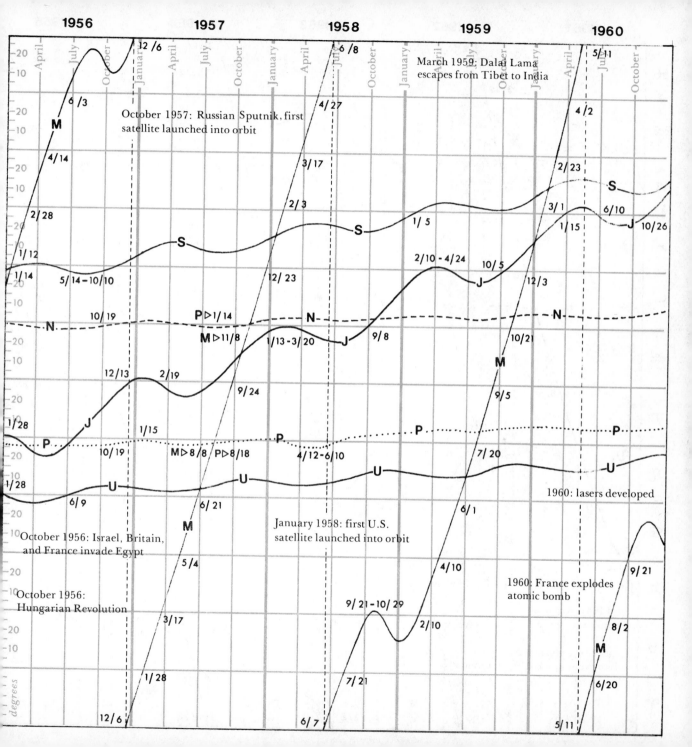

1956 **1957** **1958** **1959** **1960**

October 1957: Russian Sputnik, first
satellite launched into orbit

March 1959: Dalai Lama
escapes from Tibet to India

January 1958: first U.S.
satellite launched into orbit

October 1956: Israel, Britain,
and France invade Egypt

October 1956:
Hungarian Revolution

1960: lasers developed

1960: France explodes
atomic bomb

degrees

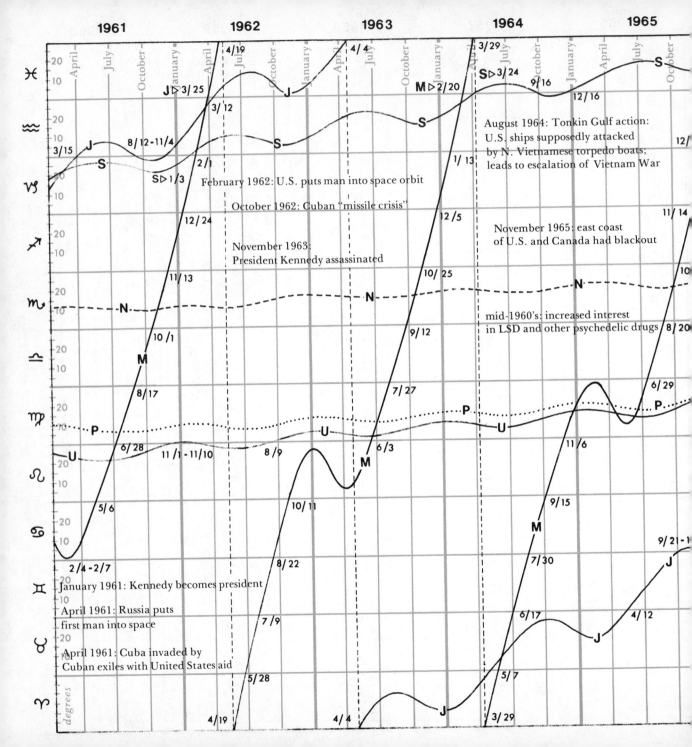

1961   1962   1963   1964   1965

J ▷ 3/25

3/12

8/12-11/4

S ▷ 1/3   February 1962: U.S. puts man into space orbit

October 1962: Cuban 'missile crisis'

November 1963:
President Kennedy assassinated

August 1964: Tonkin Gulf action:
U.S. ships supposedly attacked
by N. Vietnamese torpedo boats;
leads to escalation of Vietnam War

November 1965: east coast
of U.S. and Canada had blackout

mid-1960's: increased interest
in LSD and other psychedelic drugs

January 1961: Kennedy becomes president

April 1961: Russia puts
first man into space

April 1961: Cuba invaded by
Cuban exiles with United States aid

degrees

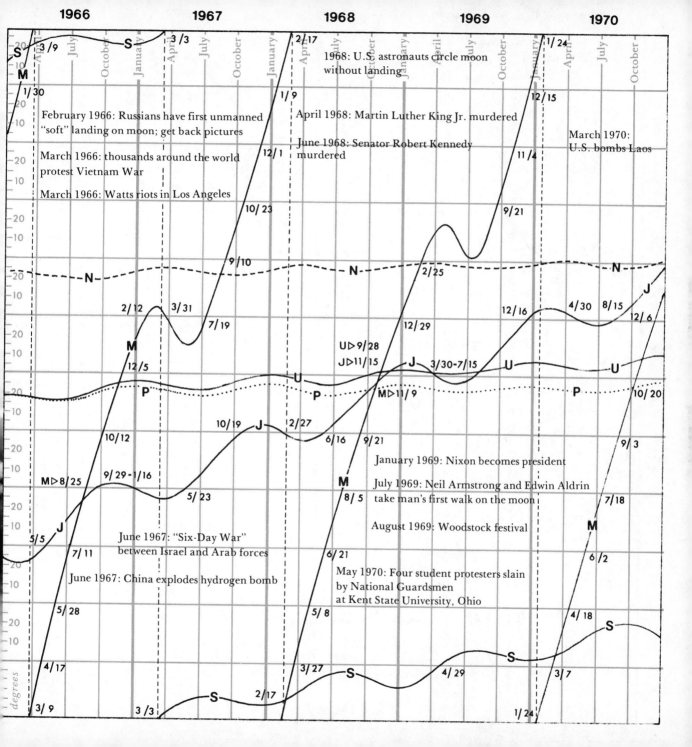

1966 1967 1968 1969 1970

1968: U.S. astronauts circle moon without landing

February 1966: Russians have first unmanned "soft" landing on moon; get back pictures

April 1968: Martin Luther King Jr. murdered

March 1966: thousands around the world protest Vietnam War

June 1968: Senator Robert Kennedy murdered

March 1970: U.S. bombs Laos

March 1966: Watts riots in Los Angeles

January 1969: Nixon becomes president

July 1969: Neil Armstrong and Edwin Aldrin take man's first walk on the moon

August 1969: Woodstock festival

June 1967: "Six-Day War" between Israel and Arab forces

June 1967: China explodes hydrogen bomb

May 1970: Four student protesters slain by National Guardsmen at Kent State University, Ohio

degrees

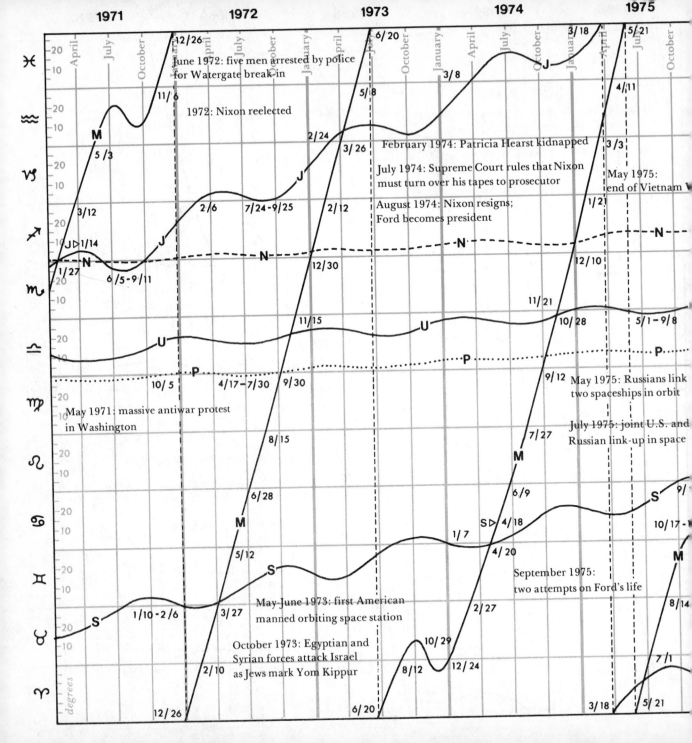

1971   1972   1973   1974   1975

June 1972: five men arrested by police
for Watergate break-in

1972: Nixon reelected

February 1974: Patricia Hearst kidnapped

July 1974: Supreme Court rules that Nixon
must turn over his tapes to prosecutor

August 1974: Nixon resigns;
Ford becomes president

May 1975:
end of Vietnam

May 1975: Russians link
two spaceships in orbit

July 1975: joint U.S. and
Russian link-up in space

September 1975:
two attempts on Ford's life

May 1971: massive antiwar protest
in Washington

May-June 1973: first American
manned orbiting space station

October 1973: Egyptian and
Syrian forces attack Israel
as Jews mark Yom Kippur

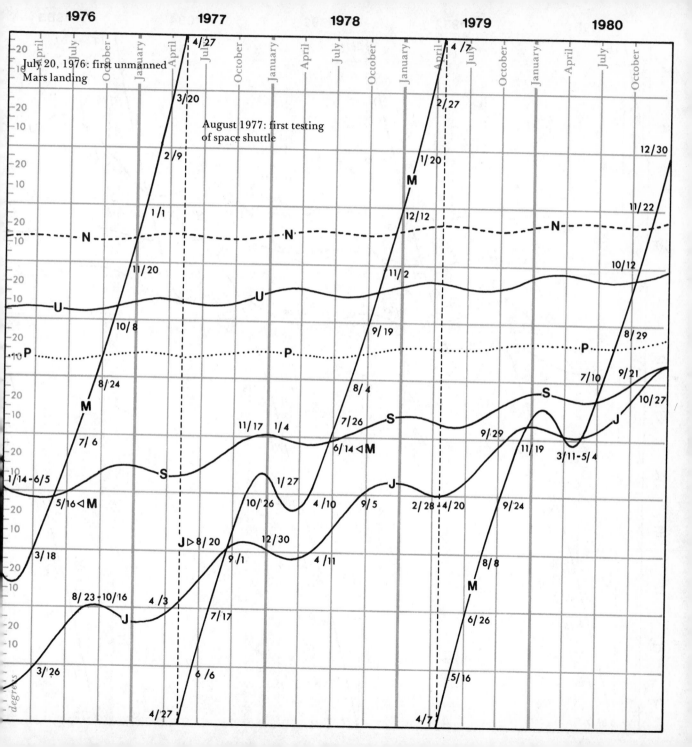

1976   1977   1978   1979   1980

July 20, 1976: first unmanned
Mars landing

4/27
3/20
2/9

August 1977: first testing
of space shuttle

4/7
2/27
1/20

1/1

M

12/30

11/22

N   N   N

12/12

11/20   11/2

U   U   10/12

10/8   9/19

P   P   P   8/29

8/24   8/4   7/10   9/21

M   S   10/27

7/26   S   S   J

7/6   9/29

11/17   1/4   6/14◁M   11/19   3/11-5/4

S   1/27   9/5   2/28 4/20   9/24

1/14-6/5   10/26   4/10   J

5/16◁M   4/11

J▷8/20   12/30   M

9/1   4/11   8/8

8/23-10/16   4/3   6/26

J   7/17   5/16

3/18

3/26   6/6

4/27   4/7

degrees

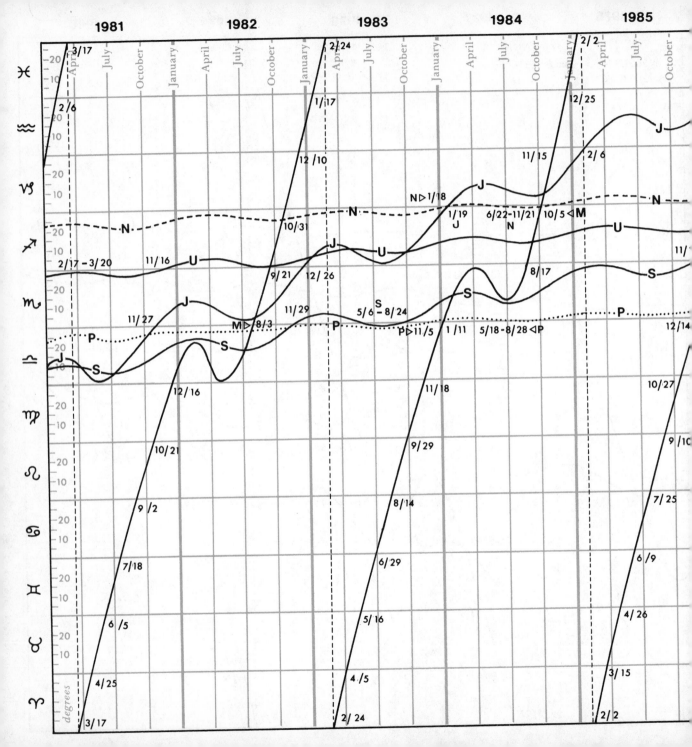

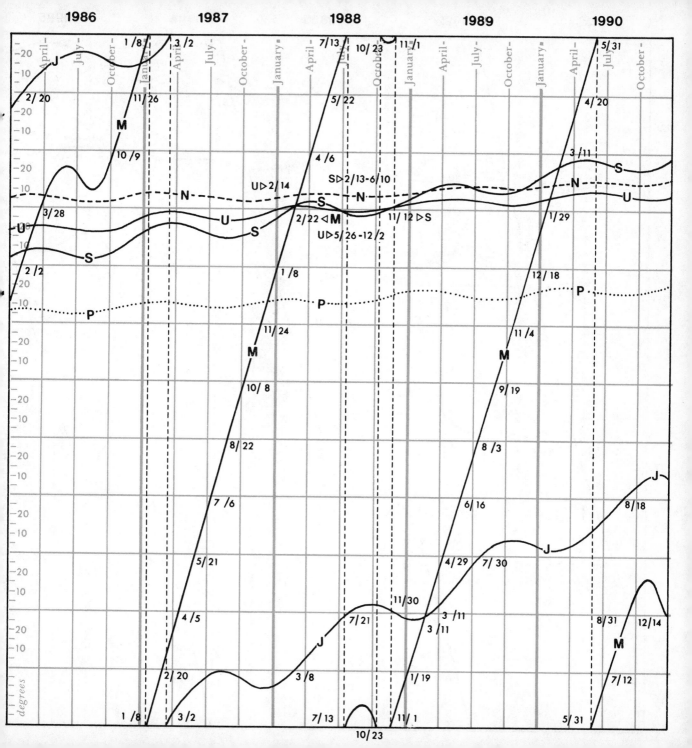

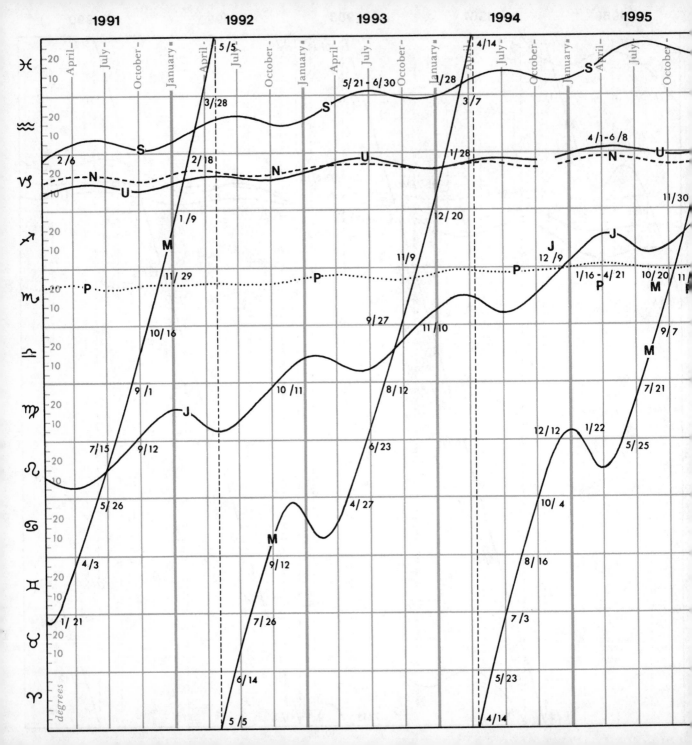

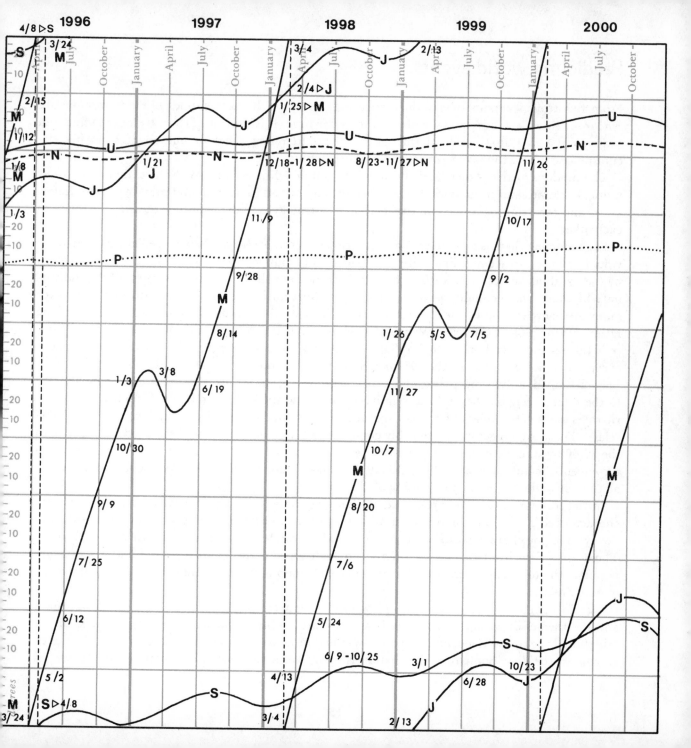

Predicting world events

From an astrological point of view the planets may not *cause* things to happen but their motions are *synchronized* with things that take place at the same time. It is the role of the astrologer to find and examine the rhythmic cycles of the universe and to relate these to human and earthly circumstances. This is the essence of astrological predicting.

The motions of the planets and the stars are composed of cycles and, in fact, describe almost musical rhythms and harmonics. Human beings, on both an individual and mass level, also follow cycles and recurring patterns, and the method of astrology is to discover how these cycles relate to each other.

Each moment there is a planetary configuration or "cosmic chord." When predicting for an individual we take into account first, what chord was being sounded when he or she was born (as shown by the natal horoscope) and further, how various themes will develop in the course of the individual's lifetime. These cosmic themes, or cycles, in effect during the life of an individual will cover many moon cycles, a sun cycle for each year that he or she lives, and quite a number of cycles of the faster-moving planets (Mercury, Venus, and Mars). Most individuals will experience 5 or 6 of Jupiter's 12-year cycles and only 2 to 3 of Saturn's 29-year cycles. A completed 84-year Uranus cycle is exceptional, as well as half of the 165-year Neptune cycle and even a third of Pluto's 248-year cycle.

Each individual, like one player in the cosmic orchestra, makes his or her particular contribution to the total effect, but beyond the relatively short time span of an individual life are the slower rhythms marked by cycles of Uranus, Neptune, and Pluto, considered separately and as they interrelate. There are longer cycles, possibly connected with planets as yet undiscovered, and also with the 26,000-year cycle of the precession of the equinoxes and the 230-million-year cycle of the sun's movement around the center of the galaxy. Of course there are even more extended cosmic cycles, all the way to the beginning and ending of the universe.

In the study of history we are aware of changing cycles over a period of centuries. These are characterized by the spirit and rhythm of the times. Even within a 100-year span we can identify slowly changing characteristics, such as the "mood" of the Victorian era or the "theme" of the 60's. These are shown by the collective opinion in such ways as the kinds of music and art that are popular, the topics and activities that dominate the public interest, even the fashions which the majority relates to.

Astrologers have made connections between the planetary cycles, particularly the slower ones, and the themes of various periods. It is as if we are all aware, at least on deeper levels, of the "rhythm of the times." Depending upon how tuned in we are, we blend with the overall themes or go against the flow. Sometimes the rhythm is faster, sometimes slower. Sometimes the "music" is more lighthearted, sometimes heavier.

The astrological study of history enables us to connect planetary and other astrological cycles with the characteristics of a period and the events within it. First we will look at the overall frame of reference and then we will examine in more detail the astrological cycles of the twentieth century as they connect with what has happened up to now and what, on the basis of this, we can project into the future.

The Aquarian age

The largest cycle that we will consider is the 26,000-year cycle of the precession of the equinoxes. For our purposes it is sufficient to know that in this cycle a change takes place approximately every 2,000 years in the zodiac sign that is in prominence. Astrologers are not agreed on the exact date of this change, but they do agree that we are now in orb of the change from Pisces to Aquarius (this cycle always moves backwards around the zodiac). It is as if the cosmic music is now going into a new key, and this major change in a very slow cycle is exerting a strong effect on the relatively faster cycles within it. In other words, *each repeating cycle of a planet is increasingly tuned into an overall Aquarian "key."*

Planet cycles

The most important planets for predicting world events: The cycles of the three outermost planets (Uranus, Neptune, and Pluto) are particularly significant in setting the stage for trends of history. The cycles of Jupiter and Saturn are also important over a shorter time span and the cycles of Mars and the inner planets, as well as the sun and the moon, work as triggers for specific events that characterize the energy pattern of the times. Eclipses of either the sun or the moon also act as triggers.

Beginnings of cycles: Planet cycles can be looked at in several ways. In one sense a cycle has no beginning and no end. Studied from this standpoint the influence on the planet of the zodiac sign it is passing through is most important. However, there are several points that can be considered as the beginning of an individual planet's cycle. The one most often used is the time the planet enters Aries. Another beginning point of significance is the time the planet reaches perihelion (closest point to the sun in the planet's cycle). Some astrologers consider that the time a planet crosses its north node is a significant beginning. The *nodes* of a planet are the points where the plane of its orbit intersects the plane of the earth's orbit. The *north node* is the point where the planet moves across this intersection toward the north in relation to earth's orbit.

Periods in which a planet is stationary or retrograde are also important.

The interaction between two planet cycles is of great significance. When two planets are conjunct, this marks the beginning of a cycle, their opposition is the midpoint of the cycle, and the following conjunction its conclusion. In world events the interaction cycles of the outer planets are especially important.

Particular zodiac degrees: As mentioned earlier, certain specific degrees of the zodiac seem to start things in motion. Some of these mark relatively permanent factors, such as the position of a particular fixed star, the node of a planet, or its perihelion point. Any degree can be temporarily sensitized if, for instance, it was the scene of the last eclipse or the last conjunction between two planets.

HOROSCOPES OF NATIONS
Astrologers who study world trends also work with horoscopes set up for the various nations, as well as for such organizations as the United Nations, the Common Market, etc. Getting the date and time the newer nations were founded is fairly easy. The horoscopes of older nations are often available from astrological tradition. The date of birth of the United States is considered to be July 4, 1776.

Transits to a nation's chart can be observed in the same way as transits to an individual's chart.

The Twentieth Century, past and future

Beginning on page 112 are charts showing the movements of Mars, Jupiter, Saturn, Uranus, Neptune, and Pluto from 1901 through 2000. These show graphically, and sometimes dramatically, the intertwining planetary movements through the century. You can see at a glance the slow advance of Pluto, beginning the century in Gemini (toward the bottom of the chart), to Sagittarius (toward the top) at the end of the century. By comparison, the line showing the fast motion of Mars shoots, like a lightening bolt, from Aries up through Pisces every two years. Slants of the other planet lines fall somewhere in between. Retrograde periods are shown when any line slants down and stationary periods are at the bends in the loops. Whenever two planet lines cross, the planets are conjunct. Other aspects can be found by using the scale on page 111 or by consulting the aspect chart on page 108.

1901-1910

You will see that at the beginning of 1901 Saturn was in Capricorn with Jupiter just about to join it. Uranus was not far away in Sagittarius. Down toward the bottom of the chart Pluto was in mid-Gemini and Neptune toward the end of Gemini about to enter Cancer. Neptune then made a brief return to Gemini before it became firmly established in Cancer in 1902.

PLUTO IN GEMINI (1884 to 1912), as we noted in the Pluto section, is characterized by basic changes in methods of communication and in ideas about deeper levels of human beings. We could also have added basic changes in ideas about mind and matter.

NEPTUNE IN CANCER (1901-1902 to 1914) is related to new appreciation of instinctual and unconscious influences.

URANUS IN SAGITTARIUS (1897 to 1904) means new attitudes toward both legal systems and universal laws; new means of travel.

URANUS IN CAPRICORN (1904 to 1912) means new approaches in business, particularly mass marketing; new attitudes toward dealing with crime; new ways to form structures.

The planet-sign influence of each of these three planets, both separately and together, can be seen in many events of the decade:

Basic changes in ideas about matter (Pluto in Gemini) and new attitudes toward universal laws (Uranus in Sagittarius): Max Planck's Quantum Theory (1900); Rutherford's General Theory of Radioactivity (1904); and Einstein's Special Theory of Relativity (1905). The basic changes in ideas about mind (Pluto in Gemini) and about deeper levels of human beings (Neptune in Cancer) were represented by Freud's developing and beginning to publish his works on psychoanalysis during the decade. Changes in methods of communication (Pluto in Gemini) included Marconi's development of the wireless telegraphy (1901) and the invention of the radio tube (1907).

New means of travel (Uranus in Sagittarius) were shown by such developments as subway systems, the zeppelin (1900), and the Wright brothers' first flight (December 17, 1903). The Trans-Siberian railroad was completed in 1906. The automobile industry was developing in Detroit, beginning about 1903, and after Uranus entered Capricorn the Model T Ford appeared (1909) and the groundwork was being laid for development of assembly line techniques. The first roller bearings, essential for high-speed vehicles, began to be manufactured in 1910.

New concepts of architectural structure (Uranus in Capricorn) were indicated by the first steel and glass building (Berlin, 1908), the initial development toward the spare, functional style that has come to typify twentieth century architecture.

In art the changes in ways of looking at matter (Pluto in Gemini) and the increased emphasis on the unconscious (Neptune in Cancer) were characterized by cubism, which began the artistic revolution leading to abstract art, the breakdown of strict representational forms. In art cubism created a different concept of form (Uranus in Capricorn) with an appreciation of the unconscious (Neptune in Cancer) which led to the development of purely abstract art.

In the area of national and international events, the time of the entry of Uranus into Capricorn saw the Russo-Japanese War (1904) and the unsuccessful Bloody Sunday uprising in St. Petersburg, Russia, in 1905. Capricorn is a sign which can lay the groundwork for future events as well as bring about the results of previous causes. The events then taking place in Russia laid the groundwork for the successful Russian Revolution in 1917, after Uranus (the planet of revolution) had entered Aquarius, the sign it "rules." During the decade from 1901 to 1910 the groundwork was also being laid for World War I.

At the beginning of the decade the outer planets (except Mars) were established in an opposition formation (more or less 180 degrees apart), with Uranus exactly opposite Pluto and Jupiter exactly opposite Neptune in January 1901. Saturn, whose orbit conjuncted that of Jupiter during 1901, was also part of the opposition pattern.

An opposition brings confrontation that must be resolved either in conflict or in a peaceful establishment of equilibrium. One resolution of this five-planet opposition pattern at the beginning of the decade was the challenge in the United States of President Theodore Roosevelt to the business "robber barons" in their virtual immunity from the law.

Not only did Jupiter and Saturn begin their conjunction cycle at the start of the twentieth century, but also each of them had just begun a Uranus-conjunction cycle, Saturn conjuncting Uranus in 1897 and Jupiter conjuncting it in 1900. A cycle of even longer duration had just begun with the Neptune-Pluto conjunction of 1891-1892.

In the United States President McKinley was assassinated on September 6, 1901, less than three months before the Jupiter-Saturn conjunction, a conjunction that takes place about every twenty years. Since the United States became a nation, every president who was elected for a term of office in which a Jupiter-Saturn conjunction occurred in an *earth sign* has died while in office, a total of seven presidents. The next Jupiter-Saturn conjunction will take place on December 31, 1980, however this time in an *air sign*.

The decade of 1901 to 1910 was also marked by a drive toward the cleaning up of political corruption on many levels: national, state, city (Uranus in Sagittarius).

On the planet charts you can find some other significant historical events of the decade to compare with planetary positions.

1911-1920

During this period Neptune and Pluto moved steadily farther apart and both moved away from opposition to Uranus. Uranus in Aquarius (the sign it rules) was one of the dominant forces of the period.

URANUS IN AQUARIUS (1912 to 1919): "Emphasis on revolution and new freedoms in many fields: personal, political, technological."

PLUTO IN CANCER (1912 to 1937): Basic changes in collective attitudes toward instinctual patterns, including deeper psychological understanding of emotions." We could have added: "Basic changes in the home and in attitudes toward one's country (both ruled by Cancer)."

NEPTUNE IN LEO (1914 to 1929): "Awareness of deeper-than-ego centers and increased fantasy in the arts and entertainment."

The revolutions and new freedoms in many fields included the accelerating breakdown of strict Victorian mores, the suffragette movement, ragtime (around 1913) and jazz (swept the United States around 1916).

In technology this was the period in which assemblyline techniques, such as the conveyor belt, were pioneered. The Panama Canal opened in 1914.

One of the major events in psychology was the publication, in 1917, of Freud's "Introduction to Psychoanalysis."

The decade was dominated by World War I and the Russian Revolution. World War I began August 1, 1914 just as Saturn came in orb of a conjunction with Pluto at the very beginning of Cancer. Whenever Pluto enters another sign, it signifies the beginning of a new push toward basic change, or perhaps conflict, in the collective mind. Politically this can sometimes be manifested by the outbreak of war, revolution, or both. At other times the change can come about in a peaceful manner. Not only did Pluto's entry into Cancer closely coincide with the outbreak of World War I, its entry into Leo closely coincided with the outbreak of World War II.

Saturn conjuncting Pluto at the begining of World War I served to bring to a head the underlying tensions that had been collecting under the surface in Europe since the turn of the century.

The Russian Revolution began in 1917. On June 24, 1917 the Russian Black Sea fleet mutinied. This was the day that Saturn entered Leo within orb of a conjunction with Neptune. Leo rules kings and Saturn brought the consequences to a shattered Neptunian ideal about the divine right of kings. Neptune also rules the sea. Uranus in Aquarius was, of course, also involved.

The area of manners and morals saw the gradual breakdown (Pluto in Cancer, Uranus in Aquarius) of strictly controlled Victorian social and sexual behavior inherited from the previous century. This was the social counterpart to the revolutionary movements on the political scene and it laid the groundwork for the roaring 20's. Dadaism, a not quite serious form of "anti-art" became the rage of the art world, while in popular music first ragtime and then jazz swept the nation.

1921-1930

The planet configurations for these years show that the three outermost planets (Uranus, Neptune, and Pluto) were more spread out from each other, with Uranus and Pluto approximately trine (120 degrees apart). Pluto spent the whole decade in Cancer, but Uranus and Neptune changed signs. Uranus first moved from Pisces to Aries (a new zodiac cycle) on March 31, 1927; Neptune first went out of Leo into Virgo in September, 1928.

The conjunction of Jupiter and Saturn on September 9, 1921, just as they were both about to leave Virgo and enter Libra, marked the beginning of a new Jupiter-Saturn cycle. The first degrees of a cardinal sign (such as Libra) are particularly important. Faster-moving Mars caught up with, conjuncted, and passed both Jupiter and Saturn in early Libra less than two months later. Mars had also conjuncted both Pluto and Neptune during 1921. This marked the beginning of events leading toward World War II. In 1922 Mussolini formed a fascist government in Italy and, in 1923, Hitler wrote *Mein Kampf*.

The conjunction of Jupiter and Uranus at the end of 1927 and the beginning of 1928 marks another interesting, astrological period within the decade of the 20's. Coming at the beginning of Aries, this meant that the two planets were starting not only new zodiac cycles but also a new cycle in relation to each other. Mars entered Aries before the middle of 1928 and rapidly made conjunctions that year with both Jupiter and Saturn. Neptune went back and forth between Leo and Virgo in 1928 and 1929, entering Virgo to stay on July 24, 1929, just before the stock market crash of October 24, 1929. Leo rules play and speculation, and Neptune in Leo had been characterized by rampant and unrealistic speculation on the stock market. Neptune going into Virgo (an earth sign) brought an adjustment toward reality. Saturn went (within a few weeks of the Neptune change) from the expansive sign of Sagittarius to the "reality" sign of Capricorn where, in February 1930, it made a last square to Uranus (the planet of the unexpected) in Aries. This square creates tension which can only be resolved by change.

Although the stock market crash came near the end of the decade to burst Neptune's Leonian bubble, this period (often called the "Daring Decade" or the "Roaring 20's") saw a major transformation of society (particularly in America). The radio, the movies, and mass tourist travel abroad all came into their own. Prohibition (1919-1933) proved to be a fantastic boon to organized crime. A new, streamlined look came into industrial design and architecture. The nation went to the movies, danced the Charleston, and idolized Lindbergh when he flew the Atlantic alone in 1927.

1931-1940

The decade began in the depths of the depression with Uranus square Pluto. Economic collapse is very Uranian and the square aspect challenged the collective mind (Pluto) to adapt to new situations. Towards the end of the decade Uranus, which moved into Taurus in 1933-1934, trined Neptune in Virgo, bringing new hopes and new ideals.

A series of new planetary cycles started at the end of 1932 and beginning of 1933, with Jupiter conjuncting Neptune on September 19, 1932; Mars conjuncting Neptune on December 6, 1932, February 7, 1933, and May 17, 1933; and finally Mars conjuncting Jupiter on June 4, 1933. Just prior to this last conjunction Mars and Jupiter came within two degrees of conjunction and then turned retrograde. Jupiter rules government and Mars rules force; thus it is not surprising that this was the month Hitler became chancellor in Germany. He gained absolute power in August 1934 (at the death of Hindenberg) within a month of a Mars-Pluto conjunction.

In America other social solutions to the same challenges were being tried with the formation of Roosevelt's "New Deal."

Pluto moved from Cancer into Leo around the time of the outbreak of World War II, signaling profound changes in power relationships on a worldwide scale. Neptune continued in Virgo for the whole period. It should be noted that Hitler's racial concepts were very Neptunian, that is, they were based on (in this case false) ideals and illusion. These were combined with Hitler's Neptunian fantasies of world domination. However, they ran head-on into the technical difficulties posed by Virgo and finally into the "balancing" of Libra (Neptune moved into Libra in 1942-1943) just as the military tide began to turn against the Axis powers.

1941-1950

Pluto continued in Leo for the whole decade, making its basic changes in the world power structures. Neptune's entering Libra in October 1942 led to negotiations for balancing out the world situation, such as the Casablanca conference between Churchill and Roosevelt a few months later in January 1943. In the same month the Russians stopped the Germans at Stalingrad, marking the highwater mark of German expansion.

It is interesting to note that Saturn and Uranus were retrograding four degrees apart at the time of the Pearl Harbor sneak attack by the Japanese. Uranus rules the sudden and unexpected while Saturn brings the results of causes previously set in motion.

Uranus in Gemini corresponded with the breakthrough in the release of atomic energy with the fission of uranium. December 1942, near the start of the decade, saw the first sustained atomic reaction. The first atomic explosion came near the midpoint (July 1945) of the period and the end of the decade (after Uranus had gone into Cancer) saw the development of atomic power to generate large amounts of electricity.

The entry of Uranus into Cancer (1948-1949) also established the new liberation of women, which had started when they filled in during the war in industry and business while the men were away fighting. Cancer rules women and the home; Uranus brings changes in underlying concepts.

1951-1960

Pluto continued in Leo until 1956-58, when it entered Virgo. Neptune left Libra for Scorpio in 1955-57. This 60-degree aspect between them (sextile), which began in the late 1940's, is to continue through the end of the century. The reason the two planets are traveling at roughly the same speed for such a long period is that Pluto, although normally slower than Neptune, is speeding up as it approaches perihelion; Neptune is slowing down as it approaches aphelion.

Uranus was in Cancer until 1955-56, when it entered Leo, just about the time that Jupiter and Mars were also entering Leo. Saturn and Neptune were within orb of a conjunction from late 1952 through late 1953. Uranus and Neptune were square each other for much of the decade. Mars, Jupiter, and Uranus made conjunctions with each other within a short period in mid-1955, followed around the end of the year by a Jupiter-Pluto conjunction as both were leaving Leo for Virgo. At the same time (January 1956) Mars and Saturn were conjunct as both were leaving Scorpio for Sagittarius, thereby squaring Jupiter and Pluto.

This was the decade that spanned the "beat generation," with its new concepts of poetry and writing, all of which placed a new emphasis on subconscious and sexual imagery (Neptune in Scorpio). The youth of the period created a new lifestyle (Uranus square Neptune) in reaction against the "middle class values" (as they saw them) of their parents. Although an "underground" movement developing since the very beginning of the 50's, the beat scene surfaced in the mid 50's, to become a national phenomenon just as Pluto entered Virgo (changes in work patterns), Neptune entered Scorpio (interest in sexual fantasies), and Uranus entered Leo (new patterns of creativity). At the same time (the mid 50's) "abstract expressionism" became the predominant art form, interacting with "beat poetry" and "cool jazz" to become a new (if loose) synthesis of the arts.

The beginning of the period saw the Korean War at its height as well as other unresolved conflicts both in the United States (this was the period of the McCarthy hearings) and in the international scene. These all became resolved in one way or another as Neptune, Saturn, and Pluto began to change signs. The Korean War came to an end in mid-1953 during a complex Neptune-Saturn interaction (see planet chart) shortly before they went into new signs.

1961-1970

Pluto was in Virgo the whole decade. Neptune was in Scorpio until 1970, when it entered Sagittarius. Uranus left Leo for Virgo in 1968-69.

The decade was dominated by the coming together, long conjunction, and slow separation of Uranus and Pluto, first in Virgo and then crossing into the cardinal sign of Libra. In late 1968 they were joined by both Jupiter and Mars at this Virgo-Libra cusp. A Jupiter-Saturn conjunction took place in February 1961 at the end of Capricorn.

This decade was overshadowed by the escalation of the Vietnamese War and by political assassinations. A secondary theme was the space race with the Russians putting the first man into space (April 1961) and the Americans landing the first men on the moon (July 1969). A lot more was happening in this lively decade with the "hippies" coming into their own, discotheques, go-go girls, miniskirts, and the relaxation of restrictions on obscenity. The interaction of Uranus and Pluto (particularly in Virgo) coincided with wholesale changes in society and myriads of new directions. In the beginning of 1969 Nixon became president with both Saturn and Uranus retrograde just into Libra, a premonition of the difficulties which lay ahead for him. Just before this there were three Mars conjunctions, all very close together, first with Pluto, then with Jupiter and Uranus, just following the assassinations of Martin Luther King (April 1968) and Senator Robert Kennedy (June 1968).

1971-1978

Neptune left Scorpio for Sagittarius in 1970. Pluto left Virgo for Libra in 1971-72. Uranus was in Libra until 1974-75, when it entered Scorpio. Through the whole decade it moves between Pluto and Neptune.

In early 1971 Neptune, Jupiter, and Mars were conjunct within a few days of each other in the beginning of Sagittarius. During the decade both Jupiter and Saturn make last trine and last square aspects to Pluto, Uranus, and Neptune in succession. Through the whole decade Jupiter and Saturn are approaching the conjunction that they make on December 31, 1980 in 9° Libra.

You can see that the emphasis of the outer planets in the first half of the 1971-1980 decade was in Libra and Sagittarius. In fact, the Libra influence continues through the early 1980's and the Sagittarius influence grows even stronger during the 1980's, when Jupiter, Saturn, and Uranus all spend time in this sign.

Both Libra and Sagittarius are connected with government, law and international relations, Libra more in the sense of weighing and balancing and Sagittarius more in basic concepts. Thus, we have already experienced, (and can expect to continue to experience) an emphasis on basic changes (Pluto), ideals and deception (Neptune), and innovations and unexpected events (Uranus) in these areas. Watergate and the continued uncovering of deception in government are examples.

The future

Using astrology for making general world predictions for the years ahead is a matter of studying the coming planetary configurations in combination with the more or less "obvious" directions in which society is heading. For example, it does not take an astrological analysis to predict that man will build large orbital satellites in space, colonize the moon and Mars, explore the rest of the inner and outer planets, and eventually aim at the stars. In the planetary positions coming up we can look for what seem likely points in time for all these things to take place.

Most "hard" scientific predictions have usually fallen short of the mark; that is, the future has always turned out to be *more* fantastic than was predicted. Or, to put it another way: "The future will not be stranger than we think, but stranger than we *can* think." The rate of advancement in science (and accompanying social changes) has accelerated to such an extent that what took twenty or thirty years in the nineteenth century now takes two or three years.

What seems to be indicated in the astrological "record" of the future is a basic transformation of society comparable (at least) in depth and scope to the fifteenth and sixteenth centuries, when Columbus and other explorers reached the Americas, Southern Africa, and the Orient and opened the way for worldwide empires which have only dissolved in our own century.

During the end of 1979 and most of 1980 all six outer planets will be arranged in four adjacent signs, from Virgo to Sagittarius. During 1980 Mars will conjunct each of the other five outer planets. As we move into the 1980's, it is clear that the outer planets are slowly gathering in the same area of the zodiac.

The "interplay" between Jupiter, Mars, and Saturn in 1979-1980, particularly when Mars and Saturn conjunct while squaring Neptune, points to a major energy or ecological crisis at the beginning of 1980. This immediately precedes a Jupiter-Saturn conjunction on the very last day of 1980 in 9° Libra, the scales, which means a new cycle of *balancing things out*. Within 1982 both will join Uranus in the 60-degree span between Pluto and Neptune, composed of the signs Scorpio and Sagittarius. Mars will be there also. In the years 1981 through 1984 Jupiter and Saturn will not only begin their own new conjunction cycle, but each will also begin new conjunction cycles with Pluto, Uranus, and Neptune. In both 1982 and 1984 Mars will conjunct each of the other five outer planets in rapid succession.

One way we can make predictions is to *go back* into the record and study the effects of the beginnings and ends of significant cycles. If we go back to 1941-42 near a Jupiter-Saturn conjunction (with Uranus involved), it seems interesting that this is where the initial breakthroughs were made in nuclear fission, which led to the atomic bomb as well as peaceful use of atomic energy.

Fission is based on the breakdown of uranium into lighter elements with the release of energy. Fusion (the same power that lights the sun) is the joining of hydrogen atoms to form a heavier element, also with the release of large amounts of energy. As a means of producing power, this can be done without releasing radioactivity to the atmosphere.

The 1980 conjunction of Jupiter and Saturn (necessity taking over from politics) and the other astrological configurations in the early 1980's may connect with a major breakthrough in practical large-scale use of hydrogen fusion technology, freeing man in the future from any lack of energy. This is because we can never run out of hydrogen (it is half of H_2O or water) and we can even "scoop up" hydrogen in outer space. It is possible, of course, that this freedom from energy problems will take other forms, such as solar energy, as well.

This freeing of man from worrying about energy will enable him to concentrate on exploration and making use of space. The space shuttle and workable space stations in orbit will be in operation by the end of the 1971-1980 decade, with a gradual acceleration of development in the early 1980's. The acquisition of unlimited power would seem particularly to connect with Pluto's passage through Scorpio.

This is not without its dangers. By 1984 even the smaller African and South American countries will have hydrogen bombs. At the same time, there will probably be manned stations on the moon or Mars, and a number of space "colonies" in between. If World War III should develop, the indications are possibly for the 1984 period (compare 1914-1915 and 1941-1942). It is definitely possible that the tensions of this period can be resolved by peaceful means, but if war comes, there are strong indications that it will be fought in outer space, since if fought on the surface of the earth, it could be the end of the ballgame. Out of this period will come a new concept of world government. This must of necessity see the end of provincialism and nationalism, with all people becoming world citizens primarily, rather than American, Chinese, etc.

Pluto indicates basic changes in underlying patterns in individuals and basic changes in balances of all types of power in the world. Pluto went into Scorpio (bringing to the surface that which was hidden) in the 1490's when Columbus discovered (or rediscovered) the "New World" at the height of the Renaissance of art and culture. The next time Pluto entered Scorpio was around the 1740's. This coincided with the intellectual revolution, often called the "Age of Reason," which laid the groundwork for the first democratic revolutions at the end of the century. This intellectual revolution was the first to challenge institutional religion in the name of logic and science. The period also saw the invention and development of the steam engine, which freed industry from human and animal power and created the Industrial Revolution in the late 1700's.

It seems significant on many levels of meaning that Pluto will next enter Scorpio (in its 248-year cycle) in 1984, remaining in the sign until 1995. For one thing, Pluto is considered by many astrologers to be the ruler of Scorpio. When a planet passes through a sign it rules, its action is intensified. Scorpio is a high-energy sign to begin with, so its effect will be profound. Also, Scorpio is the sign of Pluto's perihelion—it won't be this close to the sun again for 248 years. Pluto's orbit is so eccentric that it is closer to the sun than the orbit of Neptune when near perihelion, and Pluto will be inside Neptune's orbit from about 1978 through 2000. The point of its perihelion is around 13° Scorpio, during 1988-89. It is also moving faster at this period than at any other time.

Pluto in Scorpio can be expected to bring basic changes in many areas. These will include the understanding of individual and collective psychological drives, life after death, and sex, as well as basic theory in many of the sciences.

Neptune will enter Capricorn in 1984, where it will remain until 1998. This period can be characterized by the seeking for perfection in organization, which may include world government and also overall structures of scientific understanding and the application of that understanding. Structure and simplicity in the arts can be expected. Neptune was last in Capricorn around the 1820's, a period when simplicity and "back to nature" were idealized.

Uranus will enter Sagittarius in 1981. This planet-sign combination can mean new attitudes toward both legal systems and universal laws, as well as new means of travel. The last passage of Uranus through Sagittarius, as you will recall, was from 1897 to 1904, a period which included breakthroughs in understanding the laws of physics, as well as major transportation advances, including the Wright brothers' first flight. In 1988 Uranus will join Neptune in Capricorn, approaching their conjunction in 1993. The emphasis will be on new approaches to applying the understandings gained while each was in Sagittarius. Uranus in Capricorn will mean changes, often unexpected, in any structures (religious, government, psychological, scientific) which cannot stand up under the new insights.

These and other astrological factors indicate (despite some pessimistic predictions for 1984 by writers such as Orwell) that this period will see the beginning of a breakthrough in knowledge: an understanding which integrates spiritual and scientific concepts and is accompanied by spectacular developments in the areas of technology, communication, travel, the arts, education, and government.

A particularly interesting period can be seen in 1988-89. On February 14, 1988, Saturn and Uranus will be conjunct exactly as they are leaving Sagittarius for the cardinal sign of Capricorn. Both will retrograde into Sagittarius a few months later, returning to Capricorn before the end of the year. Saturn will proceed to a conjunction with Neptune during 1989. This unusual emphasis on Capricorn will extend into the next decade and be amplified whenever one or more of the faster-moving planets also passes through Capricorn. For example, around January 18-20, 1990, the sun, Mercury, and Venus will also be in Capricorn, Mercury approximately stationary. By the end of that month Mars will enter Capricorn, although the sun will have moved into Aquarius. Jupiter will be in Cancer, opposite Capricorn.

The essence of Capricorn is the crystal, a symbol of perfect organization. This period marks the beginning of changes in basic consciousness of the whole human race, an integration of consciousness based not on man-made laws but on awareness of fundamental laws of the universe and how these laws apply to the specifics in our world, including such areas as understanding the basic laws of physical and biological science and their applications on many levels of technology; and tapping the basic genius in man and releasing powers and abilities which now surface only rarely. This can be applied to healing, whether of the body or of the mind; communicating with other beings, whether on this planet, other planets, or in states of consciousness after physical death.

Because the planet forces are all gathered together, this period of 1989-1990 could mark a climax period not only of earthquakes but of other readjustments of the earth's surface.

The early 1990's will see the close intertwining of Neptune and Uranus for several years. This period may see the first "official" physical contact with extraterrestrial civilizations, although "psychic" contact may be made earlier. Perhaps we will learn from them a completely new (and to us now unimaginable) method of space travel.

In 1995 Pluto leaves Scorpio for Sagittarius, where it should bring even more basic changes in patterns of religion and government as well as in travel. Uranus and Neptune will be very close together in Capricorn all through the first half of the decade, conjuncting exactly in 1993. Uranus and Mars will enter Aquarius in January 1996 within a few days of each other. Neptune will enter this sign in 1998, emphasizing the dawning Aquarian Age and bringing to the point of universal application this redefinition of our role in the universe. This "Age of Man" or "Age of Enlightenment," will manifest in a world religion, not in any terms we can conceive of clearly at this stage but in terms of a total psychic and spiritual union of all mankind. This will begin the next major stage in the development of mankind.

Astrological weather predicting

Making connections between the weather and positions of the planets is very likely the oldest form of astrology. All over the world farmers, sailors, and other people who work outdoors have passed down traditional knowledge of how to anticipate weather conditions by knowing where the planets are. Farmer's almanacs, which predict the weather a year ahead, rely on astrology as a major method.

The movement of the moon is one of the strongest indications of weather changes. As it goes through its phases, there are measurable changes in electromagnetic and gravitational factors. These, in turn, seem to have effects on the elements in our atmosphere that bring more or less moisture. Researchers from the National Science Foundation, after studying weather records going back ninety-one years, discovered that chances for a heavy rainfall in the week after the new moon and after the full moon were up to three times greater than for the week preceding the new moon.

Astrologers have also observed that each zodiac sign seems to have characteristic effects on the weather when the moon in particular, but also the other planets, are transiting through it. In addition, each planet seems to have a recognizable effect on the weather when it is in a prominent transiting position.

Like any other form of meteorology, astrological weather predicting is quite complex, although there are astrometeorologists who claim more accuracy than meteorologists who don't use the planetary positions! Here are some of the basic astrometeorological techniques to let you do your own experimenting.

General forecasts for temperature trends

The positions of the planets at the time each new season begins indicate general trends in the weather for the next three months. Although this seems to apply especially to temperature trends, these general forecasts are also used to some extent in predicting wind and rain trends. To set up a season prediction chart, look in the planet position calendars for all planet positions on the *first day* of the season. As this can differ by a day or two each year, check the sun and moon calendars (beginning on page 82) for the year in which you are interested.

Season	Begins day sun enters
Spring	Aries
Summer	Cancer
Fall	Libra
Winter	Capricorn

Below is a chart of the influence of each zodiac sign on temperature, movement of air, and moisture. For each new season note what zodiac sign each planet is in at the time of the sun's movement into the appropriate sign. Then tally, for each sign occupied by a planet, whether the influence is for cold, cool, moderate, warm, or hot, using this weather influence chart. See example on following page.

		♈	♉	♊	♋	♌	♍	♎	♏	♐	♑	♒	♓	☉	☽	☿	♀	♂	♃	♄	♅	♆	♇
TEMPERATURE	cold			■	■		■		■		■	■										■	■
	cool							■	↑1 or ↓				■	■	■							■	■
	moderate		■														■				2		
	warm									■									■				
	hot	■				■			■					■				■					
AIR MOVEMENT	calm		■						■			■		■						■			
	breezy				■				↑1 or ↓	■					■		■	■	■	↑ or ↓		■	
	windy	■		■			■	■								■							■
	gusts								■											↓	■		↑ or ↓
	high winds								■	■											■	■	■
MOISTURE	dry	■		■		■	■	■	■	■				■		■		■	■		■		
	fog								↑1 or ↓													■	
	drizzle																						■
	rain or snow		■								■	■	■				■	↑ or ↓		■	↑ or ↓		
	heavy rain or snow, hail, floods				■				■									■			■		
	thunderstorms																				■		

[1] Scorpio seems to influence toward extremes, according to the prevailing trend. In other words, if the trend is toward cold, a Scorpio planet will add its "vote" toward cold, and if the trend is toward hot, Scorpio will tend that direction.

[2] Sudden temperature changes.

147

Sun entered Capricorn on December 21, 1976, about 1 P.M. Eastern Standard Time.

Planet	Sign	Cold	Cool	Moderate	Warm	Hot
☉ Sun	CAPRICORN	1				
☽ Moon	CAPRICORN	1				
☿ Mercury	CAPRICORN	1				
♀ Venus	AQUARIUS	1				
♂ Mars	SAGITTARIUS				1	
♃ Jupiter	TAURUS			1		
♄ Saturn	LEO					1
♅ Uranus	SCORPIO	1				1
♆ Neptune	SAGITTARIUS				1	
♇ Pluto	LIBRA		1			
TOTALS		5	1	1	2	2

So far we have seen that the weight of the zodiac positions is clearly toward a cold winter in the general season forecast, but you might be even more interested in weather trends for your particular area. In order to do that, it is necessary to determine the midheaven and ascendant at *your latitude and longitude* for the exact time that the sun enters the new season. This can be calculated either by a competent astrologer or by a computer service in the same way as would be done if a child had been born at this particular moment in your locality. The exact time that the sun enters a new season is available in a number of calendars and other sources.

With a horoscope cast for the beginning of the season in your locality you are now ready to make a temperature tally, as you did for the general season forecast. This time, however, you should allow more weight to any planets which are in the zodiac sign of the ascendant and its opposite for your locality, or the zodiac sign of the midheaven and its opposite (see Aspects Chart on page 108). Weight the planets in these signs as follows:

Zodiac sign of:	*Count any planet in it:*
ascendant	three times
opposite ascendant	two times
midheaven	two times
opposite midheaven	three times

(If you have a weather horoscope with the houses indicated, count three times any planets in the first and fourth houses and count two times any planets in the seventh and tenth houses.)

With an accurately made season horoscope adjusted to your latitude and longitude, it is possible, just as with your own birth horoscope, to note transits to *important points*, particularly the ascendant and the point opposite the midheaven, since these are the most important points specific to your locality. These transits during the season indicate weather changes for your locality. What kinds of changes depend both on the transiting planet and the planet or other *important point* being transited. The weather influence of each planet is given on the right side of the Weather Influence Chart on page 147.

Besides the season horoscopes, there are other astrological events that seem to indicate coming weather changes. Amount of rain (or snow) for the coming month is indicated by a horoscope set up for the time of the new moon. (New moons are indicated in the sun and moon calendars.) Again, if ascendant and midheaven of this horoscope are set up precisely for the latitude and longitude of your locality, more specific forecasting can be done.

Astrometeorologists also set up horoscopes for the time Mercury enters a new zodiac sign, as this horoscope indicates the air movement, from calm to high winds, until Mercury enters another sign.

Of course, in all weather predicting you must take into account prevailing weather patterns, since the astrological information indicutes how the season will compare with normal. In other words, even if the indications are for very cold weather, don't expect a blizzard in the tropics, merely colder temperatures than usual.

Experimentation with weather horoscopes for your own locality may show that certain planets have stronger influence than others. Observation of the transits over a period of time will tell you what to look for.

Earthquake predicting

Astrology has been used as a method of predicting earthquakes and other disasters since ancient times. In fact, the *aster* in *disaster* comes from the same root as *astrology*, and the word *disaster* originally meant " a negative influence of the stars." More recent students of the heavens, including Sir Isaac Newton as well as present-day investigators, have found astrological earthquake indicators, some of which can be coordinated with recent advances in other areas of scientific knowledge about earthquakes.

The majority of geologists now believe that the outer shell of the earth is divided up into enormous "plates," most of which are as big or bigger than the continents themselves. These plates drift slowly over the earth's surface, changing the positions of continents and oceans. This drifting movement takes millions of years to make significant alterations in geography. One of the changes that has taken place relatively recently, from a geological point of view, is the emergence of the Atlantic Ocean, between the giant jigsaw puzzle pieces of North and South America, on the one side, and Europe and Africa, on the other. The fit between the continents on either side of the Atlantic is clear on any world map and has been confirmed by mineral, plant, and animal comparisons between areas originally in direct contact.

As each plate drifts apart from past neighbors, it also drifts toward others. When two plates collide, the edges are thrown up in the form of a mountain chain. This is true of both the Alps and the Himalayas.

Earthquakes can occur anywhere in the world. But it is not surprising that the areas of most frequent earthquake activity are where two plates interact with one another. This is true of the San Andreas fault in California, for instance.

If movements of the earth's plates took place evenly, we would not notice the motion because it is extremely slow, usually not more than a quarter of an inch per year! But the irregular edges of the plates stick against each other until the pressure becomes too great. Then the plates can move with a jolt, or series of jolts. These are earthquakes. Pressure between the plates is always building up. Predicting earthquakes depends upon an understanding of these pressures as well as the factors that can trigger the sudden catastrophic release of these pressures.

In addition, there seem to be other pressures caused by charging magnetic and gravitational forces created, in turn, by the positions of the sun, moon, and planets relative to the earth. Certain of these patterns were observed to be associated with earthquakes centuries before they could be labeled "gravitational" or "magnetic." In fact, planetary positions may be connected with other important force fields that we have not yet learned to measure.

The angles of the heavenly bodies in relationship to the earth's position show the stress pattern that applies directly to the earth. Another stress pattern (known to be a factor in the eleven-year sunspot cycle) is shown by the angles of the planets relative to the sun. Sunspot cycles have been shown to be connected to a number of cycles on earth, including the frequency of earthquakes. There are more earthquakes at the peak of the sunspot cycle. Changes in magnetic phenomena shortly before and during earthquakes have been observed on many occasions as well as unusual weather patterns. Strange auroral lights have taken place at the same time. Animals often become unusually nervous several hours before earthquakes, implying that they are aware of some sort of change, perhaps in some force field that we ourselves do not sense.

Using astrology to predict earthquakes is a matter of looking for future planet positions and other such keys which have been associated in the past with earthquakes. No one factor alone can be shown to invariably indicate an earthquake. However, if a combination of astrological "strain" factors happens at the same time, it indicates the distinct possibility of an earthquake. There are also methods, as in weather predicting, to astrologically pinpoint the areas likely to be involved.

Here are some astrological earthquake factors:

1. MOON CLOSEST TO EARTH

One a month the moon is closest to the earth (called perigee) and therefore exerts a little more pull on the earth than at other times. You will find moon perigee tables from 1978 to 1980 on page 155. For other years this information can be obtained from astronomical and astrological calendars as well as almanacs.

2. EARTH CLOSEST TO THE SUN

The earth is closest to the sun (called perihelion) once a year in January, and at this time the sun's pull is stronger on it. When any planet is in perihelion, a strain factor seems to be exerted on the sun. Because of the sun's effect on the earth, this adds an earthquake factor.

3. SUN-MOON CYCLE

The sun and moon exert the strongest pulls on earth. When they are pulling from the same direction, as in a new moon, or from opposite directions, as during a full moon, the strain on the earth is stronger. This comes from the gravitational pull on the solid part of the earth as well as the increased or decreased weight of the water from higher tides. Any new or full moon (both are called *lunations*) can be an earthquake factor, but eclipses of either the sun or the moon are even more important. The sun and moon calendars on page 82 will tell you when to expect both eclipses and ordinary lunations.

4. "STATIONARY" PLANETS

Another earthquake factor is created when a planet is stationary just before it goes retrograde or stationary just before it goes direct again. Stationary periods of the planets can be seen in the planet charts beginning on page 108.

5. **PLANET ASPECTS**
Conjunctions and oppositions of all planets seem to be earthquake factors, but the larger planets (Jupiter, Saturn, Neptune) and those closest to the earth (Mercury, Venus, and Mars) are particularly important, especially when they are also conjunct or in opposition to the sun or the moon. Close squares and trines are also to be looked for, but they seem somewhat less important than conjunctions and oppositions. Planet aspects considered from the sun's position (*heliocentric*) as well as from the earth's position (*geocentric*) have been found to be earthquake factors. Planet aspects can be found from the planet graphs beginning on page 111.

6. **PLANETS PASSING CLOSEST TO EARTH**
In addition to the *angles* (aspects) of the planets with respect to the earth, there is also the period when a planet passes *closest* to the earth. This is another earthquake factor.

7. **PARTICULAR ZODIAC DEGREES**
Certain specific degrees of the zodiac seem to be earthquake factors if the sun, moon, or a planet is passing over them. Among these are the degrees the sun is in at the beginning of each season (0 degrees of Aries, Cancer, Libra, and Capricorn). Other sensitive degrees mark the location of certain fixed stars. In addition, there are some degrees which seem to be important even though they can't be pinned to anything as specific as a season or a star.

Some of the "sensitive degrees" are:

0 Aries	17 Taurus: Neptune perihelion	22 Virgo: Uranus perihelion
0 Cancer	25 Taurus: fixed star Algol	13 Scorpio: Pluto perihelion
0 Libra	29 Taurus: constellation Pleiades	25 Sagittarius: "earthquake degree"
0 Capricorn	2 Cancer: Saturn perihelion	26 Sagittarius: center of our galaxy
	15 Leo: "earthquake degree"	12 Capricorn: position of sun when earth is nearest it.

Astrologers have long noticed that any degree of the zodiac can become sensitized for a period after something of astrological importance has happened in it. The planet also exerts a gradually increasing effect on the point before it actually arrives. For example, the degree in which an eclipse of the sun has taken place is sensitive for a short period before and at least a month thereafter. Some astrologers have found that a sun eclipse degree can be important until the next sun eclipse. When a degree is sensitized, a planet crossing it can trigger the event that was set up when the degree became sensitized. Here are the principal types of sensitized degrees to consider:

Degrees of eclipses of either the sun or the moon

Degrees where a planet was stationary

Degrees where two or more of the slower-moving planets were conjunct.

When more than one of the rare and slow moving astrological factors happen at about the same time, look for the time of a more frequent and fast-moving astrological factor to trigger the earthquake.

Earthquake locations

So far we have told you about astrological methods of predicting *when* earthquakes are likely to occur. To locate *where* they might happen requires determining what areas of the earth are on the same longitude as the planets involved in the earthquake factors *at the time the aspect, lunation, etc. is exact.* This means any planets in the chart for a particular locality that are near the midheaven or its opposite point directly below the earth. Also important are planets at the ascendant (eastern horizon) or opposite it (western horizon).

Like the sun, all the planets travel once a day over the ascendant, the midheaven, and their opposites because of the rotation of the earth. When the stress patterns are already critical, the added strain of certain planets crossing one of these four points can be the last straw. Uranus at the midheaven or Saturn opposite the midheaven seem to be special triggering factors.

Here are some heavy earthquakes of the past analyzed for astrological stress factors:

April 18, 1906, San Francisco, California

Uranus was stationary (about to go retrograde) in opposition to Neptune. At the time of the earthquake Uranus was at the midheaven at San Francisco and Neptune was opposite it.

November 10, 1938, Bering Sea

A full moon eclipse had happened three days earlier, at which time the moon had been conjunct Uranus and the sun had been in opposition to it. At the time of the earthquake Pluto was stationary (about to go retrograde). Mars was at the midheaven of the area horoscope in opposition to Saturn.

August 24, 1942, Brazil
A full moon eclipse took place two days later. At the time of the earthquake Uranus and Saturn were seven degrees apart, and both were opposite the midheaven. The sun was opposite the ascendant. Mars was square Saturn and Venus was conjunct Pluto.

March 27, 1964, Anchorage, Alaska
The earthquake happened within twenty-four hours of a full moon. Mercury was conjunct Jupiter. Uranus and Pluto were six degrees apart.

    Earthquake prediction is a constantly developing science. The combination of the study of the astrological stress factors with conventional earth sciences promises a breakthrough.

Here is a map of what many scientists believe to be the present boundaries of the earth's plates. The greatest earthquake activity occurs along these lines.

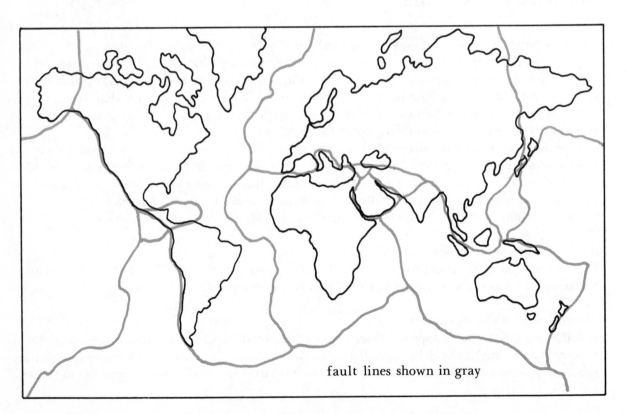

fault lines shown in gray

Moon perigee dates

DATES MOON WILL BE IN PERIGEE (CLOSEST TO EARTH)
1978 through 1980 (Eastern Standard Time)

(See earthquake predicting, page 150.)

1978

January 8	7 a.m.
February 5	4 p.m.
March 5	12 noon
March 31	12 midnight (between March 30-31)
April 26	3 a.m.
May 24	12 midnight (between May 23-24)
June 21	7 a.m.
July 19	5 p.m.
August 17	1 a.m.
September 14	5 a.m.
October 11	11 a.m.
November 5	7 a.m.
December 2	11 a.m.
December 30	5 p.m.

1979

January 28	5 a.m.
February 25	5 p.m.
March 26	1 a.m.
April 22	5 p.m.
May 18	4 a.m.
June 13	11 a.m.
July 11	7 a.m.
August 8	2 p.m.
September 6	12 midnight (between Sept. 5-6)
October 4	10 a.m.
November 1	3 p.m.
November 28	7 p.m.
December 23	11 a.m.

1980

January 19	9 p.m.
February 17	4 a.m.
March 16	4 p.m.
April 14	2 a.m.
May 12	8 a.m.
June 8	11 p.m.
July 4	11 a.m.
July 30	6 p.m.
August 27	2 p.m.
September 24	10 p.m.
October 23	9 a.m.
November 20	8 p.m.
December 19	12 midnight (between Dec 18-19)

Gardening with astrology

Using astrology for growing things is another ancient tradition found in many countries and passed down from generation to generation of farmers and gardeners. You have seen some of this astrological lore in farmer's almanacs. We know several "astrological gardeners" who have used the system for years. They all testify that it works and that when (either for convenience or experimentation) they have planted, transplanted, etc. under the wrong astrological conditions, the plants didn't do as well.

For growing things the moon is the major indicator of proper conditions. In the chapter on weather we mentioned that researchers from the National Science Foundation have confirmed that the chances of rain in the week after the new moon and the week after the full moon are up to three times greater than for the week preceding the new moon. The electrical potential of plants measures higher during the full moon, and there is a direct connection between plant growth and electrical potential.

Gardening with the moon is one of the simplest forms of astrology. It is primarily a matter of checking for both the moonphase and the moonsign and scheduling your garden tasks under the favorable phase-sign combinations. In the sun and moon calendars beginning on page 82 you can check on the moonphase and moonsign for any day up through the year 1980, as well as the hour of each change of either phase or sign.

Eight moonphases are given, but for gardening purposes the principal four phases are the ones you will use: new moon (●), first quarter (◑), full moon (○), and last quarter (◑). The period of the new moon to the full moon, while the moon's light is increasing, is called the *waxing* moon; from the full moon to the next new moon, while the light is decreasing, is the *waning* moon.

For the best moonsigns and moonphases to perform various gardening operations, see the chart on page 157 . The moon changes signs every two and one-half days but the time between one principal phase and the next is one week. The moon's travels around the zodiac and its phases are not synchronized with each other, so you need to check both for any given day.

As a rule of thumb, plant anything to be harvested *above* the ground during a waxing moon and anything to be harvested *below* the ground during a waning moon. You should also pay attention to the moon*sign* in addition to its phase, as nothing should be planted during a "barren" sign. However, barren signs are good for weeding, harvesting, etc. See page 158 for the characteristics of each zodiac sign.